W9-BUJ-961

PASSION and PROPERTY

in the HAMPTONS

"Hugely entertaining....With wit and zest...Mr. Gaines tells the story
of the embattled Hamptons through a series of deft profiles
of some of the more colorful residents."
—STEPHEN BIRMINGHAM, *WASHINGTON TIMES*

"Breezy, irreverent...amusing....Mr. Gaines has found in the stretch of
Long Island shoreline that comprises the Hamptons a place worthy of its own
unauthorized biography, replete with scandals, scurrilous characters,
assorted bacchanalia, and all manner of wretched excess."
LAURA LANDRO, *WALL STREET JOURNAL*

"The history of the Hamptons is the story of successive barbarian invasions and the indignant reaction of earlier arrivals....*Philistines at the Hedgerow* deftly fashions the biographies of the purveyors and owners of the Hamptons' choicest real estate into a narrative of surprising unity and velocity. Such a cast of eccentrics hasn't been seen since *Midnight in the Garden of Good and Evil*."
— JAY McINERNEY, *THE NEW YORKER*

"Gaines vividly paints the history of the Hamptons, from the Algonquin Indians to Martha Stewart....It's some of the best summer reading you're likely to find this season.
— G. WILLIAM GRAY, *TAMPA TRIBUNE-TIMES*

"The English farmers drove out the Indians, then the blue bloods came, bought all the prime land, and retired quietly behind their hedges and to their beach clubs. The bohemian artists made lots of noise, bared their breasts on the beach, and stole the spotlight, and now Hollywood and Wall Street reign. What is surprising is that Gaines is the first to tell the story."
— JACK OTTER, *NEWSDAY*

"If you've ever been curious about the little spit of Long Island, N.Y., where everyone from Steven Spielberg to John F. Kennedy Jr. plays in summer, Gaines's book is your ticket....It ranges from the 1658 witch trial of one Goody Garlick in East Hampton to the 1920s and 1930s playgrounds of Douglas Fairbanks, Mary Pickford, and Gerald and Sara Murphy of F. Scott Fitzgerald fame to today's knockdown real estate battles and mansions of excess."
— JEANNIE WILLIAMS, *USA TODAY*

"A satisfying comedy of manners about snobbishness and land lust among America's overachievers....Gaines knows how to tell a story, and he knows how to dish."
— CARL SWANSON, *SALON*

"Engaging....Tales of the social, ethnic, and architectural history of one of the most exclusive summer resort areas in America."
— JENNIFER STEINHAUER, *NEW YORK TIMES BOOK REVIEW*

"Even those who have never heard of Long Island's home to the superrich and the celebrated will find page-turning entertainment....Gaines depicts a fabulous cast of real-life characters, both high and low. More fun than most fiction, this is a terrific summer— or anytime—read."
— *PUBLISHERS WEEKLY*

Philistines
at the Hedgerow

Also by Steven Gaines

Obsession: The Lives and Times of Calvin Klein
(with Sharon Churcher)
Simply Halston: The Untold Story
Heroes and Villains: The True Story of the Beach Boys
The Love You Make: An Insider's Story of the Beatles
(with Peter Brown)
Me, Alice: The Biography of Alice Cooper
Marjoe: The Biography of Evangelist Marjoe Gortner
The Club (novel)
Another Runner in the Night (novel)

Philistines
at the Hedgerow

Passion and Property in the Hamptons

STEVEN GAINES

Little, Brown and Company

BOSTON   NEW YORK   LONDON

Copyright © 1998 by Steven Gaines

All rights reserved. No part of this book may be reproduced
in any form or by any electronic or mechanical means,
including information storage and retrieval systems,
without permission in writing from the publisher, except
by a reviewer who may quote brief passages in a review.

Originally published in hardcover by Little, Brown and Company, 1998
First Back Bay paperback edition, 1999

Library of Congress Cataloging-in-Publication Data

Gaines, Steven S.
    Philistines at the Hedgerow : passion and property in the Hamptons /
Steven Gaines. — 1st ed.
        p.   cm.
    Includes index.
    ISBN 0-316-30941-9 (hc) / 0-316-30907-9 (pb)
        1. Hamptons (N.Y.) — Social life and customs.   2. Upper class — New
York (State) — Hamptons — Social life and customs.   3. Celebrities — New York
(State) — Hamptons — Social life and customs.   4. Real property — Social
aspects — New York (State) — Hamptons.   I. Title.
F127.S9G5   1998
974.7'25 — dc21   98-11029

10   9   8   7   6   5   4   3   2   1

MV-NY

Printed in the United States of America

For Lynn and Bob

"Mid pleasures and palaces tho we may roam,
Be it ever so humble there's no place like home."

— From "Home Sweet Home,"
John Howard Payne, 1823, the song he wrote about his
boyhood home on Main Street, East Hampton

Contents

Philistines
at the Hedgerow

The Pasha

ONE FRIDAY NIGHT in December 1991, while dining at the home of Bruce Cotter, a retired East Hampton police lieutenant, real estate magnate Allan M. Schneider began to choke on a piece of rare sirloin steak lodged in his windpipe.

Schneider, fifty-four, was the most powerful broker in all the Hamptons — "the Pasha," as he was affectionately called by his staff — with offices in Southampton, Bridgehampton, Sag Harbor, and East Hampton and revenues approaching $100 million. His empire had grown even larger that morning when he closed a deal to acquire a fifth office, in Amagansett. The new office, plus the imposing Allan M. Schneider Agency headquarters he was erecting along the highway in Bridgehampton, would seal his domination in the Hamptons real estate market.

Shortly after signing the papers at the lawyer's office, Schneider started to drink — first with celebratory champagne, then a three-martini lunch at Gordon's restaurant — and he hadn't really quit since. Earlier in the day he had called his secretary, Rochelle Rosenberg, who gave him his messages and said, "I'll see you on Monday, Allan."

Allan answered playfully, "Maybe you will, maybe you won't."

The Cotters, one of the many local families with whom Schneider was close, had invited him over for a steak dinner to mark the occasion and, they hoped, sober him up. It was Schneider's hallmark that he was friendly not only with the wealthy Summer Colony but with the hoi polloi, the farmers and tradesmen who were the "real people" of the town. He had met Cotter soon after arriving in the Hamptons in 1968, when the lieutenant had pulled him over on Montauk Highway for a traffic infraction. Allan stunned the policeman by inviting him home for a drink. Cotter indignantly declined, but over the years Allan became a good friend to Cotter and his wife, Carol Lynn. When Cotter retired from the force, Schneider invited him to sell real estate for the firm, where he became a valued employee.

That December night at Cotter's house, Allan was cutting pieces of steak and shoving them into his mouth, several at a time, chewing and talking, very drunk and red in the face, when a chunk of meat got caught in his throat and he couldn't swallow or speak. Cotter, who was trained in the Heimlich maneuver, calmly walked around behind Schneider's chair and pulled the short, corpulent real estate broker to his feet. Then he clasped his hands around Schneider's girth and with a mighty tug pulled upward. The steak dislodged with dramatic force, shooting ten feet across the room. Schneider gasped for air and sank into his chair, his blue blazer and starched white shirt askew. He loosened the striped rep Princeton tie at his neck and looked ashamed.

"I'm so embarrassed," he said, uncharacteristically meek. He managed a wan smile to his dinner companions, showing small, ivory-colored teeth. "I'm so sorry," he repeated, looking blankly at the table in front of him. For a moment there wasn't a sound in the room. Then Allan pitched over to the side and hit the floor with such a thud, the walls shook.

2

ALLAN SCHNEIDER was a balding man with a cherubic face and the aristocratic bearing of an Edwardian lord. Princeton-educated, of good Protestant and German stock, a member of the Vanderbilt Club, he had his name and social credentials listed every year in the Blue Book, a privately published social register sold under the counter at Book Hampton to "our crowd." He owned a historical mansion in East Hampton, a cooperative apartment at Forty Central Park South in Manhattan, and an eight-bedroom retreat at Dark Harbor, Maine, one of New England's most exclusive resorts. He was also a trustee of the East Hampton Historical Society and a member of the board of directors of Guild Hall. He wore, proudly, his family crest on his pinkie ring, on the breast pocket of his dinner jacket, and on the vamp of his black velvet evening pumps.

Like all brilliant salesmen, he was charismatic, an engaging conversationalist who enjoyed meeting people. Nevertheless, there was something in his small, deep-set eyes that was coolly assessing. He was a keen judge, of value and of character. His "reading" of people, as he would put it, was his greatest gift in the real estate business. "I understand people," he was fond of saying. "I know what people want. I know *about* people." About rich people especially. He was fascinated by the wealthy, by who they were and what they liked and how they lived. He loved elegance and possessions; most of all, he loved houses.

You could see it in the way he showed houses to his clients, in the relish he took in the home's location or in some obscure architectural detail, like the "scuttlehole" trapdoor in the roof through which the occupants scurried to put out chimney fires. He knew everything about houses, from how foundations were poured to the way ceramic roof tiles were baked. He didn't just know who McKim, Mead and White were, he knew which of their houses had historical importance and which were considered, in his words, "trash." He also knew the modern masters personally — Gwathmey, Futterman, and Jaffe. Late at night, over an Armagnac, he talked wistfully about parcels of land and great beach cottages like an aging lothario recalling lost passions.

His love of business, mixed with a quick mind and a charming but superior attitude, gave him the golden touch in Hamptons real estate. For more than twenty years he ruled the market, becoming famous for listing the choicest homes with the most exclusive clientele. Schneider's firm made some of the flashiest sales in the history of Hamptons real estate. It was the driving force behind the sale of the $6 million acreage for the new Atlantic Golf Club and was the agency that sold Calvin Klein his house for $6 million. His firm twice handled the sale of Toad Hall, the soaring glass-and-steel Charles Gwathmey–designed structure with a two-story greenhouse on Further Lane in East Hampton: once when Texas art collector Francois de Menil sold the house to Seagram scion Edgar Bronfman Jr. for $7.5 million, and a second time when Bronfman sold the house to art dealer Larry Gagosian for $8.5 million.

Schneider had the authority to pull off some breathtaking deals. "When I started asking people who was the best," said Mickey Schulhof, then vice-chairman of Sony in America, who was shopping for a house, "his name was at the top of everyone's list." One day Schulhof and his wife, Paola, were being driven by Schneider to see a house for sale on Further Lane when on the way they passed an old French mansard house of white brick on Egypt Lane, near the ocean. Schulhof pointed out the house and said, "That's exactly the kind of house I want." Allan remembered that the house had only recently been sold, and he picked up his car phone and called the new owners on the spot. "Look," he said, "I know you just moved in, but if you sell my client the house, I'll sell you something else you'll like better, and you'll make several hundred thousand dollars' profit." Twenty minutes later Schulhof had his house and Schneider had a six-figure commission.

It was also Schneider's agency that sold the house that nearly bankrupted the entire town of Southampton, Barry Trupin's hideous Dragon's Head, for $2.3 million, a feat they said couldn't be done for half that amount. Despite the legend that it was Truman Capote who convinced CBS chairman William Paley to buy twenty-five acres of oceanfront land on Peters Pond Lane as a gift for the Nature Conservancy, it was actually Schneider who came up with the idea. Years later Paley's estate sold the property instead of bequeathing it as a gift. And when Jackie Onassis's sister, Princess Lee Radziwill, married the film director Herb Ross, and the pair decided to leave Southampton for the artier, more show-biz East Hampton, they turned to Allan Schneider. He not only sold the Rosses an oceanfront "cottage" on Highway Behind the Pond for $6.2 million but flipped Radziwill's old Southampton house to magazine publisher Frances Lear for $2.5 million.

Perhaps Schneider's greatest pride and joy was West End Road, his "street of dreams" in East Hampton. He took great pleasure in driving important clients to this narrow street in his gray Mercedes sedan and boasting, "I sold every house on this road at least one time." The road is less than a mile in length and is perhaps the most exclusive strip of property in the Hamptons. It is unusual not only because it is a dead end but because it funnels into a narrow promontory that separates the ocean from Georgica Pond. The houses on the south side of the street stand high above the dunes in fields of saw grass. Those across the road have an unparalleled view of the shimmering, halcyon Georgica Cove to the north, its far shore dotted with sprawling mansions and timbered boathouses.

"They used to call this the 'Trippe Strip,' " Schneider explained, a hint of a British accent sometimes seeping into his voice, "because the 'anchor' of the twenty or so houses on this road used to be the one owned by Juan Trippe, the founder of Pan American Airlines and a president of the Maidstone Club. Calvin Klein is in there now, and it's no longer the anchor. I guess you could say the first one on the right that I sold to the director Steven Spielberg is the anchor."

Schneider was gesturing to an unprepossessing white gate wide enough for only one car to squeeze by. A small placard stuck in the ground said, QUELLE BARN. Tall bushes hid from view anything other than a dark gravel drive. "It doesn't look like much from the outside," Schneider said, "but it's the only house in the Hamptons that was ever guarded by a crack team of retired Mossad, the Israeli secret service."

Without a doubt, not only is Spielberg's house the most important on the block, but the film director is probably the jewel in the crown of the Hamptons' hierarchy of celebrity. In the Hamptons there is ne plus ultra than Spielberg and his wife, "Katie," actress Kate Capshaw. He is a reluctant potentate, in residence only during the summer months and even then rarely seen in public. In fact, he is loathe to have his presence in the Hamptons publicized at all (even though he has twice invited the cameras of *Architectural Digest* beyond his gate and protective shrubbery), seeing the place as a sacred refuge.

The Spielbergs live in pristine white buildings of classic geometric shapes — one, a massive square barn attached to a huge circular silo; another, a long, low rectangle — all sheathed in rows of cedar shingles stained milky gray. At the highest point of the main building is a weather vane in the silhouette of a *Tyrannosaurus rex*, a homage not only to *Jurassic Park* but to Spielberg's abiding interest in dinosaurs. The guest house has a spine of glass skylights and three separate master bedroom suites. Since this is a child-friendly estate, each suite has its own adjoining dormitory room, designed in a ship's-captain theme, furnished with four built-in bunk beds. The artifacts of family life are everywhere: games and toys, easels and paints, musical instruments and myriad computers or state-of-the-art electronic equipment. A giant-sized TV screen disappears out of sight into the floor of the guest barn at the push of a button, so as not to detract from the beautiful views. On the walls are pieces of expensive American folk art or framed drawings and paintings by the Spielbergs' favorite artists — their children and their children's friends, making up an art gallery that is changed and edited with the care of the Metropolitan Museum of Art. Although the main building was originally decorated by Steve Ross's widow, Courtney, the newer buildings were decorated in similar Arts and Crafts style by Naomi Leff, a Manhattan decorator who also did the Spielbergs' Los Angeles home.

Steven Spielberg is a California boy who came to visit the Hamptons for the first time one summer twenty years ago to see his best friend and mentor, Steve Ross, the man who melded Time Inc. with Warner Communications Inc. into the largest media empire of the time. Ross lived for years on West End Road and practically insisted that Spielberg be his next-door neighbor. It wasn't hard; Spielberg paid one visit to the Hamptons and, like so many before him, caught Hamptons land lust. In 1983 Ross was tipped off by Allan Schneider that the widow who owned the three-acre property next door was thinking about selling, and one weekend when Spielberg was visiting, the two friends walked over and rang the woman's doorbell. They introduced themselves ("This man is Steven Spielberg," Ross is reported to have said to the startled lady) and told the woman that if she wanted to sell her house, Mr. Spielberg would be happy to buy it. "Within a week," Allan Schneider said, "they had a deal for one point two five million dollars — a steal." Spielberg reportedly didn't even lay out the money. Ross negotiated the price for him, Warner Communications fronted the money, and Spielberg reimbursed the company later.

While Gwathmey was busy renovating the barn, Spielberg was too busy to come out to the Hamptons and check on the progress, so Ross would sneak next door every week or so, check it out himself, and then call up Spielberg. "Don't tell Gwathmey I told you this," he would say, "but I think the windows are too small." The next thing Ross and Spielberg did together was to secure as much abutting property as they could get their hands on. Word spread among the neighbors that if they wanted to sell, Ross and Spielberg were collecting property like a moat. They even bought a huge chunk of farmland clear across Georgica Cove so nobody would build an ugly house in the distance and block their sunset.

Just across from Quelle Barn, through a time warp 100 years into the past, stands a primly painted white and blue-gray Gothic mansion with a small portico and an exquisite English garden. This is the mist-shrouded Grey Gardens, now the home of former *Washington Post* editor Ben Bradlee and his wife, writer Sally Quinn. The house gained infamy years before when it was the home of Edith Bouvier Beale, the paternal aunt of Jacqueline Kennedy Onassis, and her daughter, Edie. "Big Edie" and "Little Edie," as they were known, could have had a life as promising as the rest of their family, but Mr. Beale died young and left them to live in the big house by the ocean. By the mid-seventies, the two women had become charmingly eccentric. By then a spinsterish sixty, Little Edie wore Jackie's designer hand-me-downs — upside down; she was several sizes larger than her svelte cousin and had to wear the skirts with the Chanel hemlines bunched around her waist. Big Edie never left her bed on the second floor, which was littered with garbage, and the two women lived in the house with twenty-eight cats, no litter box, and a raccoon that was fed a steady diet of white bread.

The house had been built by Mrs. Stanhope Phillips in 1908 and later was occupied by Anna Gilman Hill, an internationally famous horticulturist who built the high concrete walls surrounding the gardens, to break the ocean wind. Within this courtyard she planted all pale flowers, gentle blues and grays that played against the frequent mists and gave the house its melancholy name. Under the Beales' neglect, the gardens had become a tick-infested thicket of vines and brambles, in the midst of which stood the rusted carcass of a 1937 Cadillac that once belonged to Mr. Beale and had great sentimental value to Little Edie.

The town hated the eyesore at Grey Gardens and when an oil burner repairman tipped off the fire safety officials that the burner was unsafe, the town seized on the opportunity to decide it wasn't humane to allow these eccentrics to live not only in filth but with a dangerous oil heater, and one October day the East Hampton police, the Suffolk County Health Department, and the ASPCA raided the house with a search warrant. They burst in with a photographer and reporter in tow and took pictures of what they called "evidence," including mounds of raccoon excrement. Mrs. Beale, thinking she was being robbed by stickup men, became hysterical as she was photographed in her bed. "It was a raid," Little Edie complained to the local paper, calling it the work of a "mean, nasty Republican town." She said her mother thought it was the "most disgusting, atrocious thing ever to happen in America."

The plight of the clueless mother and daughter became a national cause célèbre and eventually the subject of a fascinating film by Albert and David Maysles, called *Grey Gardens.* The attention motivated Jacqueline Onassis and a few other embarrassed relatives to cough up enough money to make the house habitable for the Beales. When Big Edie died in 1985, Little Edie finally decided to sell the place, and Allan Schneider was enlisted to find a buyer.

"It didn't take me long," he said, "because the house was a gem, really. The Bradlees bought it for the bargain price of eight hundred and forty thousand dollars." The day Bradlee bought the estate, he discovered that the legend of Grey Gardens was so great that the front door had been stolen off its hinges. It turned out that an over-zealous fund-raiser for Guild Hall, the local East Hampton cultural center, had used the door as raffle prize. The woman who won it was disturbed to learn that it had been stolen and refused to claim her prize. Bradlee only discovered what happened to his front door from reading an account in the *New York Times*. Unfortunately for him, a more troubling legacy than the house's notoriety was the stench of cat urine that had soaked into the wood of the house, forcing him to rip out a portion of the floors and walls in the east end in an attempt to get rid of the odor.

As Schneider drove farther down West End Road, the gravel top narrowed protectively and the hedgerows grew higher for privacy. The houses could be glimpsed only in the brief hiatus of a driveway, if at all. "That's Iona Dune, the writer Ring Lardner's old house," he said, "which was a play on another house called Ona Dune. One year as a joke Lardner renamed his house The Mange. Next door is the house built by his pal Grantland Rice, the prince of sports-writers in the nineteen twenties. And that's Michael Cimino's house. Four acres. He might have bought it in part with his fee for mak-ing one of the great flop movies of all time, *Heaven's Gate*." Cimino wanted to call the house Heaven's Gate as well, but that name was usurped by television journalist Judy Licht and her advertising-executive husband, Jerry Della Femina, for their own oceanfront home. Cimino sent Della Femina and Licht a letter demanding that they cease and desist using the name Heaven's Gate, to which the couple pointed out that Cimino didn't invent the expression; it was from the Old Testament. The Della Feminas stuck with the name.

Farther along, hidden up a curving drive, was the former Juan Trippe estate, which was the subject of a court battle between the Trippe heirs, who wanted to divide the eight and a half acres into smaller parcels, and their next-door neighbor, Cox Communications heiress Katherine Johnson Rayner. The grown Trippe children hadn't occupied the 8,000-square-foot estate since matriarch Elizabeth Stettinius Trippe died in 1983. They wanted to divide the property into four buildable plots and applied for a zoning board variance, which would have raised the value of the property from $6 million to $8 million. The estate was still intact when Calvin Klein and his wife, Kelly, came along to rescue it.

"I sold this to Calvin and Kelly Klein in 1991," said Allan. Klein leveled the main building and, with the design talent of Thierry Despont, had it rebuilt into an airy palace, a paean to one of his own commercials. Other than the stained dark floors, made of antique wood planks brought from a Vermont barn, everything in the house is white or muted shades of sand and gray, including sheer white drapes on every window that billow like spinnakers in the ocean breeze. In perhaps the most unusual move of any homeowner in the Hamptons, Klein filled in the large terraced swimming pool behind the house (because he said it distracted him from the vista of the dunes, ocean, and horizon) and had it sodded over. As a final touch the dunes were hand-planted with 7,000 blades of saw grass and 4,000 square feet of pine trees, to make them look as perfect as a fragrance ad. Total cost, purchase and renovation: $10 million.

Finally, Schneider came to the last on the road, perhaps the most privileged tract of land in all the Hamptons. "It is the only house in the Hamptons from which you can see both the Atlantic and Georgica Pond in one sweeping gaze," he said reverently. The huge barnlike structure was a wedding gift from Ann Cox Chambers, the daughter of the 1920 Democratic presidential candidate, James Cox, to her daughter Katherine on the occasion of her marriage to former Condé Nast publishing executive William Rayner. Mrs. Cox paid approximately $4 million for the house, buying the adjacent wetlands for an additional $3 million. With views so extraordinary, the Rayners have kept the inside of the house strikingly simple. The southern side of the living room is all sliding doors of wood and glass, an impractical touch because the damp continually warps the wood. The rooms were decorated by society designer Mark Hampton, the bleached-blond floors covered with sisal carpets and the furniture upholstered in Hamptons signature khaki-and-white stripes. Although Mrs. Rayner had a small second story added to the house, there are still only six bedrooms. Mrs. Rayner prefers a more formal country lifestyle than many, and there's a ritual time for breakfast, lunch, tea, massage, and cocktails.

Schneider always ended his tour not on West End Road but on Main Street in the village of East Hampton, pulling his Mercedes beyond the white picket fence of his own home, one of the most charming and distinguished houses in all the Hamptons. "This is the Summer White House," Allan explained, his head tilting back. " 'Tyler House,' we call it, the former summer residence of John Tyler, the tenth president of the United States. 1836 Greek Revival." Situated on a rise across the road from the manicured town green and pond, the immaculately kept four-bedroom house had deep green shutters; a low, overhung porch; and an American flag fluttering outside the side door.

The house was furnished with a museum-quality collection of antiques — Chippendale cupboards and lowboys, a $45,000 Empire dining room table, a $40,000 George III linen press and bar, and hundreds of nineteenth- and twentieth-century hunting prints. Hunting scenes were everywhere in the house, from the embroidered place settings on the dining room table to the rim of the teacups. The scent of lilies, overflowing from tall Chinese vases, mixed with the clean smell of furniture polish filled the air. In the plush master bedroom on the second floor, Allan slept in a Federal four-poster bed worth $20,000.

Even in the highly social world of the Hamptons, an invitation to one of Schneider's elegant parties was a coveted ticket. At one time or another the gamut of the inner Hamptons' hierarchy, what Schneider called the "local noblesse," was invited to a party at Tyler House, to mingle with visiting notables such as Donald Trump or Governor Mario Cuomo. Schneider gave parties nearly every week in the summer, strawberries and champagne for as many as 100 people. Other times he would give *intime* dinner parties for eight, after which he would play piano in the living room and challenge his guests to Name That Tune.

Christmas was Allan's favorite time to entertain, and under his direction the house took on a storybook quality. The florist literally decked the halls and mantels of Tyler House with holly, there were wreaths and candles in every window, and the pine trees on the front lawn were roped with blue lights. On Christmas Eve, near midnight, Schneider and a small group of close friends would bundle up in their coats and hats and mufflers and step out onto Main Street of "the most beautiful village in America," according to one register of historic landmarks. The group would wend its way past the serene pond with the Christmas tree frozen in place, along a path by the textured tombstones of the South End Burying Ground, where the town fathers were laid to rest, and into the brick-and-mortar sanctuary of Saint Luke's Church. Later, a little teary-eyed and sentimental, Allan Schneider took communion at midnight mass.

One night, after one of the many parties, when the staff was in the kitchen cleaning up and Allan was seeing a last guest to the door, the man turned to him and said, "Allan, your house is beautiful. Picture perfect! The only problem is, there's nobody sharing it with you."

Allan looked flustered. "Yes there is," he said, and shut the door.

3

IN 1969, when Allan Schneider arrived on the East End of Long Island, as the fin-shaped piece of land is sometimes called east of the Shinnecock Canal, the Hamptons were on the brink of enormous change. Until then the only phone book the Summer Colony needed was the Blue Book, and when you picked up a phone to make a call, it was still possible that a local operator would ask with a brisk Yankee twang, "Number please?"

Until then, the string of villages and hamlets that collectively compose "the Hamptons" — Southampton, Water Mill, Bridge-hampton, Sagaponack, Wainscott, and East Hampton — was home to only 27,000 year-round residents and some 6 million ducks (originally imported from Peking). But in 1951 a tiny airport was developed in East Hampton and in the late sixties a roadway from the Long Island Expressway was extended to Route 27, challenging what had kept the Hamptons safe for two centuries — its remoteness. Also, the prosperity of the postwar economy afforded upper-middle-class families vacation homes for the first time. These newcomers to the Hamptons, although wealthy by any normal standard, weren't rich enough to build the kind of grand summer "cottages" (they were always called cottages, no matter how big they were) that lined the grassy dunes of Gin and Lily Pond Lanes. Instead, they built fashionably low-key "second homes," as they came to be called. So great was the influx that between 1950 and 1960, the population of East Hampton alone grew by 68.3 percent and three out of every four new homes built were for "summer people." The migration of these common millionaires — many of them self-made in the manufacturing or retail business — was so distressing to Hamptons society that the determinedly protective local news-paper of record, the *East Hampton Star,* which for nearly fifty years had run a column called the "Summer Colony," officially declared 1969 as "the end of the Summer Colony" and did away with the heading in the paper.

The seventies were chaotic for the staid Hamptons. There was even a jingle about the neatly discernible lines that had divided them until then: Southampton was for the sporting rich (inherited wealth); Bridgehampton for the nearly rich (working on it); and East Hampton for the *really* rich (a meritocracy of the self-made). In each community the Summer Colony denizens knew one another, their children went to private boarding schools together or to summer camp in Maine, they all belonged to the same clubs: in Southampton, the Meadow for tennis, the Southampton Bathing for the beach, and the Shinnecock or the National for golf and in East Hampton, the Maidstone Club, of course, for everything.

At the same time the new wave was arriving, the Blue Book hegemony that made the Hamptons famous was breaking down — the du Ponts, Fords, Bouviers, Vanderbilts, Auchinclosses, Hearsts, Mellons, and Murrays were dying off or moving out. The cost of keeping up the rambling, unheated cottages became exorbitant, especially for the diluted resources of the grandchildren of the families who built them before there was such a thing as income tax. Thus, the legendary estates of the Hamptons began to be sold off one by one. One of the first to go, in 1949, in East Hampton, was "The Fens," a twenty-five-acre estate owned by Mrs. Lorenzo E. Woodhouse, a pillar of society and a member of the Maidstone Club, whose husband had been president of the Merchant National Bank of Burlington, Vermont. The formal, Italianate gardens were famous for their boxwood topiaries of birds and animals in trellis-enclosed compartments, and the Summer Colony was stunned when the hedges were mowed down, the land parceled off into lots, and the outbuildings sold off as individual homes. A few years later, when ranch houses were built along Three Mile Harbor, it seemed as if the end had come. "The implications," moaned the *East Hampton Star,* "are staggering."

When Allan Schneider first came to the East End, he didn't need a crystal ball to see what was happening. After being brought up in Brooklyn Heights and graduating from Princeton, he spent most of his life in New York City, visiting the Hamptons on summer weekends. He did the debutante circuit and dated his fair share; he had conquests from Dallas to Philadelphia's Main Line. After a brief stint writing advertising copy on Madison Avenue, he went on to public relations, for Mattel, where, he always joked, his greatest success was the promotion of a little red truck.

In 1969 he abruptly moved to the Hamptons. He was fed up with Manhattan, the crime and the dirt. He told his brokers that he came out for a party one Saturday afternoon, intending to drive back to New York the same night, but his beat-up old Mercedes died on him and he was forced to stay over. He spent the next day in Southampton, found it difficult to tear himself away, and stayed another night; finally on Monday morning he had to force himself to return to Manhattan. Allan had succumbed to Hampton's land lust — that inexorable gnawing desire to own a piece of the landscape — which has been bewitching visitors for centuries. By 1970 he had ditched his New York life and invented a new one in the Hamptons.

His first job was selling real estate for a small firm called the Carolyn Rose Agency in Water Mill. Schneider was a natural at the job, so proud of the first house he sold on the corner of Maple and Lumber Lanes that he framed a black-and-white photo of it and hung it on a wall in his office for the rest of his life. As he began to assess what was happening in the real estate market, he was surprised to find the local real estate business so frozen in time. In the early seventies there were only half a dozen or so brokers operating in all the Hamptons, about the same number there had been for twenty years. They were mostly mom-and-pop operations, ancillary businesses of insurance brokerages, with scratched oak desks, green metal filing cabinets, a yellowing assessor's map, and a fern shedding in the corner. Many of the salespeople were retirees, housewives, or widows, frequently tough old Yankee women in slacks and cardigans. There was no financing advice and not much of a sales pitch.

The only money to be made was through sales to the rich Summer Colony crowd, but the rich bought from only two brokers, Lyda Barclay, in Southampton, a charming Southern lady who had the touch, and Mrs. Condie "Boots" Lamb in East Hampton, who bought artist Thomas Moran's historic house and was a member of the Maidstone Club, which meant that she was on the inside. Being on the inside in the Hamptons was what it was all about, Allan decided. He joked that he was "our man in Havana" in the insular world of Hamptons real estate, a New York–style broker with an inside track in the East End. But Allan also held that the real secret was not knowing just the blue bloods but the workmen who fixed the houses, the farmers who were selling off their land, and the local builders who had their ear to the ground. So while he memorized the names of the Fortune 500 presidents and ingratiated himself over cocktails on Gin Lane, he was also just as chummy with the local police and schoolteachers. He gave cocktail parties in his modest house in Mecox, a farming area around a scenic pond; he lunched; he networked; he frequented local bars — and he loved every minute of it. He kept himself so busy that few people ever stopped to question why he was alone.

It wasn't so lonely at Bobby Van's, where Allan went to drink every night. Bobby Van's, the celebrated Bridgehampton saloon and restaurant, became Schneider's "real estate central" for much of the seventies and eighties. Bobby Van's opened the same year Schneider showed up in town. It was a roomy wood-paneled bar and grill on the north side of Main Street. The eponymous owner was a Juilliard School dropout and as good a schmoozer as he was a saloon piano player, the perfect kind of host. In the off-season, when the rest of Bridgehampton was like a ghost town, Bobby Van's was filled with people at night. The food was cheap and hearty, and the farmers and workmen ate dinner there, as did Truman Capote, who lived nearby in Sagaponack, and James Jones and Kurt Vonnegut and Willie Morris, who wrote an op-ed piece in the *New York Times* mythologizing Bobby Van's as an oasis of warmth and country bonhomie in the bleakness of the gray Hamptons winter. Allan Schneider began to spend several nights a week there too, drinking at the bar till the early hours of the morning and chatting up strangers; soon he felt he knew half the town.

It was one night in the winter of 1971, two years after Allan Schneider moved to the Hamptons, that he met Paul Koncelik at Bobby Van's. Koncelik, twenty-three, an unemployed carpenter, looked little more than a fresh-scrubbed kid, tall and handsome, with wavy brown hair and a roguish grin. He certainly didn't look old enough to have a wife and a small son and to be struggling to kick-start his own construction company. Schneider had seen him work the bar around Bobby Van's, quite the ladies' man. One night Koncelik and Schneider struck up a conversation about an Andy Warhol movie they had both seen called *Heat.* Schneider remembered all the funny dialogue from the movie — he had a talent for quoting movie dialogue, Broadway lyrics, and poetry — and he and Koncelik downed martinis and talked until nearly closing time.

Paul Koncelik grew up in the Northwest Woods, one of the last undeveloped areas of East Hampton, unfashionably far north of the highway. He was the oldest of ten kids, a gentle man whom his brothers and sisters admired. His father was a teacher at Bridgehampton High School, and several of his siblings were attorneys. Paul was a gifted carpenter, a master at his trade from the time he was a teen, able to build an entire house practically by himself. He just somehow had a hard time holding down a job. Although he was married, he prowled the local bars, priding himself on his charm and good looks. He had known lots of unusual types from the summer crowd, but he had never met anyone as fascinating, and certainly nobody who had ever taken as keen an interest in him, as Allan Schneider. "You are a diamond in the rough," Schneider would reassure Koncelik. "A diamond in the rough!"

Schneider insinuated himself into the life of Paul Koncelik and his wife, Carol. He took up the young couple like a hobby. He dined with them a couple of times a week at his house in Mecox or took them to dinner at expensive restaurants. He adored their little boy, Jesse, whom he showered with expensive gifts, and was eventually named Jesse's godfather. When Paul needed money, Schneider gave him work painting and renovating his house; when Paul wanted to build a spec house, Allan loaned him $40,000. Even when the sale fell through and the bank foreclosed, Allan forgave him the loan.

In return, all Schneider seemed to want from Koncelik was companionship. Schneider sometimes discussed his "lady friends," saying things like "Linda forgot her shoes at my place the other night." But clearly he doted on Paul, who was constantly cheered by the attention and support. As the years passed, the two drinking buddies and confidantes fell into a deep and abiding friendship.

4

RAY WESNOFSKE, the chairman of the board of Bridgehampton National Bank, lives in a French château–style house with a mansard roof, high on a ridge of land overlooking the village of Bridgehampton, a considerable chunk of which he owns. Directly below the house, workers with heavy machinery harvest potatoes from rolling farmland, and in the distance the white spire of the Bridgehampton Presbyterian Church emerges from a dark canopy of autumn leaves. Beyond it all, the Atlantic Ocean shimmers, miragelike, across a pale blue horizon.

Of the many providential moments in Allan Schneider's life, one of the luckiest was in 1969 when Wesnofske, the scion of the South Fork's premier farming family, called the Carolyn Rose Agency and by chance got Schneider on the phone. "My father had given me a piece of property," Wesnofske remembered. "My wife and I decided to sell our old house and build a new one. I called the Carolyn Rose Agency and Allan showed up to look at my house. My wife, Lynn, and I enjoyed him very much. The guy was brilliant. He had a photographic memory and he could remember everything people said. He knew every house in Bridgehampton and not just who every farmer was but the names of his wife and children."

At one time Ray's dad, Remi Wesnofske, farmed or leased more than 1,000 acres of South Fork farmland, buying when it was cheap. Now, in Ray's custody, the land was making the family rich. Ray Wesnofske was no country-bumpkin farmer either; he was a Cornell graduate, an imaginative businessman, and a clever real estate speculator. Many of the other landholders who got rich in the Hamptons housing boom of the past thirty years were from families like Wesnofske's, the children and grandchildren of Polish and Irish immigrants who owned valuable fields south of Montauk Highway, the fertile, flat farming area closest to the ocean.

Beginning in the mid-1800s, the Hamptons had become the destination of an exodus of Polish and Irish farmers who came to America looking for fertile soil to till. Arriving first in Brooklyn and Queens, they worked their way eastward, to Hicksville, like the Wesnofske family, then to the East End, drawn by the legend of the Bridgehampton loam. The so-called no-fail soil is perhaps one of the most unusual natural blessings of the Hamptons. The result of a glacial moraine rolling over the surface of the East End 6 million years ago, the soil is nearly stone-free and very mineral-rich. This unusual soil is also porous and spongy, with little runoff on the flat terrain, so it holds water like a camel's hump and needs little irrigation except in dry spells. So plentiful is the groundwater that the entire population of the Hamptons still depends on it for its drinking water.

It was the Poles who began to plant large fields of potatoes, the food of midland Europe, fat and heavy Katahdin, Chippewa, and Cobbler potatoes. Before the Poles, the crops had been mostly fruits and other vegetables. They tilled the land of others, first as hired hands, then by leasing, and finally by buying up tracts. In 1908 there were six Polish families in Southampton; in 1918 there were 331. The Irish farmers were originally servants who bought out the little shanties they lived in and started to farm. By the end of the century, immigrant Polish and Irish farmers owned an estimated 70,000 acres of land.

These farms did well for two generations, until competitive prices from industrial farming and easy refrigerated truck routes from the Midwest changed the economics of the business. World War II hurt the farmers further still, and things got worse as taxes soared in the sixties and seventies and vacant land was taxed at its "highest and best use," which of course was for real estate development. The farmers' children had to pay estate taxes on the land when they inherited, a financial time bomb. Rather than burden their heirs with huge taxes they would be unable to pay, the farmers began to sell off half an acre here, an acre there. Years later, working farms were given a tax break if the farmers would forever dedicate the land to agricultural use, rendering it unavailable for resale. The attrition rate of working farms in the East End was dramatic. In 1875 there were 218 farms in East Hampton; in 1935, only 117. By 1940 there were only 55 farms; and in 1966, only 20 in what was once the greatest agricultural resource of New York State.

The Wesnofske family was smarter than most farmers, and they began to farm less and speculate in real estate more. Allan Schneider became Ray Wesnofske's personal real estate broker, finding him properties and giving him the edge in a fast-moving market. "He'd hear about a property for sale that was a good buy and he'd call me up and say, 'You must buy this! You must!' " That's what happened in 1975 when a small two-bedroom farmhouse on Montauk Highway in Bridgehampton, most recently a marble and tile showroom, came up for sale at a good price. "He kept pressuring me into buying it," Wesnofske said. " 'What am I going to do with that building?' I asked, and he said, 'You are going to rent it to me.' " Schneider had rancorously outgrown being an employee at the small Carolyn Rose Agency, where he had become the top earner, and wanted to strike out on his own and keep all the profits. He felt the time was ripe in the Hamptons for a sleek, modern real estate office to open, one that would cater to the nascent upscale market, something that looked and felt chic, not dowdy, something called the Allan M. Schneider Agency. "I don't think it's necessary for someone to all of a sudden have a lobotomy when they start dealing in country properties," Schneider said, "to suddenly put on Oshkosh B'Gosh shoes and sit around a cracker barrel in a sweater with holes."

Wesnofske bought the building, and Schneider had it painted pristine white, the shutters deep hunter green, the same dark color he chose for the walls of his office, which he decorated with tasteful rows of equally spaced framed Audubon and hunting prints. Out front he hung a shingle on a signpost and parked his Mercedes by the front door. "From the day he opened the door of that first office," said Wesnofske, "it looked like he already made a million dollars' profit." As time went by, Wesnofske noticed that Allan gave the impression that he owned the building, and Wesnofske, who was amused by Schneider's airs, let it pass. Over the years, Wesnofske became Schneider's silent partner and closest business ally.

Schneider built his business by creating a brilliant salesforce of local people, "discovered" from other walks of life. He'd meet people, get to know them, and one day unexpectedly ask, "Did you ever think about selling real estate? I think it's worth talking about." His first "discovery" was Peggy Griffin, a Bridgehampton housewife who drove a school bus part-time. She also happened to be a Hildreth, one of Southampton's founding families, and she was trusted and admired by the local farmers with land to sell. Next came Price Topping, from another founding family, one that owned horse farms. Paul Brennan, whom Schneider first met when Brennan was thirteen years old, was the son of an Irish farmer whose father owned one of the largest farms south of the highway in Bridgehampton, ripe for being chopped up and sold. In East Hampton he enticed Charles Bullock, a Maidstone Club member with a house on Lily Pond Lane, into running the East Hampton office, and in Southampton he hired Richard Harris, the retired owner of a shipping line, who provided entry into the Southampton Association estate owners and the Meadow Club. Schneider was a brilliant tutor to his discoveries and nourished his sales staff, referring to them as his "family."

Perhaps Schneider's cleverest innovation was to open up multiple offices, one for each village, and cover the Hamptons octopus-like; first in Sag Harbor, then East Hampton, Southampton, soon Amagansett, each office identically outfitted with hunter green shutters, billiard-table green walls, and rows of beautifully framed hunting prints. He opened shop every morning by nine o'clock sharp, always dressed in a starched Oxford shirt, suit and tie, with fox-hunt-motif cuff links and tiepin. Salespeople were expected to dress appropriately as well, and he could not tolerate clutter on desks. "Get rid of those cardboard coffee cups," he would scream, aghast. He never complained if an employee used the company charge account to order fresh flowers for the office.

Although he was good to his "family" and engendered a loyal staff with long-term relationships, he did not suffer fools gladly and, after one of his famous three-hour lunches, could turn cutting and nasty. "He would hunt you down and dismantle your personality," one of his brokers said. It was no wonder that when the receptionist in his Bridgehampton office saw his car pulling up in the parking lot, she shouted out, "Here he comes!"

The distinctive green ALLAN M. SCHNEIDER, REAL ESTATE BRO-KER shingle, with a silhouette of a three-story white farmhouse, began to appear on the front lawns of the finest estates in the Hamptons. It became a status symbol to have the Schneider seal of approval on a home, and he could pick and choose which houses to spend his time marketing. Although a spate of other brokers sprang up out of nowhere, from 1975 on Allan Schneider "owned the Hamptons," said Robert Keene, Southampton's official historian. "His name was the magic word." He reached another milestone in 1981 when he signed an exclusive agreement with Sotheby's International Realty to represent its interests in the Hamptons, and now a second picture joined the one on the wall of the first little farmhouse that he sold. This one was of Amanda Burden, the daughter of Babe Paley and wife of Carter Burden, alighting from a private helicopter in the field just next to the Allan M. Schneider office in Bridgehampton, clients now literally dropping out of the sky for him.

5

IT WAS ALSO IN 1981 that Schneider solved his "empty house" problem. That spring Paul Koncelik arrived at Schneider's Mecox house, teary-eyed with the news that his wife had asked for a divorce. In the ten years Schneider had been his close friend and supporter, things had not gone well for Koncelik. His drinking had worsened, and for some years he and his wife had lived separate lives — Koncelik on one side of the house, Carol on the other.

"Well, it's her loss," Schneider said, consoling Koncelik and fixing him a drink.

"I was very upset about the divorce," Koncelik remembered of that night, "and Allan knew I was in a low slump. I was very down. I had nowhere to live, and Allan said, 'Okay, Paul. I'll rent a little house for you to live in.' So he rented a little house for me, and I wound up staying there only one night." The other nights Paul and Allan got very drunk together — Paul would pass out in the guest room. Eventually, "Allan asked me to move in with him because he was fond of me."

Koncelik knew what he was doing, even as he got entangled in the sterling-silver web of Schneider's life. He began to feel a little embarrassed by the implication of the situation, as Allan tried to polish his "diamond in the rough." He bought Paul a Dunhill suit and sent him to real estate school. He gave Paul a car to use — leased to the company — and a gas credit card. He had Koncelik put on the company health plan and made him a signatory on all his local charge accounts, including ones at the grocery, drug store, and liquor store.

When the Mecox house got too small for the two of them, Schneider moved them to a series of rented houses on Further Lane in East Hampton, each one grander than the former, until in 1983 he bought Easterly, a gracious shingled farmhouse at Hither Lane and Cross Highway, just down the road from Brigadoon, the famed estate of Evan Frankel, for $300,000. He spent more than a year and nearly $1 million in improvements before they moved in; while Easterly was being renovated, they traveled to Nantucket and Key West.

They drank more than their share; and inevitably the drunker Paul got, the more he hated himself. Some nights he would stalk off, leaving Schneider shattered, sitting alone in the house. Other occasions the real estate broker would wait for Koncelik to come home for dinner, only to wind up eating alone from a tray in front of the TV set. Allan could swear off the booze for a month or two and get the toxins out of his system, but Paul found it impossible to stop, even for a day — and Allan made it easy for him to continue. He also made it easy for him to come back. After one spat Schneider took him out to the garage, where a green 1953 MG was waiting. "Oh, look what we have here!" Schneider cried in mock surprise and handed Paul the keys — but not the title.

Allan finally admitted to Paul that there had once been someone special in his life, a man he knew from the city named John Phillip Nagel, who was married to a wealthy woman. Nagel, Schneider explained, bought a Georgian-style mansion on the ocean in Wainscott on Schneider's advice, but the house was in danger of being washed away by storms. Nagel had no insurance against beach erosion, but he did have fire insurance — when the house burned to the ground, he was accused of arson. Nagel was never convicted, but his life was ruined, his marriage was in shambles, and he later killed himself in a hotel room in Baltimore.

Paul Koncelik felt sorry for Schneider. "There was no one closer to him than I was," Paul said. "He didn't let anybody else but me inside." And so, as odd a couple as they were, they made a life together for ten years. "I was there for him when he got off from work to lay his thoughts on me," Paul explained, "and [to tell him] what I thought about different things, and he'd run things by me, about his business. He would say, 'Stick with me, Paul, you are going to be a very wealthy man.' "

Dr. Watson

BUY EVERYTHING in sight! Hock your gold teeth!" Allan Schneider told anyone who would listen to him. As the go-go eighties stock market pushed the Dow Jones toward the 2,000 mark for the first time in history, freshly minted millionaires were being pumped out daily. They were the cream of the baby-boomer generation: spoiled young urban professionals — stockbrokers, lawyers, junk-bond kings, financiers, and self-styled corporate raiders. This crop of brash "Masters of the Universe," as Tom Wolfe called them in *Bonfire of the Vanities*, was seeking not only second homes but an arena in which to compete socially. For them, the Jersey shore was too bourgeois. Connecticut was hot and buggy. But the fabled beaches of the Hamptons, a society unto itself only two hours from Wall Street, seemed just perfect. To own a home in the blue-blooded Hamptons was to have *arrived*. And so, pockets stuffed with cash, a generation of arrivistes invaded the East End in numbers never before seen.

Since they couldn't develop a caste system based on breeding ("Their money is so new, the ink is wet," Schneider sneered), the newcomers determined status the only way they knew how to — on the basis of possessions. The battle cry of the buyers in the eighties was "south of the highway." In the Hamptons, property value and social status are defined by location relative to Montauk Highway. Route 27, as it is also known, is a nondescript two-lane blacktop stretching west to east, thirty-seven miles long from the Shinnecock

Canal to Montauk Point. It is the jugular vein of the Hamptons, the only road in or out. It cuts a swath through class lines and the hearts of the status-conscious. For the past 350 years, the highway has been the boundary against which all land is valued.

This peculiar arbiter of status was originally the cart path of the Puritan settlers, who also moved their cattle and cows through its mud and over its deep wheel ruts. The road was laid out to be far enough inland from the ravages of the ocean (approximately two or three miles) for it to be protected from nor'easters and hurricanes — and to skirt the chain of ponds and kettle holes. Even when railroad tracks were extended to Montauk in 1894, they paralleled the highway (but were far enough north of it so as not to frighten the horses). The Indians had taken a less inland route and built a log bridge across Sag Pond. The bridge was so significant to the settlers that they even named the area Bridgehampton.

This former cart road has become a major vexation to people in the Hamptons; crowded, dangerous bumper-to-bumper traffic sometimes backs up for miles. Every summer the same tired jokes are told about drivers growing beards while waiting to make a left turn. One year New York magazine infuriated homeowners north of the highway by publishing maps of alternative routes through residential neighborhoods. Only the greenest Hamptonites complain about the traffic, it is said, with renters being the worst, spending all Saturday talking about how long it took them to get there the night before and worrying the whole next day about how long it will take to get back. The prevailing wisdom in the Hamptons is that if you have to work on Fridays in the summer, or be back in the office on Monday morning, you're not successful enough to live there.

But more than being an inconvenience, the highway is also dangerous. The only hospital is in Southampton, and the constant traffic makes it nearly impossible for ambulances and emergency vehicles to pass. In the sixties a plan was put forward by the state

Department of Transportation to build a new, $50 million, four-lane highway about two and a half miles inland of the present one; it would have completely bypassed Southampton, Bridgehampton, and East Hampton, letting out east of Amagansett. An organization called Halt the Highway insisted that bigger and better roads would only bring more traffic, not less, and that easier access would turn the Hamptons into yet another Long Island bedroom community.

"But we've already *been* discovered" was Schneider's opinion. "We should plan for it." Yet in 1974, after environmental groups claimed that the runoff from the new highway would adversely affect the natural aquifers (which supply all the drinking water for the Hamptons), the East Hampton town supervisor asked that the highway bypass be struck from the state budget, and the idea was killed forever. Traffic on Montauk Highway in the summer is a deadly bane to daily life in the Hamptons.

But foremost, the highway has remained an important real estate landmark. Over the centuries, as stronger houses were built, storms were no longer reason enough to build homes far inland, and because the land south of the highway was limited — as opposed to the tens of thousands of acres available to the north — this narrow band of property became the most prestigious and desirable, increasing its value tenfold. While north of the highway was mostly wooded, south of the highway boasted the kind of luminous landscapes that made the Hamptons legendary: shingled farmhouses and red barns surrounded by flat fields, swatches of green and toffee-colored farmland interrupted only by a pond just beyond the ocean's reach.

Some of the stigma about living north of the highway has been diminished, since there are many beautiful waterfront vistas facing Peconic Bay. Still, over the years living south of the highway has acquired a mythical aura. It is reputed that the temperature is always ten degrees cooler in the summer or five degrees warmer in the winter, or that the highway creates an invisible wall over which the humidity will not pass, or that there are fewer bugs. ("Ocean breezes when there is no air a quarter of a mile inshore," says a turn-of-the-century brochure for a rooming house, "and at this spot, no mosquitoes.") Indeed, because the land south of Route 27 is closer to the cooling breezes of the Atlantic, the temperatures are lower and the air feels less humid in the summer, and the converse is true in the winter; it actually does snow less south of the highway because of the proximity to the salt air. But most reputed benefits of living south of the highway are pure hogwash; there are not only mosquitoes south of the highway but also flies and ticks, and none more privileged than those to the north.

One's location relative to the highway — and when one arrived there — is sometimes discernible through one's telephone prefix. In the mid-eighties, when the phone company used up its ten thousand combinations for the two main telephone exchanges, 283 for Southampton and 324 for East Hampton, it added 287 and 329, respectively. New houses north of the highway were more likely to be assigned 287 and 329. So terrible was this numerical stigma that summer renters turned down houses that had the déclassé exchanges. Brokers were amazed to be told sometimes that the sale of a house was contingent on whether the seller would include the phone number as part of the deal; the phone company reported being offered bribes for the old exchange. One Southampton hostess in a 287 rental printed the 283 number of a secretarial service on the RSVP of her party invitations rather than give her shameful home number. The summer that Calvin Klein rented while his house was being renovated, he put up with phone calls for the previous occupants so as not to lose the house's 324 exchange. He lucked out when he got a 324 for his house on West End Road, as did Ron Perelman and his then spouse, TV gossipeuse Claudia Cohen, who were fortunate enough to inherit the previous owner's 324 exchange when they bought a Lily Pond Lane house. "Thank God," Cohen said drolly. "This means we won't be socially ostracized."

Worse than a 287 or a 329 exchange, however, is 288, the prefix for Westhampton Beach, or "Wronghampton," as it is sometimes called. Snobs like Schneider don't even consider Westhampton a part of the Hamptons at all, since it is on the western side of the Shinnecock Canal and is basically a modern creation of developers who gave it its "-hampton" name. It is considered a predominately Jewish community (although in reality it is probably no more Jewish than East Hampton is) and also suffers from a dearth of big-name star power (since Bob Fosse died, its most noted resident is Marvin Hamlisch). One summer a Westhampton man accused the Southampton restaurant basilico of anti-Semitism, claiming it refused his reservation because he had a Westhampton exchange. The owners of the restaurant denied it, but the issue was taken seriously enough to be reported in the *New York Times*.

Allan Schneider played to the weaknesses of the status seekers, and the summer renters were perhaps the most desperate. "Own or rent?" is a typical gambit at a Hamptons cocktail party, and although renters are paying through the nose for the privilege of a temporary residence at the seaside resort, they are dismissed by owners as second-class citizens. ("North or south?" is the next most frequently asked question.) Allan loathed dealing with rentals and turned them over to his salespeople, but he always cautioned, "This year's renter is next year's buyer." Smiling beatifically, he would tell a young couple hoping to rent for $25,000 for the season, "For fifty thousand dollars you get a wonderful house, a divine summer, and lots of new friends between May and September."

As the stock market continued its upswing, real estate prices began to skyrocket. In 1980 the price of an acre south of the highway jumped from $75,000 to $125,000, and by 1990, $250,000 for an oceanfront acre was not uncommon. A shiny new four-bedroom house on a potato field in Sagaponack, with a heated swimming pool and Har-Tru tennis court, that would have cost a whopping $300,000 in 1978 was commanding at least $800,000 five years later. When a buyer said that he wanted to buy a house for $200,000, Schneider chortled and said, "Forget it. This isn't Flushing."

The Wall Street money also ignited the greatest speculative housing explosion on Long Island since Levittown was built at the end of World War II. There just weren't enough existing mansions for all the hungry new money, so new ones were rushed onto the market by the thousands. The eighties' real estate boom became the ruination of two of the most beautiful hamlets of the Hamptons, Bridgehampton and Sagaponack. They had been relatively forgotten communities, overlooked in the desire to live in the more fashionable Southampton and East Hampton. But it was Bridgehampton and Sagaponack (which comes from the Indian word meaning "land of the great ground nuts [potatoes])" that had the desirable expanses of potato fields. Within the space of a few years, the sweeping fields began to look as if they had developed a pox. New arrivals used their homes as calling cards, erecting thousands of what they saw as architectural "personal statements."

The roots of this kind of house can be traced to 1965, when Charles Gwathmey, then a student of architecture without a license, designed for his artist father, Robert Gwathmey, a cedar-clad house of basic geometric shapes in a field in Amagansett. So beautiful was Gwathmey's house that it won over even the staunchest tradition-alists, and it became an icon of the kind of grace a modern house could command on an open field. It also became the kind of house to which every two-bit architect and nouveau riche millionaire as-pired. There was only one Gwathmey, but lots of imitators; before long everywhere you looked, there was a modern house being framed up on a potato field — each one a geometrically shaped Bauhaus rip-off. Even with three-acre minimum plot sites, the 10,000-square-foot modern and postmodern houses, pool houses, tennis courts, and swimming pools seemed to abut like status shrines lined row on row. The implications of what the *East Hampton Star* had called "staggering" twenty years before was now simply disastrous.

Paul Goldberger, architecture critic of the *New York Times*, described the glut of new homes as "architecture of shrill egotism — whose arrogance says as much about its owner's aesthetic tastes as about the extent of their responsibilities to the land on which they have settled." Parsonage Lane in Sagaponack, which ran through the center of large tracts of rich farmland, became so defiled with multimillion-dollar homes as to render the landscape unrecognizable. The Hamptons natives renamed it "Parvenu Lane." The rest of the hamlet is carved up with pocket communities built on dead-end streets, pretentiously called "closes" and often named after the builder's granddaughter or niece. One of the most grievous examples of the narcissistic assault on the fields stands on Fairfield Pond Lane, down the road from the house formerly owned by author John Irving and only half a mile from the Sagaponack dunes. A wealthy local man built a house made of corrugated steel. The rippled structure, which looks like the home of the tin woodsman from *The Wizard of Oz*, is surrounded by a moatlike pool, six feet wide, crossed by a paved footbridge. The house, galvanized and shiny, catches and reflects the brilliant Hamptons sun like a magnifying glass, and is visible for miles around as a burning mirror of light. The hapless couple who owned the property next door were blinded by the tin house at certain times of the day and spent $40,000 on trees and landscaping to cut off the view. But within months it was all dead: The house reflected the sunlight with such ferocity that it scorched the new landscaping to death.

2

WITH MULTIPLE OFFICES and a well-trained sales staff of more than seventy employees, the Allan M. Schneider Agency was like a tsunami rolling over the Hamptons real estate market. Schneider worked at it with zest. Bright and early every morning he was in his Bridgehampton office, crisp and sharp no matter how late he had been up or how much he had had to drink the night before. He supervised every deal that went through the company's many offices via a network of "managers," often fielding fifty phone calls a day from his salespeople, advising, cajoling, teaching. His mouth watered as he read the county clerk's transfer of deeds, and he tracked not only the sales of his own offices but those of every other broker. With his remarkable recall, he became a walking resource of every house, vacant lot, and fishing shack for sale on all the East End.

As the money poured in, Schneider began to live in a grand manner. In 1988 he bragged to *Manhattan Inc.* magazine that he had spent $1 million the previous year supporting his lifestyle, which included maintaining a pied-à-terre with a book-lined library on Central Park South in Manhattan. In a stroke of reverse chic, he also bought a five-bedroom vacation home in the WASP fortress of Dark Harbor, Maine, a house that once belonged to Lee Fencers, the owner of the Marshall Field's department stores. He began to spend every August in Dark Harbor to get away from the crowds in the Hamptons, and he would flatbed his Mercedes and white MG Roadster up to Maine and ferry his weekend guests, including Paul Koncelik, back and forth on a privately chartered plane.

He became much more pretentious now that he was rich. At the office he insisted that coffee be served to him and his clients on a Paul Revere silver tray, with hunting-motif china; at home only Absolut martinis were poured for guests into nine-ounce chilled Baccarat crystal stem glasses. He bought Noël Coward's cigarette lighter for his coffee table and a Lakeland terrier named Duff, that bit people. While he could be petulant and demanding, he was also boundlessly generous with his friends and employees. It tickled him to invite friends to go shopping with him at an exclusive store and then insist that they pick out something for themselves as a gift. At Christmas his bonuses to salespeople were better than those of any other agency in the Hamptons, and even his household staff received Hermès wallets stuffed with $100 bills. There was no employer more understanding when asked for an advance against next month's pay, and many of Schneider's close friends even say that they felt a sense of security in knowing him, that they could turn to him in an emergency and borrow five or ten or twenty thousand dollars without his ever bringing it up until they were ready to pay it back.

In May 1987 he and Paul moved into the historic Tyler House at 127 Main Street, which he bought from Ted Conklin, the owner of the American Hotel, for $700,000, over a few martinis. Conklin had purchased the old house two years earlier from the Riverhead Building Supply Company, which had taken it over when a contractor defaulted on a $550,000 bill. Conklin had made the place livable. It was an old-fashioned country home, with a formal central dining room, den, spacious living room, and four bedrooms on the second floor. Schneider spiffed up the entrance by adding Greek columns and in the back built an elegant pool house with sphinxlike statuary. A Manhattan decorator created the dominion of a WASP dreadnought. Schneider also acquired a doting housekeeper, Eula Ellsworth, who polished and cleaned and looked after him like a jealous mother. To complete the picture of a country squire, he hired a full-time French chef, Jean-Claude Lacosse. The young Frenchman was thin and effeminate, with a large nose and a thick Parisian accent. He was only slightly less grand than his employer, and Schneider especially liked the way Jean-Claude pronounced his name, "Mr. Schnei-dare," making him sound very Continental.

Even with his tremendous success, Schneider was outspending his income, leveraging considerable debt for his major purchases. A man of less pride might have cut back on his high living when in 1987 the Hamptons real estate market came crashing to a halt only seven months after he moved into Tyler House. On October 19, in what was the biggest calamity since the great crash of 1929, the Dow Jones plunged 508 points. Two years later the stock market took another historic dive, this time for 190 points. The impact on Hamptons real estate was about the same as jamming a crowbar into the spokes of a speeding bicycle. The rental market was the first to crash, down 3c percent the summer of 1988, and then the speculative housing market nosedived. Brokers scrambled for customers, and the fields of Sagaponack and Southampton were strewn with half-finished gargantuan homes, abandoned midstream by either their speculative builders or would-be homeowners who suddenly couldn't support a 10,000-square-foot house with Corian countertops in the kitchen. South of the highway became the Hamptons version of Tobacco Road, with mansions standing empty on muddy, unlandscaped lots, signs hand-painted on pieces of plywood nailed to the front door, HOUSE FOR SALE, CALL OWNER.

Schneider thought it unseemly — and bad for business — to fuss too much about the recession. Things would turn around before long — and he was right. In the long run, the crashes of 1987 and 1989 were but blips on the real estate radar screen. But in the interim, between all the houses and offices and employees,

Schneider started to fall behind in his bills. There were telltale signs, like one night at the Laundry restaurant when his American Express card was declined. The caterer had to wait for his check, and he told the plumber, who gossiped to the oil delivery company; eventually half the town knew Schneider was overextended. He began to borrow large sums of money to cover his debts — often from Ray Wesnofske, sometimes as much as $20,000 at a clip — but as soon as a real estate deal closed, he'd pay it right back. Schneider became adept at juggling creditors, but toward the end of the 1980s money was so tight that he even borrowed $6,500 from Paul Koncelik, wiping out the unemployed carpenter's savings account.

Paul Koncelik had been along on Schneider's incredible ride the past ten years, but being stuffed into the jump seat hadn't been very kind to him. He was still adorable and entertaining, although now his dimples were hidden in deep smile lines and his frame had disappeared under a layer of pudgy edema. Koncelik hadn't worked in years, despite the desk that sat waiting for him at the Allan M. Schneider Agency. Things would not have been so bad for him, perhaps, if every night didn't end in a blind drunken rage, bellowing at Schneider, who was mean and goading. Koncelik, in turn, seemed hell-bent on embarrassing the proper broker. One night he arrived at Schneider's $10,000 table at the Hampton Classic Horse Show so drunk that he fell face forward into his food. Another time he appeared at Tyler House in the middle of a cocktail party and, marching up to Schneider, bellowed something about "sucking cock!" Allan was so stunned and mortified that he let his martini glass tilt, all the vodka pouring out.

Increasingly the disagreements would dissolve into fisticuffs, ending with Schneider shouting to Jean-Claude, "Call the police! Call the police!" After these rows Koncelik would pack his one suitcase, throwing the rest of his belongings in a garbage bag, and drive into the woods, where he would sleep it off. Then a few days later, in need of clean clothes and a bath, he'd sheepishly turn up at Tyler House under the disapproving eye of the housekeeper.

The ultimate blowout was set off when Koncelik had the temerity to ask about Schneider's last will and testament — or lack of one. Schneider never wrote a will or assigned a power of attorney, afraid it would bring him bad luck. Koncelik brought up the issue because loyal Jean-Claude had been diagnosed with AIDS and had recently made out a will leaving all his earthly possessions to Schneider. Koncelik began to think that he had spent nearly twenty years at Schneider's side, as his companion as well as his bane, and wanted to make sure he would get some of the riches Schneider had promised him over the years. "You know, you're not that much older than me, Allan," Koncelik said to him one night in November 1991, "so maybe we should get it in writing. You know, I'm only eleven years younger than you, and longevity runs in your family."

Schneider tossed him out that night, vowing that this time he would not let Koncelik back in. Desperate to stick to his word, he rented a small house for Koncelik in Sag Harbor and had his company pay the bills. "Maybe this will be the best thing for him," Schneider said wistfully as Koncelik came to pick up his belongings. "He'll never get better living here." It broke Schneider's heart to see him leave, and he made sure to send over brand-new Ralph Lauren sheets and towels so that Paul would be comfortable. But Paul never actually lived in that house. Sometimes he slept in the guest room at Tyler House, and sometimes he just disappeared. Schneider really didn't care anymore. He just wanted him gone. He hadn't seen Koncelik for several days that December day in 1991 when he was celebrating the contract signing for his new Amgansett office.

Schneider was coming off one of his famous three-hour lunches at Gordon's restaurant when Bruce Cotter saw him in the street in East Hampton at about 5:30. Cotter realized that Schneider was too drunk to drive, so he suggested that Schneider come home with him — his wife, Carol Lynn, would cook them up some steaks for dinner.

3

ALLAN SCHNEIDER was declared dead at Southampton Hospital at 8:30 P.M., December 6, 1991, although most likely he was already dead on the floor of Bruce Cotter's dining room. The autopsy revealed that a second piece of steak, almost four inches long, was caught farther down his throat, half chewed in his drunken state. The Heimlich maneuver had managed only to revive him with enough air left in his lungs to apologize before he died of a massive heart attack.

By daybreak the next day, Saturday, Paul Koncelik was cut off from any access to Allan Schneider's estate by the more prudent senior members of Schneider's business. He was asked to return the 1991 Pontiac Grand Am that the company leased for him and to turn in the gas credit card too. He had to hitchhike to Williams Funeral Parlor for Allan's funeral, where he showed up, his clothes rumpled, reeking of alcohol. The alarm codes were changed at Tyler House, and Koncelik was once again without his own home. "There was a general closing of the ranks on Paul," said Mark Sanne, Schneider's new chef.

The news of Allan Schneider's death was a bombshell in the Hamptons. It was greeted with a combination of morbid fascination and ill-disguised schadenfreude. It was not without irony that

Schneider, well known for his gluttonous love of food and drink and money, had ended this way. And even more ironic was that Schneider's death would quickly unravel a carefully embroidered life.

Not having a will turned out to be a foolish challenge to fate for Schneider. Because he was intestate, by law everything would go to his next of kin: his parents.

Parents? Over the years Allan had given the impression that they had died somewhere in Salzburg, Austria, in the family castle. But his parents turned out to be very much alive, albeit nearly eighty years old and living in an apartment in Tamarac, Florida. "Allan's purgatory," said Rob Barnes, the architect who had lunch with him at Gordon's that final day, "would be that his image was almost instantaneously destroyed the moment his parents showed up."

Sol and Celia Schneider arrived in East Hampton two days after Allan's death, about as bereaved and baffled as any two people in their late seventies could be. They had lost a son with whom they had rarely exchanged a word in the past twenty years and had no idea of what to expect. Allan's father had polio as a child and walked with braces and two canes. Peggy Griffin remembered when they first saw Allan's mansion on Main Street, Celia Schneider asked in a whispered voice, "Whose mansion is this?"

"This is your son's mansion," Griffin told her.

The elderly couple went from room to room, very slowly, shaking their heads in disbelief at the silver and china, the hunting prints, the antiques, and the Chippendale sofas upholstered in Scalamandré silks. They asked again and again in amazement, "Who does all this belong to?"

"It belonged to your son," Peggy Griffin told them. "Now it belongs to you."

But the most stunning revelation of all for the elderly couple was that their son's funeral service was being held the next day at Saint Luke's Church.

"But Allan is Jewish," Celia said.

He was not only Jewish, he wasn't an only son. Allan had a half brother, Harvey, who was part Hispanic and had married a woman with six children. Allan despised Harvey, who worked in the restaurant business, and refused to acknowledge any association with him at all. It also became evident that Allan didn't grow up in a brownstone in Brooklyn Heights overlooking the Lower Manhattan skyline, but in an apartment building in Flatbush, where he attended P.S. 193, and then Midwood High School, where under his graduation photo his predicted profession was "thespian."

Yet perhaps the most astonishing revelation was that Allan Schneider had no cash. He was running a $150 million operation without any cash reserves, juggling money from deals on the table on a day-by-day basis. The court-appointed coexecutors of Schneider's estate, Ray Wesnofske and Sol Schneider, discovered that Allan had been doing this high-wire act for years. Tyler House had several mortgages on it, one of which hadn't been paid in six months, and he had managing to leverage the house's debt to $1.2 million — more than it was worth. One quick remedy would have been to sell off some of his real estate holdings, but an inventory of his other property proved to be surprising. The eight-bedroom house in Dark Harbor turned out to be rented. So was the apartment at Forty Central Park South. The elegant office complex that Schneider was building on Montauk Highway in Bridgehampton — well, that actually belonged to Ray Wesnofske, who had bankrolled it for Schneider. What saved the estate were two life insurance policies, one for $1 million and another for $500,000, which kept it from immediate bankruptcy.

Schneider, it became clear, had lied about almost everything, from attending Princeton (it's possible he took some courses there) to who sold which property on West End Road. As it turned out, although his office had indeed sold Calvin Klein his house, almost every broker in the Hamptons had had a hand in the sales of the other houses on West End Road. As people put bits and pieces together, it became clear that Schneider was a master of juggling truths. The day after his death, three local caterers were comparing notes and discovered that Schneider not only left them with unpaid balances but, in a typical move, had hired all three for his Christmas party in a few weeks. That way he could play them against one another for the best price, and at the last minute cancel two. The caterers, of course, would have been apoplectic. "Schneider choked," said caterer Brent Newsom, "so he wouldn't have to tell us."

Schneider's death precipitated a small crisis in the food chain of the real estate business in the Hamptons. One of the many ironies of Schneider's story was that although his personal and financial life might have been in shambles, he had left behind a well-oiled real estate sales empire with a corps of the best-trained brokers in the business. There was literally tens of millions of dollars' worth of pending business on the table, and without anyone at the helm, the agency was up for grabs. With no heir apparent strong enough to unite the powerful players, internecine warfare broke out for control among the top brokers. There was an immediate splinter as five of the star salespeople in the East Hampton office, led by Charles Bullock, formed Dunemere Associates Real Estate, a competing agency that continues to represent exclusively the lucrative high end of the real estate market in East Hampton. Another contingent of six managing partners, including Peggy Griffin, Schneider's original employee, and Peter Hallock, a star player from the East Hampton office, banded together and made an offer to buy the use of the Allan Schneider name for $1 million from Allan's parents, who gratefully accepted the deal and left for Florida. Presumably,

Schneider's maligned brother will become the eventual beneficiary of his estate.

4

A MONTH AFTER Schneider's death, Paul Koncelik brought suit against the estate in Riverhead Surrogate's Court. In sworn statements, Koncelik claimed that he and Schneider had "lived together as emotional and physical companions" for ten years and that he had given up a lucrative career as a builder to become "Doctor Watson to Allan's Sherlock Holmes." Koncelik claimed he was available to Allan "for his business, social and personal needs. . . . He went out and made all the money, and I was basically his man Friday, his Doctor Watson. He adored me." More important, Koncelik claimed, Allan had promised Paul that he would get all the antiques and half the house.

How could Paul Koncelik have been Schneider's gay lover for ten years without half the town knowing it? Well, there were rumors, but because Koncelik had been married, no one knew for sure. "Allan Schneider was very high profile," said Koncelik's attorney — and younger sister — Theresa Quigley, trying to explain to the press how a homosexual lover had materialized seemingly out of nowhere. "His image did not include being a homosexual. He tried to come off as Mr. WASP. He was in total denial. He denied he was Jewish and he denied he was homosexual."

"He was in triple denial," corrected Paul Brennan. "He denied that he was Jewish, that he was gay, and that he was an alcoholic too."

Koncelik's attorneys made a motion to freeze the assets of the estate until its distribution could be determined, but the court ruled that the contents of the house could be liquidated. In late June 1992, in what might be called Allan Schneider's last big gala, Sotheby's erected a festive white tent and held a public auction of Schneider's personal possessions on the lawn of Tyler House. Nearly a thousand curious bargain hunters came to rummage through the scraps of Schneider's life; so many people showed up that the police towed away cars blocking Main Street. The sale of 347 items brought nearly $400,000. The house was put on the market too, eventually being bought in 1993 by Alfred Morgan, the owner of the White Rock soda company, for $1.35 million.

In October 1993, nearly two years after Schneider's death, a nonjury trial was held in Surrogate's Court in Riverhead before Judge Ernest Signorelli. Twenty witnesses were paraded before the judge over a six-day stretch, including Koncelik; his brother; his son; his brother's girlfriend; several brokers from the office; Mark Sanne, the chef; and Schneider's protective housekeeper, Eula Ellsworth. Every sordid detail of Schneider's personal life was brought out at the trial, including his prodigious spending and drunkenness. But no one was tarred as unmercifully as Paul Koncelik, who was portrayed as a "severe alcoholic" and gold digger. He sat at the plaintiff's table, mildly drunk, and listened to the details of how many times he had been thrown out in the street by Allan's cruelty and whim, and how Eula Ellsworth had put his belongings in a garbage bag in the back hall closet until Koncelik would come to collect them. When asked if he had anything in writing from Allan promising him the antiques or half the house, Koncelik said, "I never asked for anything in writing. I'm sure if I had, he would have done that. But, in fact, that wasn't my nature."

Aside from Koncelik's own family, only the chef, Mark Sanne, who is openly gay, felt strongly that Koncelik was without a doubt in a spousal relationship with Schneider and had a just claim.

But the court disagreed. On December 2, 1993, Judge Signorelli

handed down a ruling against Koncelik that served as a harsh con-
demnation. "Allan Schneider was revealed to be a strong individual,
manipulative in nature," Signorelli wrote, "and known to make vague
unfulfilled promises to close friends and associates." He called the
nature of Koncelik and Schneider's relationship "amorphous." He
called Koncelik's claim that Allan had given him the antiques as a
gift "deficient." "Apparently," the judge wrote, "the frequent arguments which took place between the two of them was precipitated
by their excessive drinking habits, and the respondent's undesirable
work ethic." Paul Koncelik has "failed to substantiate his claim."

Now publicly shamed and degraded, Koncelik found the next
three years nightmarish. Without Schneider to anchor him, he
drifted from place to place, drunk most of the time. A talented carpenter, he was able to find work but was frequently too sick in the
morning to show up. His large and loving family tried interventions
and residential treatments to help him, without success. In the spring
of 1996 he managed to sober up for a few months, but on June 1 of
that year the lease on the house he was renting expired, and with
no place to move he started to drink again. "His world was that
fragile," said his sister Theresa Quigley. On a Monday afternoon,
June 24, Koncelik was driving his Honda Civic on Swamp Road in
the Northwest Woods when he passed out at the wheel and ran into
a tree, killing himself instantly.

The following week, one of his sisters, Leah, wrote a letter to
the *East Hampton Star*. "My brother's weakness, failings, and poverty
were there," she wrote, "for everyone to see and judge. But, through
it all, he retained one shining virtue: his loving heart, his kindness.
He never judged, never competed, and never rejoiced in others' pain.
He was a kind man, and his kindness now clothes him in glory."

Allan Schneider remains a legend in the Hamptons. His namesake agency, manned with the same people he discovered and trained,

continues to be the single biggest player in the Hamptons real estate business, with an estimated $200 million a year in revenue. He not only substantially changed the face of the landscape, but his own life was in some ways a metaphor for the new Hamptons: a stage upon which nouvelle society could invent itself.

Lord of the Manor

ALLAN SCHNEIDER did not live in the Summer White House!" insisted Robert David Lion Gardiner, the sixteenth lord of the manor, his hands fluttering from his lap like gray birds startled from the brush. "Jeannette Rattray got it wrong! This is the Summer White House. I have the letters written to this house by the *president of the United States* to prove it!" His voice began to rise with anguish, and his British accent became more clipped as he spat out the address, "One Twenty-seven Main Street. Although, of course, it wasn't called One Twenty-seven Main Street then." He rolled his watery blue eyes up into his hooded lids in exasperation, as if he could just shake Jeannette Rattray by the shoulders. The only trouble is, Jeannette Rattray, the former owner of the *East Hampton Star,* has been dead for sixteen years. "Tear it down, tear it down," he chanted. "Nettie Rattray just wants to tear it down."

The air of Gardiner mansion is filled with dust motes lazily drifting in the yellow light streaming through the deeply set windows. Gardiner, eighty-five years old, was splayed on a cracked leather sofa in a small sitting room. His energy unfailing, he is vigorous for his age. His complexion is ruddy, but the years have set his long features into a sneer. He seemed indifferent to his appearance. He hadn't shaved with care (or perhaps at all), and tufts of white hair sprouted in patches on his face and heavy jowls like feathers on a poorly plucked chicken. As he pushed his arms into the sofa for balance, his cuffs rose to reveal a gold Rolex wristwatch and his buttoned navy blue blazer strained open to show a patch of dingy white shirt.

"In any event, how do I know I can trust you?" he demanded of a visitor seated to his right on a hard-backed chair. "You say you want to see Gardiner's Island, and yet you could be a socialist, against inherited wealth! Or you could be like that bitch from *Vanity Fair*!"

Gardiner's Island lies nine miles off the coast of East Hampton, a primeval gem, nearly 3,500 acres of lush Eden with twenty-seven miles of pebble beaches and towering cliffs. "Treasure Island," they call it, "the Sandbar of Sorrow." It is the never-never land of private estates in America. The shape of an elongated starfish, often enveloped in mist and fog, it is a sanctuary not just for wildlife but from time as well. It is blessed with the finest existing untouched white oak forest in America, plus dense thickets of cedar and chestnut trees, from which no wood has been cut for three centuries. Four freshwater streams provide abundant water for herds of white-tailed deer, and wild turkeys scatter through its fields and grape marshes. The island has historical buildings that date to the 1600s with names like T'Other House, where British prisoners carved a checkerboard into the floor, and a mansion house with secret passages to fake tombs in the cemetery. Captain Kidd buried treasure there, and an accused witch lived on the island for many years.

If going to Gardiner's Island is like stepping through a time warp, very few ever get invited to take that step, except for academics, historians, anthropologists, or occasional visiting dignitaries with an interest in forestry, like Prince Philip, who visited the island in 1974. The Gardiner family stopped hosting benefits on the island thirty years ago, and no one dares drop by unannounced either. Notices run in the *East Hampton Star* warning would-be trespassers that the island is private. The curious circle the island in their boats, close enough to see the PLEASE LEAVE signs. The caretaker with his shotguns and a pack of hunting dogs is less polite. Perhaps the island's best protection are the estimated 1 million ticks that inhabit the brush, carriers of debilitating Lyme disease.

"It's *late* in the *season* to see Gardiner's Island," the autocrat said huffily. Gardiner's words come out italicized, accompanied by an imperious sneer, which is why around East Hampton they sometimes call him the "sixteenth lord of the grand *manner.*" "It's the end of August, and on September third I'm joining my *wife,* Eunice, in San Diego. She was bitten by the *tick,* you see. She cannot be exposed to a possible second infection and she's had to go to San Diego to recuperate with friends. It's *exhausting,* taking people to the island, but as the sixteenth lord of the manor, it's my responsibility. I *bothered* to learn the family history. I had that mission in life, to be a custodian. I am the living product of *four hundred years of American history!* The Fords, the du Ponts, the Rockefellers, they are *noveaux* riches. The Gardiners" — he swallowed hard and repeated each syllable of the name carefully — "*Gar-din-ners* are the oldest English family in New York State. It's a *dynasty.* Gardiner's Island is the first English settlement in the state of New York! Elizabeth Gardiner, daughter of Lion Gardiner, was the first English child born in the state of New York. We *founded* the town of East Hampton. We are part of his-sto-ry."

Clearly, Gardiner is a man possessed of the holy spirit. He speaks of his ancestors not only in the royal "we" but as if they were in the room with him. He has memorized his entire family genealogy, sixteen generations' worth, as well as his relatives' professions, bankrolls, and birthplaces; which ones were drunkards and which were whoremasters. But most of all, he knows their resourcefulness, their luck, and their fortitude; how they fought pirates and Indians; how they even fought one another, the decent always triumphing over the greedy. He doesn't just love the lore of the Gardiner family, he is enslaved by it.

According to Gardiner, his ancestors were always at the crux of history, like Forrest Gump, in the "right time at the right place," by chance seeing Napoleon's casket being carried through the streets of Paris, or Mussolini's body hanging from a meat hook. Gardiner himself tells of once playing the piano for Enrico Caruso. "It was at the former Herter place called The Creeks," Gardiner said. "Very badly built. Just stucco on lathe. The Herters were good friends with my parents, and one summer when I was a little boy they rented their house to the great tenor Enrico Caruso. He was married to Dorothy Park Benjamin — society — and my mother knew her. One afternoon we were invited over there for tea and I went into the big studio and there on the stage was a Steinway grand piano. I sat down and played *Il Trovatore* and suddenly I heard a beautiful tenor voice and it was Caruso singing along with me."

His eyes focused on a portrait of his benefactor and aunt, Sarah Diodati Gardiner, painted by Adele Herter. Her largesse is the cause of much of his wealth and all of his grief. "They say I have an eight-million-dollar trust but, you know, I have eighty-five million dollars *outside* of the trust," Gardiner said. "Money I made on my own. I didn't inherit it, no, I got up in the morning and I paid a nickel and took the subway to work every day at a Wall Street bank, the Empire Trust Company, for seventeen dollars a week, that's how you do it." He now owns a forty-two-acre shopping center in Islip and recently sold his ten-room Fifth Avenue apartment in Manhattan. "Of course, eighty-five million dollars is nothing in East Hampton these days; Mr. Perelman, who now owns The Creeks, is worth billions. I understand these days you have to have a fortune of three hundred and forty million dollars to even be listed in *Forbes,* and all my fortune put together is about only a hundred and thirty-five million dollars.

"You see, I attend to all my own business affairs," he said. "Not like my cousin Winnie, who had his first scotch at two o'clock

in the afternoon and died broke." Whitney Gardiner Jr., a handsome playboy of the forties and fifties, and his wife were known as
"Manhattan's most streamlined couple" in the social columns. Winnie is the black sheep of the family, the one who nearly lost the island out of family hands (in which it had been held for 298 years).
In 1937, when the island was about to be put up at public auction, it
was saved just in the nick of time by Sarah Diodati Gardiner, then a
seventy-five-year-old spinster, who shelled out $400,000 for it. She
left half to Robert Gardiner, the other half to his sister, Alexandra.

She also once owned the mansion in which Gardiner sat. Right
in the middle of the village of East Hampton, set back from the
street down a circular drive behind a tall privet, the house is built
of whitewashed Georgian stone, its walls three feet thick, the roof a
beautiful patina of weathered tan Lucovvici tile, "the same tile used
on the Vatican," Gardiner pointed out. Because the walls are so thick,
in a Gothic touch ornate security bars are sunk into the stone, the
bars covered with "real gold leaf, not gold paint," said Gardiner, "so
thin a craftsman has to blow it on them when the air is still."

This house is a replacement of the original wood house built
on the six-acre site in 1835 by local architect John Dimon and con-
sequently owned by intertwining tributaries of the Gardiner family.
That house, along with 123 prized fruit trees, was damaged in the
great hurricane of 1938. Gardiner's aunt, Sarah Diodati Gardiner,
from yet another branch of the family, this one with an Italian strain,
had the house torn down and replaced with the huge stone one. As
formidable as the mansion may be, in 1953, when Sarah Gardiner died
and left it — plus a $40,000 trust — to the town as "the Gardiner
Memorial Building for literary and artistic purposes," the town declined to run a huge white elephant for vague literary and artistic
purposes, so the house passed through private hands into those of
Robert David Lion Gardiner.

"And how do I know you'll get it right?" he demanded of his

visitor. "First Nettie Rattray got it wrong! Then that *bitch* from *Vanity Fair*." He raised his nose in the air as if he'd just whiffed something awful. Of all the thousands of articles written about the Gardiner family, two disturb him greatly. One is a dead-on, and equally as deadly, 1992 *Vanity Fair* piece written by Leslie Bennets, which commented about Gardiner that "if it were not for his royal bearing you would think he was a derelict" and questioned Gardiner's regard for daily hygiene. He had spent the entire day on the island with Bennets, "wining and dining" her, according to him, and the last thing he said to her as he deposited her on the dock in East Hampton was "Don't do a hatchet job."

The other article that so riles him — angers him even more than the one in *Vanity Fair* — is an old clipping by Jeannette Edwards Rattray, the late editor and publisher of the *East Hampton Star*. She was a ubiquitous Queen Mother figure in the village. She not only owned the newspaper with her late husband but was also descended from one of the town's very first families. Joshua Edwards settled in the village in 1650 — technically a few years before even the Gardiners moved there, a distinction she never let Robert Gardiner forget. Rattray was the closest the town ever came to having a social arbiter or society columnist. For nearly forty years she wrote a weekly chronicle of her activities in the *East Hampton Star*, basically a gossip column called "Looking Them Over," which she pointedly signed, "One of Ours." She was a writer of some charm and grace, and much of the worthy material written about social life in East Hampton over the past hundred years comes from her pen.

Robert Gardiner would have liked to be her friend and ally — but no, who does she pal around with but Evan Frankel! At one point Frankel owned more of East Hampton than anybody else in history except Lion Gardiner himself. And then, worse, years ago Rattray wrote that she had visited with the widow of President John Tyler at the Summer White House, 217 Main Street, the house that

Allan Schneider later bought. Allan Schneider seized upon Rattray's debatable facts and capitalized on them, repeating over and over that he lived in the Summer White House. This made Gardiner frantic, and although he forced Rattray to retract the error, people still think, much to Robert Gardiner's eternal anguish, that Allan Schneider's grand house was the real Summer White House.

"Jeannette Rattray says she met the president's widow in that house," Gardiner said, burning, "but she actually met the widow of the president's *son* — John Alexander Tyler! Then, after having in headlines that I was wrong, Nettie wrote, where the Lost and Found department is, in tiny little diamond type, 'I was mistaken.' The trouble is, if anyone caught her wrong, Nettie Rattray had it in for them, and she'd crucify them.

"This is how it happened that this house became the Summer White House," Gardiner said, settling back, his eyes half closed, entering a trancelike state, like a virtuoso preparing to play his instrument. "In the 1840s, my aunt Julia Gardiner was a great beauty — 'the Rose of Long Island,' they called her. She had large round eyes, hair pulled back severely in a bun, and a saucy figure." Gardiner explained that in 1844 Julia accompanied her father, state Senator David Gardiner, as part of a large congressional delegation that had been invited aboard the USS *Princeton* to witness the firing of the Peacemaker — the greatest gun ever cast in America, which they said would end all wars.

"There she was, corseted, small-waisted, with a pushed-up bosom, showing cleavage — the big skirt from the best dressmakers in Paris, all embroidered, lovely jewels," said Gardiner. "It was hot, and shortly before the firing of the gun, my aunt Julia said to President Tyler" — and then, in a startling transformation, Robert Gardiner *became* coquettish Julia Gardiner and spoke in a falsetto — " 'I'm afraid of the gun, Mr. President, I can't stand the noise. I'm scared of it and I'm ... I'm dying of the heat. Mr.

President, would you take me below and give me a glass of champagne?' "

Gardiner sneered at the thought of the president, "the silly old goat, in his striped trousers, tailcoat, and top hat," taking the girl belowdecks. "Julia was younger than the president's daughter — the first Mrs. Tyler had died in the White House. Julia was looking at him with her famous mascara eyebrows, flirting with him, and they were drinking the champagne, when a roar and a rumble went through the ship! A tremendous cloud came into the cabin, and a sailor rushed downstairs and said, 'Miss Gardiner, your father has been killed!' " The sailors had overloaded the gun, and when it was fired, it exploded from the breech shaft and went into shrapnel, instantly killing the secretary of state, the secretary of the treasury, the secretary of the navy, and Julia Gardiner's father.

"It would have killed the president too, but my great-aunt was flirting like mad with him," Gardiner said. "When she heard her father had been killed, she swooned into the president's waiting arms — where else? — and woke up in the White House. The rest is history," Gardiner said smugly. "Of course, she was also a bitch, and she cheated on the president too, with Sam Houston. The state of Texas was practically annexed in her bed!

"In any event, in the summer of 1845, when the president wanted to escape the heat of Washington in July and August, he stayed here, at the home of Julia's widowed mother. He then wrote a letter to this house thanking his mother-in-law for letting him stay here," a letter Gardiner said he has in a vault. "They came to this house, not Allan Schneider's house," Gardiner said, shaking his head. "How could they have gone to Allan Schneider's house when Tyler was *dead* by the time Nettie Rattray visited there? How! How —?" The thought incenses him. "It was the wroooooong generation!" he whooped.

"Here, look!" he said, propelling himself up off the sofa. "Here!" He commanded a visitor's attention to a long wood trestle table covered in Colonial treasures. "This is the oldest sideboard in New York State," he said, stroking its surface, as if the sideboard proves everything he'd been saying, "and over here is a Queen Anne desk of full mahogany. It's got hidden compartments to secret away rubies and jewels from pirates." He fumbled with drawers and secret niches. "We are survivors!" he sang out as the hidden compartments came into view.

He next moved through a dark hallway, past the dining room and a collection of Chinese exports from the 1700s ("But of course the gold service for eighty-four is in a vault at the Bank of New York!") and into the living room, where, going faster, he pointed out the rugs, the floor, the walls, the satin-lined doghouse, a painting from the Diodati palace, and a Hans Memlinc that he "bought from the Krupps." His narrative became too dense to grasp as names flew by — Delanois, Migéon, Tuart — incomprehensible except for the aside "These chairs are made by Madame du Barry's own chairmaker. She was pretty dumb, but she was a famous cocksucker."

Gardiner entered the grand foyer, where an imposing curved staircase to the second floor is lined with the portraits of the Gardiner family, lords of the manor all, their brides, and children. At the foot of the staircase is a small portrait of an alabaster-skinned woman from another time, the emeralds in her necklace the same color as her eyes. The painting is distinctly the work of Dalí, but its surrealism is constrained to a vivid portrait of an ethereal redhead with high cheekbones, an Audrey Hepburn neck, and thick red hair tumbling voluptuously to her shoulders. "This is my wife, Eunice, painted by Salvador Dalí," Gardiner said. The portrait is under-sized because Gardiner bargained Dalí down $5,000 from his usual $25,000 commission.

Gardiner married Eunice Bailey Oakes in March 1961 when he was fifty-one years old. Until then he had lived with his mother. Those who knew Gardiner considered Eunice a surprising choice

for a confirmed bachelor. She was a petite, one-time British model
and the widow of William Pitt Oakes, the son of Sir Harry Oakes,
a Canadian financier. They wed at Saint Thomas Church in a high-
profile wedding with eighteen ushers in top hats and tails. The
Vanity Fair article that Gardiner so detests reported that on the receiving line of his wedding, two guests were overheard to comment, "I understand our host is looking for volunteers tonight." In
explaining why he and Eunice never had any heirs, Gardiner said
that he had his sperm tested, "and they wiggled," and left it at
that.

"It was a great society wedding," Gardiner said, relishing the
memory before Eunice's portrait. "I had the reception at the Colony
Club, which is very restricted, only four hundred guests allowed.
It was the wedding of the season. The orchestra that played at
the White House played, and I took my bride out on the dance
floor and started the waltz, and Eunice had these fabulous jewels
on, a million dollars' worth, a tiara and diamond earrings, and she
wore a magnificent gown and my mother's wedding veil, all Brussels lace with petals of roses. . . ." Although the couple were quite
social when they were first married, appearing at balls and dinner
parties in New York and East Hampton, for the past ten years
Eunice has disappeared from view and has become something of a
mystery.

Gardiner broke from his reverie and took his visitor through
open French doors, onto a brick patio. Beyond it is a lovely palladium
more than 100 feet long, lined with statues on tall pedestals and a
backdrop of dark green arborvitae. East Hampton could be 3,000
miles away back there, it is so quiet and peaceful. At the far end of
the walk there is a small hedge and, a ways off, an old tile swimming
pool, the blue water glass-flat except for the tiniest ripple of bugs
tapping the surface. "Those new people put the pools right near
their houses," Gardiner sneered. "They're so proud, 'Oh, look, we

can afford a pool!' " To the right is a small stand of unusual trees. "This is the biggest ginkgo tree in America," Gardiner said, caressing a deep-green leaf the size of a fan. "And those over there are varnish trees from China," he said. "The Gardiners brought these trees from China to Sag Harbor. The sap from this kind of tree is what makes the varnish on Chinese furniture so gorgeous."

Gardiner looked around and sighed. He was quiet, finally, for a moment. Then he brought up Evan Frankel, the man who was Jeannette Rattray's friend. "He lived in the old McCord house on Hither Lane," Gardiner said, "and put a swimming pool in the basement somehow. Frankel called himself a 'squire,' but that was just a nickname." He squinted into the sun. "He was an insufferable man, Frankel, rude for absolutely no reason, and a snob, but even Evan Frankel, when he came here, said, 'Now, this is *old money.*' " Gardiner relished the words, whispering them again, "*Old money.*"

The thought of Evan Frankel's validation pangs him, and suddenly he cried out, "Jeannette Rattray! No! No! No! No! No! Erase it! Erase it!" The words fell dead against the stone house. "Erase it! Erase it!" He motioned wildly to the house, to the trees, to the statuary. "But Nettie Rattray can't tear it down. It's four hundred years of history. You can't tear that down. Like the three-foot-thick walls. You can't change the fact that we started this town."

2

GARDINER HAD locked up the mansion and clambered into his lumbering eight-year-old Cadillac, which he was driving erratically down Main Street, the windows shut and the air-conditioning off. He seemed as oblivious to the August heat as he was to the people Rollerblading or to the Range Rovers sharing the street with him. Coming round the back of Town Pond, he drove his huge automobile up onto a sloping knoll and parked it at such a steep angle that the force of gravity nearly tore the driver's door off its hinges when Gardiner opened it. He hoisted himself out of the car and made his way past an old iron gate into the cemetery. He pointed out the graves of his ancestors as he weaved his way among them. "See, here are the graves of my mother and father," he said, gesturing to two tombstones side by side, the Gardiner crests pitted with age. "There is the grave of Senator Gardiner, who was killed on the USS *Princeton*, and this is my great-great-grandfather, Captain Averill Gardiner — his house is the one the Ladies Village Improvement Society is in — and here is my grandfather, with a duplicate of the tomb of [Sextus] Africanus, the tomb of the Roman emperor, which I'm having duplicated for my own tomb on Gardiner's Island."

Ahead is Lion Gardiner's unusual grave. He lies in a neo-Gothic sepulchre under an ornate sandstone tomb designed by James Renwick, the architect of Saint Patrick's Cathedral and Grace Church. Eight pillars support a rectangular stone roof with a shingled pattern, under which is a carved stone bas-relief of Lion Gardiner clad in the accoutrements of knighthood, his hands folded on the scabbard of a sword. He wanted to be buried on Gardiner's Island, his namesake homestead, but he dropped dead unexpectedly of a heart attack in East Hampton the summer of 1663 at age sixty-four, and in those days they didn't have refrigeration. Before the townsfolk could get him back to the island, his stomach began to swell from natural gasses — and it was decided to bury him quickly in town. Years ago, when the body was exhumed, it was discovered that he had been buried seven feet deep, facing west, so he would rise facing his friends on Judgment Day. His ivory-white skeleton showed that he had had a strong jaw and large forehead, and his curly copper-toned locks were still intact on his skull.

The heavy traffic on Main Street that sunny summer day seemed to fade from view. Vines and natural grasses had grown up around the edges of the tomb, and Gardiner fell upon them, shouting, "Look! Here!" He knelt and pulled at the weeds with shaking hands. "I was here last week and it was covered with vines. It looked deliberate. My family has left thirty-six thousand dollars for the care of the cemetery, and Lion Gardiner's grave was covered deliberately — not only with vines but with a big bush! Someone must have planted it! Why, this town is like Peyton Place! It looks deliberate to me! This is so that she could say, 'You know the Rattrays are the old family here, and the Gardiners are just common nouveau riche parvenu.' Crazy! Absolutely nuts! . . . They did it so you couldn't read this inscription."

Gardiner pushed himself to his feet and began to scratch away at the carved inscription on the tomb with his jagged thumbnail, scraping like an emery board at the hardened lichen. "Here it is," he said, growing excited. "Here is what it says!" He breathlessly recited fragments of the long inscription, ". . . an officer . . . English army . . . an engineer . . . why he was sent . . . fortifications, you see! He was fighting in Holland in the Thirty Years War . . . Gardiner's Island — Look! — of which he was sole owner and ruler." Gardiner was triumphant. "Born in 1599! How can you not say he was the first? And Nettie Rattray says, 'One of the first . . .' Here! Look! 'Lord. L-O-R-D of the island.' I mean, I did not make it up!" He began to dig again at the offending weeds with the determination of a terrier.

The man at whose grave he dug, Lion Gardiner, was the town's first de facto mayor, fixer, real estate broker, and probably the first recorded case of a white man succumbing to Hampton's land lust. Gardiner was a huge man for his time, six feet two inches tall, wiry and tough, with a silky red beard and mustache upturned at the ends. His exploits are almost mythological. He was a military engineer with a shrewd eye for self-promotion. In 1635, when he was thirty-six years old, not a young man in the 1600s, he hired out his services to Lord Saye and Lord Brook to build a palisaded fort and moat in Connecticut to protect English settlers from the rancorous Pequot. He was a respected but controversial commander. He had married the enemy — a Dutch woman, Mary Willemsen Duercant, whom he had brought to the New World with him from Holland. The Dutch in New Amsterdam threatened English expansion to the south and had become bitter adversaries of the Crown. Gardiner had a child with the Dutch woman as well, a son, the first white child born in the state of Connecticut.

Gardiner also had a reputation as being an apologist for the Indians. To be sure, he wasn't above surrounding his fort with a lawn of wooden boards through which sharp nails had been driven so any approaching Indians would impale themselves, but he much favored another tactic some found suspect: friendly negotiation. He was one of the few Puritans who believed that the natives were more than pagan beasts, fit mostly for slaughter. For Gardiner, they were misled souls, all God's creatures, open to redemption but ripe for exploitation. In fact, Gardiner was rather charmed by the Indians' exaggerated sense of honor and even bothered to learn their language. He was outspokenly against fighting with the local tribes and certainly more furious with the Massachusetts Bay Colony for sending trained mercenaries to butcher the Pequots than he was with the outraged Indians who attacked him in retaliation, shooting him with poisoned arrows, from which he barely recovered.

The Pequots were a particularly nasty crew, with an army of thousands of bloodthirsty braves who dispatched their victims by force-feeding them chunks of their own flesh and then wore the toes and fingers in a headband. The Pequots were the greatest obstacle to the British in appropriating more land in Connecticut, and so in 1637, despite Lion Gardiner's protests, the British sent a regiment of soldiers to exterminate the entire tribe. The soldiers set upon them at their encampment at Mystic and turned it into an inferno. They torched the huts and incinerated the braves who stayed inside or shot and hacked to death the old men, women, and children who ran screaming from the burning village. By day's end nearly the entire Mystic tribe had been murdered, and only a handful of survivors were scattered across Connecticut and Long Island. So shocking and stupidly unnecessary was the obliteration of the tribe, according to Gardiner, that he later wrote a book about it, *On Relation of the Pequot Warres*.

A few days after the killing at Mystic, Lion Gardiner was fascinated to learn that Wyandanch, the great sachem of the Montauk, was headed across the sound in a canoe so big that it was paddled by thirty braves. Wyandanch had requested a meeting with Gardiner, who he heard was sympathetic to the Indians' plight. Among the Algonquin tribes, Wyandanch was considered the big banker, the head of the Indian Federal Reserve. The Montauks had cornered the market on the manufacture of money — wampum — which was made from the plentiful periwinkle and conch shells found along the beaches of the Hamptons. All year long the Montauk squaws strung wampum while the men hunted and fished. They were the richest tribe in the nation, and their wampum was so valued that it was regulated by the English Crown as a means of trading.

But Gardiner also knew that the Montauks' great wealth had made Wyandanch a shakedown target: Every time trouble was afoot with another tribe, instead of going to war, Wyandanch paid a bribe. The Montauks had become so well known for paying off the bullies that Long Island was dubbed Paumenoke, the "land of tribute," by the other Indians. Of all the tormentors of Wyandanch and the Montauks, the Connecticut Pequot tribe had been the worst.

Wyandanch and Lion Gardiner laid eyes on each other for the first time in the great hall of Saybrook Fort. Gardiner and the soldiers could smell Wyandanch and his men 100 feet away. Hygiene was unknown to the Indians: they never bathed, they were bare-assed, and they wore only a small loincloth over their genitals. They were always nearly naked, even in the bitter New England winter, when they would slather their bodies in a putrid animal grease to help them retain body heat. The chief was a fierce-looking Indian with a tough, muscular body and a burned-umber complexion. He had a flat, moonlike oval face that he kept painted in brightly colored designs of blue and red and yellow. The intricacy of the design, enhanced and modified every day, was of great pride to him, as was the roach of black hair that ran from his forehead down the nape of his neck, the rest being singed away with hot rocks. Around his waist he wore a display of wampum to show his wealth, not unlike wearing a Rolex in the Hamptons today. A pack of young wolves, which his tribe had half domesticated and raised as pets, dogged his steps wherever he went, yapping and nipping at strangers.

Although the Pequots had been his tribe's lifelong enemy and he was well rid of them, Wyandanch was just as disquieted about the white men's ruthless power to obliterate an entire tribe in a single day. The Indian's opening gambit with Gardiner was "Are the English angry with *all* Indians?" to which Gardiner replied, "No, only Indians who kill Englishmen." Wyandanch suggested they make a deal. The English would not kill his tribe, and in return he would make a vow of friendship and goodwill to the English. He would pay tribute with wampum — and incidentally keep him abreast of the Indian plots and treachery against the white men. In effect, Wyandanch was buying himself the protective services of Gardiner in return for snitching on other Indian tribes. Gardiner had one condition; he said the only way he could trust Wyandanch was for the chief to bring him the heads of any Pequots who had managed to escape to Long Island from Mystic. A few days after Wyandanch returned to Montauk, a package arrived at Saybrook Fort: the severed heads of five Pequots in a sack. Wyandanch and Gardiner had a deal.

They were unlikely buddies, the opportunist British engineer who spoke in Elizabethan English and the proud Indian chief who ate with his hands and believed in black magic. At Wyandanch's insistence, Lion Gardiner became the Hamptons' first weekend guest when he stayed overnight in Wyandanch's Montauk lodging, a twenty-by-thirty-foot rectangular wigwam heated by a fire in the middle. Wyandanch and his houseguest slept head to toe on a hard wooden bench with the rest of Wyandanch's family along the perimeter. Gardiner discovered Wyandanch to be a loving husband and doting father. He had married an Indian queen, a princess of the Algonquins, with whom he had a daughter, Heather Flower, famous among the Indian tribes for her great beauty. The Montauks turned out to be a gregarious tribe who enjoyed gossip and visiting with neighbors. They took full advantage of the splendors of the South Fork and moved the location of their village from season to season, spending the summer closer to the cooling breezes of the ocean, the winters in the protection of the forest. Although Gardiner got used to the Indians' smell and total lack of hygiene, he could never accept that Wyandanch was exposed. "How can you go around bare?" Gardiner asked Wyandanch when he knew him well enough. Wyandanch, who couldn't understand why Gardiner refused to paint his face, said, "You go around with your face bare all winter, don't you?"

When Gardiner turned forty, he wanted to settle down and build his fortune. He toured several potential homesteads with Wyandanch, settling upon an island between the arms of the North and South Forks that the Indians called Manchonake, "the island of death," after a battle between the Montauks and the Pequots so fierce that not a man was left standing on either side. The island was virtually prehistoric, a world untouched by civilization, except for a tobacco crop that the Montauks had once planted and which still grew wild. Gardiner told Wyandanch that he wanted to buy the island, but Wyandanch didn't understand what selling the land meant. The land was the Indians' universe, like the stars in the heavens — it couldn't be transferred. But the chief was eager to please his white friend, and the island was a small part of the vast holdings of Wyandanch, so he "sold" it for a gun, a few bottles of rum, a black dog (the first dog the Indians had seen that wasn't a wolf), and ten cloth coats. Now Gardiner was doubly happy: he would have his own island, and the Indians would no longer be bare.

He named the island the Isle of Wight, but it would always be known as Gardiner's Island. He was careful to obtain a grant from the British Crown for five pounds a year. He lived there in feudal splendor, bringing with him from Connecticut a staff of workers and farmers to run his own private fiefdom. Over the generations there were sometimes as many as 100 servants on the island at a time; although these helpers were called his "tenants," they were really his vassals. Their labor was complemented by hundreds of black slaves called "bound boys" who lived in long, low quarters that had a pharmacy at one end where laudanum was made to keep them stoned and submissive. A man given to certain pretensions, Gardiner's coat of arms was plastered on everything, including the buttons of the servants' uniforms. It was also on Gardiner's Island in 1641 that Gardiner's wife gave birth to his daughter, Elizabeth, the child whom Robert Gardiner referred to ad nauseum as the first English child born in the state of New York.

It was an isolated existence on the island, to say the least, and dangerous as well, exposed on all sides to surprise attacks from marauding Indians and later from pirates too. But life on the island could also be idyllic, and its natural bounty of venison, fowl, shellfish, and tobacco made Gardiner rich in trade. Fourteen years went by as Gardiner and his family prospered, years marred only by the ongoing byzantine plots of the Connecticut Indians, foiled time and again by Wyandanch's subterfuge. The aging Montauk sachem had become a trusted ally over the years, but his friendship with

Gardiner had also made him reviled by the tribes of Connecticut, who justifiably branded him a traitor.

In 1648 Wyandanch excitedly reported to Gardiner that nine white men had "planted" themselves down around the mud hole east of Georgika's pond — this is, of course, Town Pond of today — and were cutting down trees and digging holes to build houses. Wyandanch's braves wanted permission to kill the strangers, but Wyandanch told them that they must not kill white men except in self-defense and that he would consult with Gardiner about what to do. Gardiner made some inquiries and learned that the nine men were a disgruntled offshoot of the families that had settled Southampton eight years before. John Hand Sr., John Stretton Sr., Thomas Talmadge Jr., Robert Bond, Daniel Howe, Robert Rose, Thomas Tomson, Joshua Barnes, and John Mulford had come twenty miles east to start a new community because Southampton had already grown too congested for their taste. They complained that within one year eleven families who lived there had grown to twenty-five. They intended to start their own community that they were going to keep from getting too crowded by giving every landowner veto power as to who could buy in after them: "Noe man shall sell as no one wants" was the way the town charter put it. This new town was to be named Maidstone, after their ancestral village in Kent, England.

Seizing the moment, Lion Gardiner presented himself to the group of nine men as the only authorized real estate broker for the Indians — as well as the muscle behind the promise that the settlers wouldn't get scalped in the middle of the night. Gardiner brokered a deal whereby Wyandanch sold the nine men 30,720 acres of land — the land from present-day Town Line Road in Sagaponack all the way out to the tip of Montauk — for twenty coats, twenty-four mirrors, twenty-four hoes, twenty-four hatchets, twenty-four knives, and one hundred little drills for making wampum called muxes. Thrown into the deal was an arrangement that the Indians, who knew it would take the settlers two or three years to put in their own crops, would sell them enough corn, squash, and beans to get them through their first few winters. They would even teach the white men how to use the oily menhaden fish as fertilizer.

In return, Lion Gardiner would never have to lift a finger in the town again, neither grinding grain nor collecting whale blubber for oil. He was exempt not only from labor but from onerous town planning board rules as well, the only man in town allowed to have front steps down to the street. He was entitled to his own chapel and his own mass at church, and he could appoint the minister. He was also tax-exempt, and his sole obligation to the government was to present one sheep to a representative of the Crown on every May 1.

The restrictive settlement policy of Maidstone's founding fathers was the first of many land-conservation plans to fail in the Hamptons. "Noe man" was ever voted unacceptable, and within a year of the "planting" of the town, the nine original families had burgeoned to thirty-four and its name had been changed to East Hampton. Many of the thirty-four were refugees from the isolation of Gardiner's Island who longed for life in a larger community. Eventually, in August 1653, Lion Gardiner himself moved off the island, mostly for safety from Indians and pirates, and built himself a fine house smack in the center of town, as well as one for his beloved daughter, Elizabeth, just across the street.

The same month that Gardiner moved to the village with his family, Wyandanch's own beloved daughter, fourteen-year-old Heather Flower, was to be married to the young sachem of another tribe at a wedding feast held in Montauk. It was the biggest Indian social event in years, and all the tribes under Wyandanch's subjugation sent sachems and braves as emissaries. It took the Montauks weeks to prepare for the celebration. A knoll was cleared in the forest, where a feast of roasted fowl and fish was served. Later the bride was lifted in the air in a litter entwined with garlands of flowers and carried down to the beach, where a giant bonfire was lit.

In the absence of alcohol, the celebrants spent hours working themselves into a frenzy of delirium by screaming and contorting their faces, a ritual to ward off the evil gods from the wedding party. Deep into the night they spun and screamed by the heat of the fire, until they were exhausted to the point of collapse. It was then, out of the darkness, that they were set upon by Narraganset braves, who with lightning speed butchered with spears and knives more than thirty exhausted Montauk. They sadistically stabbed to death Heather Flower's bridegroom before her eyes and then sliced off his scalp and took it with them as a prize. They also took Heather Flower herself, along with fourteen other women in the bridal party, much to her father's torment.

Ninigret, the Narraganset chief, announced that he would not kill Heather Flower; instead, he was holding her for ransom. He wanted 700 fathom of wampum — more than 50,000 beads, a fantastic sum in those days, even for a rich Indian like Wyandanch. Unable to ante up so many beads, he turned to Lion Gardiner, whose daughter was almost exactly the same age as Heather Flower, for help. Gardiner agreed at once to loan Wyandanch the rest of the ransom. He also bravely insisted that he himself undertake the dangerous task of retrieving Heather Flower from Ninigret, lest the treacherous chief murder Wyandanch and keep the ransom. Vowing to his friend that he would bring the girl home, Gardiner set out on a perilous journey. Accompanied by only a few armed men, he went first by small sloop to Connecticut and then by horse and on foot deep into the Narragansets' territory. There was no word from Gardiner for more than a week, until one afternoon his sloop appeared on the Long Island Sound horizon, Heather Flower and the fourteen members of her wedding party safely in his care.

The old Indian chief was wild with gratitude and expressed his thanks by giving Lion Gardiner a gift so generous that it is almost incomprehensible: the 90,000 acres of Long Island from Southampton to Brooklyn. In the written deed for this gift, Wyandanch dictated about Lion Gardiner: "In our great extremity, when we were almost swallowed up by our enemies ... he appeared to us, not only as a friend but as a father ... in giving us his money and his goods, and ransomed my daughter and friends." Wyandanch signed the deed with a stick-figure drawing of himself and Lion Gardiner holding hands. To mark this friendship, the Montauks held a great ceremony, at which the two men cut their fingers and became blood brothers.

The intrigue, murder, and bloodshed between the Montauks and Narragansets went on relentlessly for ten more years. Yet it wasn't genocide that eventually killed most of the Indians, but disease. In 1658 a pestilence of measles and smallpox, against which the Indians had no immunity, killed two-thirds of them. One of the few survivors was Wyandanch himself, who lived through the plague only to be poisoned at the hands of one of his own kind, probably an Indian who could no longer bear his allegiance to Lion Gardiner and the dominance of the white men. At Wyandanch's death, a grief-stricken Lion Gardiner wrote in his diary, "My friend and brother is dead. Who will now do the like?"

Wyandanch's grave has never been found, but it is somewhere beneath the streets and fields of East Hampton or Montauk.

More than 300 years and many generations of Gardiners later, the 90,000 acres Lion Gardiner received from Wyandanch has been sold off, traded, or squandered, until now all that is left in the hands of the Gardiner family are the house in East Hampton and the spectacular, unreachable island in the bay.

Gardiner's Island

ROBERT GARDINER leaned into the wind as he steered his mahogany boat, *Laughing Lady,* into the chop. In the distance, Gardiner's Island was a small crescent of green. "There's Lion's Head!" Gardiner shouted, the sea stealing the rest of his words from the air. He pointed starboard at a rock erupting into Gardiner's Bay that perhaps, fancifully, might look like the head of a lion. He was wearing the same navy blue blazer and baby blue leisure pants, with a salmon-colored dress shirt and white collar. "Of course, it's all very well to say how wonderful it is to *own* an island," he shouted to his passengers. "What people don't understand is how expensive Gardiner's Island is to keep up. People have no *idea.* It costs nearly *two million dollars a year* to run. So when people say to me, 'It must be so wonderful to own an island,' well . . . wonderful, yes, but you have to be able to *afford* it."

It was the Saturday of Labor Day weekend, the peak of the end-of-summer frenzy in the Hamptons. Despite predictions of a possible glancing blow from a nor'easter, it was a clear, sunny day, and the famous light ricocheted across limpid blue skies. Behind Gardiner, receding with the rest of the flat mainland, roads were thick with luxury cars, the restaurants were fully booked, and lines had already formed at the counters of gourmet food shops. The subtle hysteria of the summer renters, who had to clear out of their rentals by the stroke of midnight Sunday night, gave the Hamptons a frenetic, if slightly desperate, celebratory air.

Gardiner was on his way to give his last tour of the summer of Gardiner's Island, indeed, what might be his last tour ever. He is, as he is fond of pointing out, eighty-five years old and will be lying in a grave on Gardiner's Island "soon." In three days he was going to close up his mansion in East Hampton, retrieve his wife from San Diego, and go on to Palm Beach, where they spend winters in Gardiner's condominium building "filled with billionaires."

But today he was in all his glory. He was a walking historiography, an indefatigable tour guide and minister preaching the glory of the Gardiner clan. Today Gardiner had what he likes best, a captive audience. Packed in the *Laughing Lady* with him, and in a second, larger boat following close behind, were two dozen historians from various small towns in the Suffolk County Historical Society. Each summer, as part of his responsibility to the family legacy, Gardiner escorts historians and academics on rare tours of the island. The middle-aged historians and their spouses might have been mistaken for any group of American tourists just departed from a bus in front of the Colosseum in Rome, dressed in their comfortable clothes, canvas caps, and sensible walking shoes. Earlier, on the dock in East Hampton, they had slathered themselves with sun block shared from passed containers and had drenched their clothing in the insecticide DEET to protect them from the island's notorious ticks. Shoulder to shoulder, crossing Gardiner's Bay with Instamatic cameras hanging around their necks, they expectantly awaited their tour of the Colonial Jurassic Park.

"I can't keep household servants on the island because it's too lonely," Gardiner shouted, although a married couple who live in a small cottage are paid caretakers of the island year-round. "There is only direct current, and the television doesn't work properly. There used to be an underground telephone cable, but a fishing boat tore it out thirty years ago. People don't understand how complicated the full underpinnings of the island are to run. Tankers from Connecticut have to bring oil to fill the underground tanks. It costs *fifty thousand dollars* a year just for oil. Trucks have to be transported to the island on immense barges. We have twenty-seven miles of dirt road — laid out in the 1600s — which we have to clear every year by ourselves, and yet we pay a huge road tax to East Hampton. Yes, a road tax to East Hampton! Not only that, but I pay a school tax! And we're *miles* from the nearest dock! That kind of taxation was what the Boston Tea Party was about."

What Robert Gardiner didn't mention is that he pays for none of this, none of the taxes and not a penny of the $50,000 for the oil. The entire $1.8 million it currently costs to run the island each year is footed by Robert Gardiner's bitterest enemies: his niece, the pale, blond, aloof Alexandra Creel Goelet, fifty-six, and her fantastically rich husband, Robert G. Goelet, sixty-seven, with whom he uneasily shares the island.

For fifteen years Robert Gardiner and the Goelets have been enmeshed in a series of bitter, bizarre lawsuits over the island's up-keep and its future, during the course of which Gardiner has charged that the Goelets have stolen valuable paintings belonging to him, that they put his portrait in an outhouse (the island has no outhouse), and that Robert Goelet attempted to murder him by running him over in the presence of two historians to whom Gardiner was giving a tour. Whatever happened that day, the historians are suing for $20 million, claiming they were hurt in a car accident while Gardiner was driving. In another incident heard before the New York State Supreme Court, Gardiner alleged that Goelet menaced him by slamming the door of the manor house in his face, saying, "If you come through this door, I'll bash your brains in. I could crush you to death. I hate your guts."

The feeling is clearly mutual. How Robert Gardiner found him-self sharing the island with his niece and her husband in the first place is like some Chekovian nightmare to him. When Gardiner's grande dame aunt, Sarah Diodati Gardiner, died in 1953 at age ninety, she left the island jointly to Robert Gardiner and his sister, Alexandra Gardiner Creel, with the stipulation that it remain in family hands when they passed away. In 1990, when Gardiner's sister died, her share of the island passed to her steel-willed daughter, also named Alexandra, who married Robert Goelet. Alexandra and Goelet were a duo made in naturalist heaven. He was a past president of the American Museum of Natural History, the New York Zoological Society, and the New-York Historical Society; she studied environmental science at Barnard and is a graduate of the Yale School of Forestry and Environmental Studies.

He is also very rich. It is of endless aggravation to Robert Gardiner that Goelet's family is almost, but not quite, as old and important as his own. The Goelets arrived in America in 1676, a mere forty years after Lion Gardiner. The family mansion in Newport, Ochre Court, was at least as grand as the Gardiner mansion in East Hampton, and their family mausoleum, worthy of a resting place for Zeus, was designed by McKim, Mead and White. Robert Goelet himself, called "the good Bobby" by family members (there are sixteen generations of male family members named Robert, a situation that confuses the family itself), was born in France on a "family shooting place called Sandricourt which comprises a respectable château and ten thousand acres," he once recounted. He attended boarding school in Normandy, Brooks School in Massachusetts, and graduated from Harvard University. He was also a dive-bomber in the U.S. Navy.

Goelet's family has owned some of New York's most prestigious chunks of real estate, including the land beneath the Ritz Carlton Hotel, the Lever Building on Park Avenue, and all the land under the Fulton Fish Market. In the early 1800s the family owned all the land contiguous from Union Square to Forty-eighth Street and Fifth

Avenue. Curiously, for a family that helped found Chemical Bank (a Goelet has always sat on the board), not many New Yorkers have ever heard of them. They are not the kind of people you find on the pages of *Women's Wear Daily*. They are not just secretive WASPS, they *abhor* attention and publicity. The family is almost clannish in its aversion to public identification. They have even managed to remain invisible in Manhattan business. The family doesn't have offices in an office building with other companies; it operates its far-reaching real estate holdings from an unmarked townhouse on East Sixty-seventh Street just off Fifth Avenue. Although Robert Goelet has run the family business and sat on the board of Chemical Bank, he has for the most part lived the life of a country gentleman, a fishing buff and expert in wildlife and forest fauna. He was older than fifty when he married Alexandra in 1976, much the same age as his nemesis Robert Gardiner was when he married.

"Bastard!" Gardiner spat out at the mention of Goelet's name. Gardiner claims that not only is Goelet an attempted murderer but he is the destroyer of the Gardiner legend. Given a chance, Gardiner swears, Goelet will fell the primeval forest and destroy Gardiner's Island. "When I'm gone, he is going to sell that island off," Gardiner warned, his voice quaking with rage, and "develop it into a golf course and condominiums." Although Gardiner's prophecies sound far-fetched, it is true that Gardiner's Island is zoned for five-acre housing. It could be developed into a fantastic private retreat of huge mansions with individual docks and a small, private landing strip. It would be the unbeatable baby-boomer address, where some Wall Street turk could build a manse on the very spot Captain Kidd buried his treasure. "Just think," a forlorn Gardiner said at the thought. "Just think."

The possibility of the development of Gardiner's Island sends a chill up the collective spine of the East Hampton town fathers and conservationists, and Robert Gardiner swears that Goelet is evil enough to do it. As proof, he points to the fact that the Goelets have been assiduously buying up rights to the island from the only other possible heirs, Alexandra's brother, J. Randall Creel Jr., who died in 1988, to whom they paid $300,000 to relinquish any claim on the island, and his two sons, to whom the Goelets reportedly paid only $5,000 each. Goelet has repeatedly denied he has any intentions of developing the island when it eventually falls into his hands and points out that he's spent nearly $20 million to keep it in good care.

Perhaps the most diabolical of Gardiner's plots to foil Alexandra and Robert Goelet from getting the island all to themselves was for him to produce a male heir. Clearly, although his sperm "all wiggled," after years of marriage to Eunice without producing an heir, a natural-born child was not in the cards. So Gardiner decided to adopt a member of the Gardiner clan. After years of researching the Gardiner bloodlines, he found a very distant but certifiable Gardiner heir, Gardiner Green Jr., fifty-two, a wealthy cousin many times removed, from Laurel, Mississippi, who had made money in the oil business. Gardiner proposed to legally adopt Green and leave him his share in Gardiner's Island. Green, who looked like a smiling Jimmy Carter, was happily married and had two children. He was chairman of the board of a local museum in Mississippi and drove a Rolls-Royce. He was bemused with Gardiner's scheme and reluctantly agreed to come up north to meet his distant relative and take a grand tour of the island and manor house.

While Green was making up his mind, Alexandra and Robert Goelet sued Robert Gardiner in New York State Supreme Court to prohibit him from adopting an heir, claiming it a fraudulent means of depriving them of the island, and Gardiner paid nearly $1 million in legal fees to defend his rights. The court eventually found in Gardiner's favor, but the legal battle was for naught. After some consideration, Gardiner Green Jr. declined the privilege of becoming the seventeenth lord of the manor and incurring

its costs, and he has never seen or heard from Robert Gardiner
since.

In another scheme that backfired, in 1977, when the trust left
by Sarah Diodati Gardiner to support the island ran low, Gardiner
stopped paying his share of the upkeep, unable or unwilling to, saying he was trying to force the island into the safe hands of New
York State receivership, which would protect it as a historical place.
In 1980 the Goelets took over the entire support of the island and
sued Gardiner, asking New York State Supreme Court Justice Marie
Lambert to ban him from the island since he wasn't paying for its
maintenance. Lambert — whose name enrages Gardiner just behind
Jeannette Rattray's and Leslie Bennets's — concurred and banished
Gardiner from his beloved island for twelve years.

Those dozen years without his ancestral turf were torture. No
monarch suffered more greatly in exile than Gardiner, except during
the summer of 1989, the island's 350th anniversary, when he paid over
half a million dollars toward his share of the upkeep for the privilege of usurping the Goelet's residence for three months. It was well
worth it to him, he gleefully remembered. "The Goelets couldn't
go" that summer. "They had to hire Faye Dunaway's house in East
Hampton. They were furious." Gardiner battled the Goelets through
the courts until, in 1992, a New York State appellate court overruled
Marie Lambert's decision and decided that since Gardiner was one
of the island's true owners, he couldn't be banned despite not paying
for its upkeep, and he was given limited access and use.

When he first returned to the island in 1992, he said, "I got
down on my tummy and hugged it." He claims he discovered that
while he was gone, the Goelets had thrown his linens and blankets and towels into an outbuilding, where they had been "eaten by
rats and rained on," and that he was forced to drive all the way to
Caldor in Bridgehampton and buy $2,000 worth of linens to replace
them. His niece was furious at his return, calling him a "freeloader."

Gardiner can now visit the island only under special circumstances and by prior arrangement, like the autumnal shoot he leads of twenty hunters to thin out the deer, or the twice-a-summer tours on which he is permitted to take a group of historians, like today. At those times the Goelets are obligated to clear out of the manor house and make themselves scarce, presumably somewhere off the island, safe from the wrath of Robert Gardiner.

2

FOR THE MOST PART, the historians knew none of this bitter feud as they crossed Gardiner's Bay, watching as the verdant island came up before them. Gardiner edged *Laughing Lady* to a small dock in a sheltered cove with surprising skill. The second boat, manned by Gardiner's assistant, was close behind. As Gardiner spryly alighted from the boat, the joy and excitement of being on the island was apparent on his face. The caretaker waited for him and his guests with a flatbed pickup truck, rigged with bench seats in the back like an army transport, and a ten-year-old Chevrolet suburban jeep with the words ROBERT D. L. GARDINER, GARDINER'S ISLAND monogrammed on the doors. The two-tone jeep has no license plates, and the inspection sticker expired five years before, but as Gardiner reminded his passengers, it doesn't matter, because there is no law on Gardiner's Island except for himself.

"Over in Bostwick Forest," he said, "there's a hanging oak. We hanged a man here for murdering his brother on the island. We had a legal right to, we ruled this island." In fact, legend holds that four men were hanged on the island for various crimes, all of them black.

Gardiner led the way, driving his own jeep, flying up the hilly dirt road like a kid in a go-cart. His passengers in the backseat were

trounced around unmercifully, and farther behind, the people following in the open flatbed truck driven by Gardiner's assistant were
holding on to the sides for dear life. Gardiner came to a stop in front
of the thirty-eight-room manor house, modeled after the Governor's
Palace in Colonial Williamsburg. What is lovely about the three-
story, dark-brick house is how easily it stands on the island without manicured landscaping or elaborate gardens. The grass around
the yard and dirt driveways is scrubby, and not a flower in sight has
been planted by hand, only by nature, save for the red geraniums in
a 300-year-old try-pot used to cure whale oil.

This is the fourth manor house, the three previous ones having
been reduced to smoldering rubble. The first was burned to the
ground by eighty Spanish pirates in 1728, who were so angry not
to find the family jewels, "cleverly hidden down the well, hung on
a string," said Robert Gardiner, that they slashed the hands of the
third lord of the manor, John, Lion's grandson, and left him tied
to a tree. The second house burned to the ground in 1774, a fire
caused by someone smoking in bed the tobacco that once grew on
the island. The third house, a grand Georgian mansion 173 years
old, burned on January 24, 1947, while Sarah Diodati Gardiner
was leasing the island as a hunting retreat to Winston Guest, the
multimillionaire polo-playing sportsman. Sarah Diodati Gardiner
supported the island for years by turning it into an executive resort.
Previous to Guest the island had been leased to Clarence Mackay,
the silver-mine millionaire, and to Baron von Blixen Finecke, the husband of Isak Dinesen. Winston Guest built an airstrip on the island
and flew in hunting aficionados from all over the world, including
UN Secretary-Generals Dag Hammarskjöld and Trygve Lie, Indian
diplomat Madame Pandit, and Ernest Hemingway. Extraordinary
shooting parties were held at which 300 wild turkey were taken in a
morning's shoot, and the men took lunch at a stand in the woods,
brought to them by liveried servants.

The night the third house burned, only the writer Van Campen Heilner was in residence, and he escaped in his nightclothes from a second-floor roof, but a Pekinese dog perished in the flames, as did many of the house's historic antiques. Robert Gardiner, then a young man, rushed to the island the next day to see the damage and found it a ruin. Wandering through the charred timbers, he stumbled upon the remains of a secret closet that he had only suspected existed, from which floated the shreds of silk dresses that had been hidden away for centuries. It took Sarah Diodati Gardiner fourteen months to rebuild the house at a cost of $1 million, having to ferry every piece of wood, every brick, and each workman to the island by boat from the mainland.

It is in front of this rebuilt manor house that Gardiner's guests paused for a brief lunch. Gardiner's assistant helped carry an upholstered armchair out of the house for him to sit on, and delicatessen sandwiches brought from the mainland were produced from a corrugated-cardboard box. Several bottles of domestic champagne, floating in a chest of watery ice, were poured into paper cups. The historians settled under the shade of a broad oak that stands on the front lawn and contentedly ate their sandwiches and sipped their drinks while Gardiner, with Gardiner's Bay a milky cuticle on the horizon behind him, told his audience that the one building they would not see was the cottage of Goody Garlick, the woman accused of killing Lion Gardiner's darling daughter, Elizabeth, with witchcraft. The cottage is long since gone, Gardiner said, but the story remains as good as the day it happened.

"You *had* to believe in witches in Puritan days," explained Gardiner, "because Cotton Mather said that to deny witches was to deny evil and was to deny God. But Lion Gardiner didn't believe in witches, and he was the one who wound up saving Goody Garlick's life."

Goody Garlick's 1658 witch trial in East Hampton was the trial of the century for the town, no doubt. It took three months to conclude, and a great deal of the testimony still exists verbatim in the town records, dialogue dutifully recorded by hand. But more than just the workings of a seventeenth-century witch trial, the transcripts reveal what a mean little Calvinist town East Hampton was. By all accounts, Goody Garlick had it coming. She had a bitter disposition and was universally disliked by her neighbors. Goody (married couples were addressed as "Goodwife" and "Goodman" at the time) Garlick worked as a servant on Gardiner's Island for twelve years before she and her husband, Joshua Garlick, were able to afford their own place in East Hampton. Not long after moving to town, they became entangled in numerous slander lawsuits.

Ironic as it might seem in light of present-day East Hampton's litigious culture, between 1650 and 1665, the first fifteen years of the town's existence, slander was the single most common lawsuit in East Hampton. Sociologists say that societies in formation sometimes use slander lawsuits to establish pecking order and status among themselves. Perhaps that's why almost every adult member of the thirty-five or so families in town was involved in a slander suit, even Lion Gardiner and his wife, either as a plaintiff or defendant or witness. The townsfolk challenged one another in court over perceived slurs that now seem bizarre. One of the most exhaustively documented on record centers on whether Goodwife Edwards was bragging when she told her neighbor, Goodwife Price, that she brought her petticoat with her to East Hampton all the way from London. Never mind that nobody ever saw this petticoat or that Goody Price had already had her tongue put in a "cleft stick" for speaking badly. Goody Edwards sued Goody Price for calling her a "base lying woman" and received damages of twopence after tying up the town court with testimony for several weeks.

In 1658 Mary Gardiner's servant, John Wooley, sued one of his mistress's friends, Goodwife Hand, for saying he had made a "bow-wow" sound behind Mrs. Gardiner's back, mocking her. Mrs. Gardiner — she was the only woman in town important enough to be called "Mrs." in lieu of "Goodwife" — was revered as the town's first lady (and resented as a Dutch woman), and Wooley's suit against her friend Goody Hand turned into a full jury trial, with half a dozen witnesses testifying on either side. After several days of trial and testimony, Wooley was awarded ten shillings plus court costs from Goodwife Hand for his tarnished character.

But the slander lawsuits didn't reach their apotheosis until Goody Garlick was nearly burned alive for being a witch. By 1658 Goody Garlick's reputation had already been sullied when her twenty-something indentured servant, Daniel Fairfield, was caught masturbating with three other men — two of whom were married and over forty years old. The four men were brought to the church meeting hall and tried before three magistrates — one of them the father of one of the accused — on charges of "spilling their seed." The entire town turned out for the trial, and the four men were found guilty of being "notorious masturbators," but "not deeming the offense worthy of loss of life or limb," the magistrates determined that two of them be pilloried in punishment and that the ringleader, Daniel Fairfield, be publicly whipped.

Goody Garlick refused to take Fairfield back into her household, a wise move since immediately thereafter he sparked the second-biggest scandal in the town's history by seducing not only the Reverend Mr. James's maid but the Reverend Mr. James's daughter as well. "Acting filthy," they called it. Fairfield's eventual fate, alas, was never consigned to town records.

But Goody Garlick's was. In February 1658, twenty years of ill will against Goody Garlick bubbled to the surface when Lion Gardiner's fifteen-year-old daughter, Elizabeth, fell ill with a high fever and in her delirium accused Goody Garlick of bewitching her. One afternoon the child bride told her husband, "Love, I am very ill of my head"; her nursing baby was taken from her, and Elizabeth was put to bed. Her fever raged out of control, and at one point she opened her eyes wide in terror and shrieked, "A witch! A witch!" Her mother was summoned and begged her child, "Who do you see?" Elizabeth said that Goody Garlick was at that very moment standing at the foot of her bed, pricking her with pins.

Elizabeth continued to accuse Goody Garlick through the night to several neighbors who took turns sitting vigil. The neighbors also reported a mysterious presence in the room that night, a "black thing," at the foot of the bed, and deep in the night came a hollow and mournful sound from the fireplace. The next day Elizabeth went into convulsions and died in her father's arms.

For the next three months, anybody in the town of East Hampton who ever had a grudge against Goody Garlick was given the opportunity to vent his or her spleen in court. Garlick's neighbors recounted volumes of horror stories about her alleged witchcraft. Goodwife Edwards in particular held the court mesmerized when she testified that years before, while nursing her newborn infant, as soon as Goody Garlick wandered by and said how pretty the baby was, Edwards saw "death in the face" of the infant, who never opened its eyes again and died days later. After months of intermittent testimony, it was suggested that the only sure way to find out whether Goody Garlick was a witch was to hold her underwater in the Town Pond to see if she would drown.

Lion Gardiner would have none of this. He appeared at the courtroom and forbade the magistrates to allow anyone to harm Goody Garlick. He said that his daughter died of sickness, not an evil spell, and that only the heathen Indians believed in witchcraft. Gardiner saw to it that Goody Garlick was brought to a more sophisticated court in Hartford, Connecticut, where they knew more about witches than in East Hampton. Gardiner himself, along with armed guards, accompanied Garlick and her husband to Hartford. None of the witnesses ever appeared, and Gardiner was able to arrange for the charges to be dismissed.

"Lion Gardiner returned Goody Garlick to East Hampton himself," Robert Gardiner explained to the historians sitting in the shade at the manor house. "She had to spend the rest of her life with the neighbors who had accused her. One version of her story has it that she returned to town and made the best of it, the other is that Gardiner gave her a cottage on this island, where she lived her last years in disgrace. Wherever she spent them, they were long years. Town records show that Goody Garlick lived to eighty-seven, and her husband to over a hundred."

3

THE INTERIOR of the manor house is decorated in taste so low-key as to be bland. There are unremarkable upholstered chairs and anonymous slipcovered sofas flanked by dark-wood occasional tables. The wallpaper pattern is leafy and unobtrusive. The dining room is large but gloomy, the table and chairs polished and dark. Nature prints and old oils adorn the walls, each of whose significance Gardiner dutifully recited. Often the tour was too comprehensive. He even insisted that his guests follow him down to the basement to see just how large the fuse boxes are or to touch the hot-water tanks to see how warm they feel. Bounding up the cellar steps like a young man, Gardiner shouted, "Now, my bedroom!" and darted up to the master bedroom on the second floor with the two dozen visitors trudging after him.

The master bedroom is essentially a dowdy room with faded peach-colored walls and a handmade multicolored hook rug on the floor. There is a double bed with a clean white duvet and a headboard tufted in a salmon-colored fern-print fabric. The historians spread out around the room, looking at the personal articles lying about, at the history books on the mahogany bedside tables, at the women's clothing in the closets. They peeked in the bathroom and at the objects on top of the dressers. As Gardiner spun one of his tales about an uncle who married Hungarian royalty, he plopped down on the bed, clasped his hands behind his head, and put his muddy shoes up on the white duvet. The historians knew a photo opportunity when they saw one and their flash cameras went off in a rain of strobe light.

Next to the bed was a small wire cage with a carpet remnant inside. "Is that for your little pet?" one of the historians asked Gardiner. He glanced at the cage warily and said, somewhat reluctantly, "Yes." The present location of Gardiner's pet was not pursued, but a more savvy visitor might have realized that Gardiner didn't have a pet, that the cage was for the pet of Alexandra and Robert Goelet, and that the clothes in the closet didn't belong to Gardiner but to the Goelets, as did the bed and duvet that Gardiner was intentionally muddying with his shoes. The historians were unwitting collaborators in a gross invasion of privacy of the Goelets' bedroom. Yet the only clue that alternative occupants of the manor house even existed was a large handwritten sign on a blackboard in the kitchen that said, THESE THINGS DO NOT BELONG TO MR. GARDINER.

Later, Gardiner's guests loaded themselves back into the overcrowded vehicles for a tour around the island. Gardiner's suburban careened into Bostwick Forest at breakneck speed. The 1,200 acres of forest are as lush and green as something in a Grimm fairy tale. The jeep flew by herds of unperturbed deer grazing in sunlit glens, and he passed a flock of wild turkeys in a ravine of rich dark grapes. The low tree branches whiplashed into the open windows of the jeep. He made various stops, including the highest point on the island, where the white-bearded David Gardiner, the sixth lord of the manor, cried aloud to the wind in his isolation in 1734. ("No one," he wrote in his diary. "Rien.") He pointed out the low wooden building where the "bound boys" were quartered and made to say their Sunday catechism to the lady of the manor, and to T'Other House, where sick British sailors had been bivouacked.

Finally, he came to another unique claim of Gardiner's Island, the spot where Captain Kidd buried treasure in 1699. John Gardiner, Lion Gardiner's grandson, was roused from his bed one night by Captain William Kidd and forced to watch as his men buried gold and jewels on the island. John Gardiner was a huge man, called "the Powerful One" by the Montauks. He knew of Kidd before that night. Kidd wasn't a pirate at all, but a well-known businessman who owned a fine home on Wall Street and a pew in Trinity Church. He had gone into the ugly but perfectly legal business of bounty hunter of the seas. He had letters of marque from the Crown permitting him to raid the ships of French and African privateers on the high seas, then bring the spoils back to London and divvy them up with his backers.

In 1699, after one particularly good score — a ship carrying the dowry of the sultan of Madagascar — Kidd was on his way home to London when he heard that he had been declared a pirate by his partners. He decided that instead of returning home to London to certain trouble, he would set out for Boston, where he could clear his name. On the way it occurred to him that it might be prudent to hide the treasure until the matter was settled, and stumbling upon Gardiner's Island as he pushed northward in his six-gun ship, he thought he discovered the perfect place to hide it. He woke John Gardiner in the middle of the night and forced him to witness the burying of fifty-eight rubies, several sacks of gold ducats, bars of gold and silver, and a sultan's ransom in emeralds and pearls. Kidd warned that "If I come back for this treasure and it's not here, I'll have your head or the head of your sons."

Allan Schneider stands in front of a $100,000 East Hampton summer rental.
(© 1990 *Newsday*)

Tyler House, Allan Schneider's "White House" on Main Street. (Credit Lee Minetree)

Allan Schneider in the living room
of the Summer White House,
feeding his ill-tempered dog, Duff.
(Property of Rochelle Rosenberg)

Grey Gardens, now the home of former *Washington Post* editor Ben Bradlee and his wife, writer Sally Quinn. The house came to infamy when it was the home of Edith Bouvier Beale, the maternal aunt of Jacqueline Kennedy Onassis, and her daughter, Edie.

On the way to Gardiner's Island, a tattered Jolly Roger flaps in the wind as the lord of the manor, D. L. Gardiner, spins his tales.

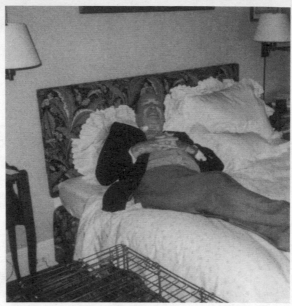

Robert Gardiner makes himself comfortable in the bed of his niece, Alexandra Creel Goelet, and her husband, Robert G. Goelet.

Lion Gardiner's Gothic sepulchre under an ornate sandstone tomb designed by James Renwick, the architect of Saint Patrick's Cathedral and Grace Church.

The East Hampton home of Robert D. L. Gardiner, the "real" Summer
White House, with its fortresslike walls.

Adele and Albert Herter in their later years, with daughter, Lydia,
who lived in the "Happy Hour" house on the grounds of The Creeks.
(Courtesy of the Santa Barbara Historical Society)

Albert Herter in costume for one of his famous tableaux at The Creeks. (Courtesy of the Santa Barbara Historical Society)

Ted Dragon in costume for Bach French Suite for Paris Opera. Danseur E'toile, 1951. (Courtesy of the Ossorio Foundation, Southampton, N.Y.)

Alfonso Ossorio, circa 1966. (Courtesy of the Ossorio Foundation, Southampton, N.Y.)

Group sitting on steps of The Creeks, circa 1954. Seated left to right, Ted Dragon with poodle Horla, the Polish poet Kasmir Wierzynski, Alfonso Ossorio, Josephine Little with infant Abigail, Halina Wierzynski, Joseph Glasco, Jackson Pollock. (Courtesy of the Ossorio Foundation, Southampton, N.Y.)

Ted Dragon in sitting room at The Creeks with Ta-Yu, circa 1976. (Courtesy of the Ossorio Foundation, Southampton, N.Y.)

Aerial view of The Creeks, East Hampton, New York, circa 1984.
(Courtesy of the Ossorio Foundation, Southampton, N.Y.)

Jean Dubuffet and Alfonso Ossorio in
front of sculpture by Ossorio, "In, Out,
Up & Down," 1973. (Courtesy of the
Ossorio Foundation, Southampton, N.Y.)

Kidd never came back to Gardiner's Island. He didn't have much luck clearing his name in Boston; he was arrested and sent to London, where he was tried and convicted. They hanged him in 1701 — not for piracy but for killing one of his sailors by hitting him over the head with a wooden bucket. The governor of Massachusetts, Lord Bellomont, who had a detailed list of the treasure, was most eager for John Gardiner to dig it up and return it, which he did. However, one diamond somehow remained in Gardiner's portmanteau, and his wife snatched the stone for herself, a large, uncut dull diamond, which was later set and worn in a ring, but has been lost to the tyranny of time.

4

THE HISTORIANS' PATIENCE was also lost to the tyranny of time. It was late in the afternoon, they had been Gardiner's wards all day, and they were eager to return to the mainland for the long drive home in the holiday weekend traffic. On the way to the boats Gardiner stopped by the manor house to pick up the coolers and supplies from lunch when he at once noticed something that perked his interest: Parked next to the house was a jeep that hadn't been there earlier. He stopped his own vehicle at the front door and, without a word to his mystified guests, hurriedly disappeared.

Moments later, like hornets exploding from a disturbed hive, Alexandra and Robert Goelet and their namesake children, Alexandra, nineteen, a student at Middlebury College, and Robert Jr., sixteen, a sophomore at a New England prep school, burst through the front door of the house. They spilled out the door, with Robert Gardiner behind them in hot pursuit, screeching after Robert

Goelet, "How dare you ask me if I went upstairs when I had a perfect right?"

The Goelets look stunned to discover two dozen people staring blankly at them from the two vehicles on their lawn. One of the historians asked loudly, "Who are *those* people? Do *those* people live on the island? How are they going to get *home?*"

They were a handsome family, the Goelets, considering that they were cringing. Alexandra is a beautiful woman in her fifties, managing a youthful elegance, as does her sixty-six-year-old husband in his khaki slacks and blue Oxford shirt. It would be impossible to divine how very rich they are by just looking at them. They had spent the day at a beach on the far side of the island, assiduously avoiding any confrontation with Gardiner, who was supposed to be gone by five o'clock. But now they'd returned to find not only that he was still there, complete with audience, but that there was mud on their bed upstairs.

At the sight of the two dozen strangers gawking at them, the Goelets scattered in four directions. Gardiner went after them one at a time, trying to pick them off and confront them, but they evaded him. As though in a Keystone Kops movie, he began to chase them around the house—in one door, out the other. First he cornered Alexandra Sr., then her daughter, then he went after Robert Sr. The historians, uncomprehending, began to unfold slowly from their cramped quarters in the truck and jeep to watch the show.

"And you say that I'm making it up!" Gardiner shouted at Goelet, who was now ducking around the far side of the house. "I'm not making this up!" Gardiner howled. "*You're* the one who's making it up!"

Alexandra Goelet, the strain showing on her face, politely canvassed the confused historians as if nothing were happening, asking if they had enjoyed their day on Gardiner's Island. "Who's she?" one of the wives asked, her patience at an end, and Alexandra just smiled. "We want to go home," one of the men in the jeep told Alexandra.

"What do you need to leave?" Alexandra asked the man.

He pointed to Gardiner. "That man."

"We'd love to give him to you," she said, managing a wry smile.

"Why don't you get lost?" Robert Goelet was now saying to Gardiner. "You're just upsetting yourself."

"Why don't *you* get lost! You tried to kill me! Before two witnesses you tried to run me over."

"The implication being that I'm a lousy driver?" Goelet asked with a sardonic laugh.

This mockery caused Gardiner to shriek, *"You said that I had no right to go upstairs! How dare you say that?"*

A silence fell over the scene as Goelet simply walked away.

Gardiner decided his last best hope was his nephew, Robert Jr. A handsome teenager with large brown eyes and sandy hair, gangly at six feet five inches, who his father hopes will not get any taller, he was also the only member of his family who didn't run from his uncle. Although he was clearly embarrassed with the audience of strangers watching, he managed to maintain his dignity as he stood his ground, his hands jammed into the pockets of his khaki pants.

"Will you hear me out?" Gardiner implored the boy, and with a wan smile on his face, the young man resigned himself to a few moments. Gardiner began to speak hurriedly, like a man begging for his life before a lynch mob. He asked the boy to have lunch with him, that there was something important he had to tell him. The legacy must not die. The Gardiner legacy is too rich, too worthy. It's a fantastic legacy, and it's *his*, for one day he will be the seventeenth lord of the manor. There are witches and pirates, and the man who founded the town of East Hampton ... But Gardiner is too upset to impart all this, and all that came out were fragments, pieces of his dreams, "The first English child ... the lord of the manor ..."

After a few minutes of listening to his uncle's rant, Robert Jr. excused himself. He said that he had to return to prep school in Massachusetts that week, and that it would be impossible to schedule a lunch. Gardiner's shoulders fell in defeat as he turned to walk away, but his nephew watched him contemplatively as he left.

This brief moment over, Gardiner returned to his jeep and got behind the wheel. "That never happened before!" Gardiner exclaimed, not very convincingly, to his passengers about the altercation. He turned over the engine. "What a mess!" There was silence in the jeep. "What a mess," he repeated, and set off for the pier and *Laughing Lady* and escape.

"Well, for the Historical Society this was not a good day," Gardiner said in summation. "But at least I had enough champagne to go around, I think, good French champagne."

He stopped the car at the dock, and all the doors flung open simultaneously, passengers fleeing to the waiting boats as Gardiner muttered behind them, "What a mess! What a mess!"

The Creeks

THE CREEKS, Ronald O. Perelman's fifty-seven-acre estate, is the cynosure of Hamptons nouvelle society. It is "the most important house in East Hampton," Allan Schneider declared to the *New York Times,* and for once he wasn't exaggerating: The Creeks is perhaps the most important house in *all* the Hamptons. Not only is it the largest privately held estate but the copper-topped, two-story Mediterranean villa, with its half a dozen guest houses, outbuildings, and 2,000 feet of Georgica Pond front, is the crown jewel of all the sprawling mansions that grace the shores of the most coveted location in the Hamptons. The 290-acre tidal pond is a willowy fingered estuary separated from the assault of the Atlantic Ocean by a wide, white strand of East Hampton beach. The water is brackish, opened to the nourishing waters of the ocean each fall by a trench dug with a shovel, and its views are arguably the most superb on the South Fork.

Past and present luminaries with homes on the pond include film directors Robert Benton and Steven Spielberg; communications executive Christopher Whittle; Donald Petrie, a partner in the banking firm Lazard Frères; former New York Yankees general managing partner Robert Nederlander; and author and heir to the Uris building fortune, B. H. Friedman. Most of the pond's west side is made up of a private enclave called the Georgica Association, which up until the fifties had no Jewish or gay residents (it now has both). The association is an exquisite encampment of narrow roads with speed bumps, where dogs run free in open fields and there is a beach cabana and tennis courts for members.

Only thirty of the seventy houses around the pond have ocean views, and the waiting list of interested buyers for those houses is prodigious, including actor Tom Hanks and his wife, actress Rita Wilson; Barbra Streisand; media entrepreneur Barry Diller; and impresario David Geffen. Pondfront property is so coveted that art dealer and cineaste Arnold Glimcher spent an estimated $1 million reclaiming a swampy area so he could build a house with a pond view. Prices start at about $3 million for one of the smaller houses that previously served as servants' quarters for the large homes. What little undeveloped land there is sells for more than $2 million an acre. It is rare that houses on the pond are put up for rent; on any given summer only two or three houses are available, and a recent listing asked $500,000 for "the season" — Memorial Day to Labor Day — for an eight-bedroom house with a six-car garage, screening room, "kitchen garden," and two pools.

Gracious-living doyenne Martha Stewart proved what a good shopper she was by snatching up a $3.2 million travertine-and-glass house that Gordon Bunshaft, the Skidmore, Owings and Merrill managing partner, built for himself and his wife, Nina, on the pond as a weekend retreat in the sixties. (Bunshaft was the first Jew ever to own property on the pond.) When Nina died in 1995 the modestly sized, 2,600-square-foot house passed into the hands of the Museum of Modern Art. This was the only residential house that Bunshaft, who built some of Manhattan's greatest skyscrapers, ever designed, and so has tremendous historical importance as well as its prime location on the pond. Of course, it was the antithesis of Martha Stewart's Victorian style. It has only two small bedrooms and a galley kitchen without even a window; its sleek rectangular minimalist design dictates furniture sans chintz slipcovers. Stewart also already owned an elaborately gardened, thirteen-bedroom shingled gray mansion with teal blue (a color coined "Martha Stewart blue," in a paint available from Sherwin-Williams) trim on venerable Lily Pond Lane in East Hampton. Not satisfied with the classic design of the Bunshaft house, Stewart immediately filed plans to build a four-foot-deep lap pool and a separate studio.

Most of the Georgica Pond houses have pedigrees. The house now owned by Dr. Richard Axel was previously owned by art collector Ben Heller, was built in the 1800s by New York society physician Dr. Tod Helmuth Jr., and rented by artist Alfonso Ossorio his first summer in the Hamptons. In the sixties it was bought by art dealer Leo Castelli, who shared it one summer with Elaine and Willem de Kooning until the artist and his wife bought their own house on Springs Fireplace Road. But none of the houses on the pond have the provenance of The Creeks. Isadora Duncan danced in its theater. Jackson Pollock attacked a piano with an ice pick in the music room. Enrico Caruso dozed one summer away on its deck chairs. The estate's parklike grounds, with $5 million worth of rare specimen trees, have been called "the eighth wonder of the horticultural world" by the American Horticultural Society. Forty-six species of wildlife live along the estate's two and a half miles of private roads, and in the summer the magnificent ospreys, who nest atop towering pitch pines, lazily float just above the pond's calm surface, casually plucking perch from the clear waters and carrying them back to their mates.

The Creeks' current owner, billionaire Ronald O. Perelman, is a former Philadelphian who cobbled his estimated $3.5 billion fortune from his father's modest $12 million business complex. Perelman assembled an eclectic and always glamorous portfolio of companies that have included Revlon, Inc., Consolidated Cigar Corp., Marvel Entertainment Group, and the behemoth foodstuff conglomerate Pantry Pride. He purchased The Creeks in late spring of 1992 at a bargain price — $12.5 million. He bought it in a hurry, as he was rebounding from an expensive divorce from gossip columnist Claudia Cohen, who walked away with a reported $80 million cash settlement as well as half of the couple's $8 million estate on Lily Pond Lane.

Because of Perelman's wealth and paranoia — or perhaps simply because its entrance and exit are located prominently on Montauk Highway — The Creeks is the most heavily guarded and secure compound in the East End. This is particularly unusual in a community where year-round residents leave the doors to their homes unlocked and the summer crowd feel safe enough to park their foreign sports cars with the tops down on Newtown Lane while they pick up a pizza at Sam's. The only other house known to employ guards is Steven Spielberg's Quelle Barn. Several of Perelman's burly security men sit ominously behind the steering wheel of twin green Jeeps parked just off the highway on The Creeks' private roads. All security wear white polo shirts with Adirondack green logos that say, *The Creeks.* On the pond side security guards patrol the waterfront on foot, and one of them with a gun showing in his shoulder holster warned a couple canoeing on the pond not to come closer than 100 feet to shore. Perelman hates that his security and privacy are compromised on the pond side by transient boaters who rent canoes from a nearby surf shop and gain public access to the pond on the highway and then paddle around to gawk at his house. Famously short-tempered and controlling, Perelman reportedly demanded to rent all the boats in the shop for the entire summer to get his privacy, and when the owner refused to accommodate him, he asked to buy the store. (Ironically, Perelman owns Coleman, the well-known camping-goods company that manufactures canoes, of which Perelman keeps dozens on hand for his own guests.) So annoyed is Perelman by the possibility of boaters (or reporters or photographers with telephoto lenses) paddling by his house that he has floated little buoys in front of his property to mark off an area, as if that part of the pond belonged to him. This so incenses Perelman's neighbor and longtime pond resident B. H. Friedman that Friedman periodically rows through Perelman's barricade to show that he will not be intimidated from public waters.

The richer Perelman has become and the greater the notoriety, the more futile his Orwellian attempts to control his environment. In late August 1995 Perelman's caution backfired when his security chief and a maintenance man tried to extort $500,000 from him by threatening to blow the whistle on an eavesdropping device Perelman had planted in the house, which they claimed he was going to use to listen in on guests attending a fund-raiser for Senator John Kerry. Perelman contended that the device was only used to monitor the safety of Samantha, his daughter with Claudia Cohen. The case is not resolved.

By the summer of 1996, it appeared that Perelman's need to control everything around him began to unhinge his marriage to his third wife, Patricia Duff, the former wife of Tri-Star chairman Mike Medavoy and stylishly blond Democratic Party fund-raiser, whom Perelman married when she was pregnant with their daughter, Caleigh. The couple were in a limousine in Chicago on their way to the Democratic National Convention when Perelman learned that Duff had disobeyed him by attending a party for Vice President Albert Gore without him. Perelman jumped out of the limousine in a rage and took his Gulfstream jet back to New York, stranding her at the convention. The following Saturday, after he had calmed down, Duff arrived at The Creeks to talk things over, and Perelman had her searched. A tape recorder was found in her pocketbook, which she hadn't turned on but that her lawyer had suggested she bring. Duff left The Creeks in less than an hour, and two years later she and Perelman quietly divorced.

All this family drama has leaked its way out of The Creeks despite a strictly enforced veil of secrecy. Since staff turnover is high (mostly because Perelman frequently fires people), each member of the corps of maids, cooks, handymen, cleaning and grounds maintenance crews, and landscapers is asked to sign a confidentiality agreement. It is also said that the household staff is asked to make themselves scarce if they see Mr. Perelman in passing. Each Friday at a roll call for the staff, a set of dicta and rules are handed out to every employee. Perelman, who is an observant Jew and keeps a kosher household, has standing orders that no food, not even candy bars, may be carried into the "kosher buildings" on the estate. (Sheds and barns are considered nonkosher.) There are two pantries off the kitchen, one for dairy plates and one for meat, as well as four individual stainless-steel refrigerators, separated for dairy and meat. On the frame of most every door at The Creeks, from the front door down to the linen closets, there is a gold mezuzah.

The Creeks was remodeled by Peter Marino, the designer of Barneys department store on Madison Avenue and Andy Warhol's townhouse. Calling the black circular pool that had been part of The Creeks fame a "birdbath," Marino had it torn out and a rectangular one put in. The Creeks is decorated in a simple, unpretentious style, in colors of white, cream, and hunter green, with sisal rugs on the floors and overstuffed, slipcovered furniture. The art on the walls, ever changing, is by the biggest names of the modern art world — Lichtenstein, Schnabel, Bleckner. On every table is a telephone with several lines, a cigar, a cigar clipper, a lighter with the logo of MacAndrews & Forbes, Perelman's umbrella company, and a pen and cream notepad with the hunter green logo *The Creeks.* Most guest rooms have their own refrigerators with snack foods, as well as a list of activities that can be arranged, including horseback riding and screenings in the estate's own movie theater, created out of a vast artist's studio. The movie theater has its own candy counter and popcorn and soda machines; instead of seats, there are fifty chaise longues made of teak, each with a forest green cushion and red wool blanket bearing the Revlon logo. Behind the screen is a stage on which stands a professional drum kit, which Perelman plays along with practice tapes.

There are no guest bedrooms in the main house. The second floor consists of two nurseries and the master bedroom suite. Perelman's bedroom suite has its own sitting room and fireplace, and not only his-and-her bathrooms but his-and-her offices. Across from a comfy double bed with a plump duvet stands a large-screen television, as well as smaller TVs on the night tables next to the bed. Perelman first saw the pale green marble that covers his bathroom walls and floors in a hotel in Italy. When he learned that the quarry where the marble came from had been closed, he bought the bathrooms from the hotel and had the marble shipped to The Creeks. Perelman also has a room-sized, walk-in closet, lined with floor-to-ceiling shelves and drawers, each labeled with the name of a designer: Ralph Lauren, Calvin Klein, Yves Saint Laurent. Some garments are brand-new: slacks hanging in neat rows; pairs of blue jeans, in several different sizes, many still with price tags hanging on them; and more than a dozen pairs of sneakers of every purpose and brand.

In the Hamptons, Ron Perelman is both envied and despised. For the baby-boomer billions, he's the one to beat — the richest guy with the best house. But for many others, he is a figurehead of impending doom, the personification of big, new money, Hollywood pretensions, and political flirtations — turning a gentle place into an armed camp. For them, the worst aspect is that The Creeks was so rich in culture and history that even the richest man in New York State has managed to cheapen it. To buy a house is one thing, to inhabit it is another.

2

IF THE POND ever really "belonged" to anyone, it was to Jeorgkee, a wizened Montauk who lived and fished on its shores most of his life. In the 1600s he signed on as a whaler with a Dutch hunting company. There is little more known about this Indian, except that by the time the pond became part of a parcel bought up by Puritan settlers in 1648, it was already known as Georgika's Pond.

By the 1770s the parcel of pondfront land that became known as The Creeks was called Sheep Point, a grassy dune where a rugged army captain and farmer named John Dayton took his sheep to graze. Dayton was a stalwart descendant of one of the original founding families of the town of East Hampton, eight generations removed. The bearded good captain, who was an experienced fisherman as well as an army officer, paid one pound an acre for a seventy-acre tract, a good value for land at the time even though the pond was inconveniently located two miles from the safety of town. He built himself a two-room farmhouse close to the muddy road that led to and from East Hampton village, about where the gatehouse to The Creeks stands today.

Dayton had not lived at Sheep Point long when one snowy February night during the Revolution, while the British still occupied Long Island, English soldiers tried to plunder the house for food. No sooner had Dayton slipped his little son, Josiah, clothed in only a nightshirt, out the back door, telling him to run quickly into the woods for safety, than a bullet whizzed past his head and shattered his weaver's loom. The farmer began to return fire feverishly, running from window to window, calling the names of an imaginary regiment, "Nathanael! Joseph! Simon! Wake up men and come to arms!" The ruse scared off the marauders, and at daybreak Dayton found copious British blood soaked in the snow. It wasn't until later that he learned his son had made it safely to a neighbor's house.

That afternoon, while Dayton was working in the barn, a British major appeared on horseback and accused Dayton of killing one of his soldiers the night before; the man whose blood Dayton had found in the snow had later bled to death. Dayton, enraged, grabbed a pitchfork from a bale of hay and told the major that he would "rip [his] guts out and string them along the cow-yard fence" if he didn't hightail it off his farm. The British officer retreated and was never heard from again.

Eventually, living in a damp house primitively insulated with seaweed and corn cobs took its toll on John Dayton's joints, and by the time he was in his fifties, he was virtually crippled with severe rheumatism. One particularly bitter winter, doctors gave him up for bedridden. Determined to prove them wrong, Dayton painfully dragged himself out of bed one night and, dressed in only his nightshirt, pulled himself up on his horse and rode slowly through the frigid night to the gut where the ocean joined the pond. There, with the help of his son, Josiah, now a young man, Dayton dipped himself three times in the freezing water. Then Josiah wrapped his father in a blanket and took him home to bed. The next Sunday, so the story goes, Dayton walked sprightly into church, a new man. He said the shock of the cold had cured him — frozen out his rheumatism — and now he was able to "run, jump, and wrestle," as good as any man. Indeed, he lived another thirty years, into his eighties.

It was Josiah Dayton's grandson, Edward, who sold Sheeps Point out of family hands for the first time. In 1894 he deeded the seventy-acre tract over to Mary Miles Herter, who paid $10,500 for the land and farmhouse, "a large advance from the original cost," noted the *East Hampton Star*. The powdered and perfumed Mrs. Herter was the trim, rich widow of Christian Herter Sr., of Paris and New York, the man who had practically invented the trade of society interior decoration. For a fee of approximately $100,000 (the equivalent of $3–4 million today), Christian and his brother, Gustave, decorated mansions of Civil War profiteers and robber barons around the world. The Herter brothers designed rooms for President Ulysses S. Grant in the White House and ornate mansions for Mary and Mark Hopkins in San Francisco, Milton Slocum Latham of Menlo Park, and J. Pierpont Morgan's elaborate New York Midtown manse. They were the leaders of the "aesthetic movement" of America's Gilded Age of design. They created the hyperluxurious look that Edith Wharton captured in her novels: furniture inlaid with mother-of-pearl, cascading crystal chandeliers, opulently heavy rugs and drapes, and hand-carved moldings. Since no store-bought furnishings were good enough for the Herter brothers, they simply manufactured their own. They opened their own looms and brought weavers from France to make their own tapestries and rugs. They manufactured their own furniture, including chairs that were wrought with such brilliant craftsmanship that they are now considered priceless and are on display in museum collections around the world.

Christian Herter's pièce de résistance was William H. Vanderbilt's block-long mansion on the corner of Fifth Avenue and Fifty-first Street, opposite Saint Patrick's Cathedral. Herter designed the sumptuously baroque interior, down to the design of the hardware pulls on the doors and the marquetry around the woodwork. In 1882, after creating a worldwide sensation with his work on the Vanderbilt mansion, Christian Herter was so rich that he was able to retire to fulfill his lifelong dream of becoming a painter — only to die of tuberculosis a year later at age forty-four. He left his wife, Mary Miles Herter, with a vast and unexpected fortune, $10 million, the equivalent of ten times that today.

Mrs. Herter bought Sheep Point on Georgica Pond not for herself but as a wedding gift for her rather extraordinary son, Albert. He was a sandy-haired, handsome boy, six feet two inches tall, with a proud, Germanic face. Educated by private tutors in Paris and New York, Albert was a sweet young man, kind and friendly. He was also in some ways the personification of his father's style of decorating, a man who lived his life with ornate flair in pursuit of good taste. He was a brilliant painter, a gifted writer, and as talented an interior decorator as his father. His personal style was markedly flamboyant, and he sometimes wore a red fox-hunting jacket to drama school classes or a swank dinner jacket at home. He smoked cigarettes in an ivory-inlaid cigarette holder to keep his fingers from nicotine stains and stayed up late into the night writing memoirs and musicales. His greatest gift, however, was painting murals — vast, dramatic, tableaux of heroic battles, some of them fifty feet long with hundreds of characters.

In the 1890s, while studying art at the Académie Julian in Paris, Albert, then twenty-two, met Adele McGinnis, twenty-four, the beautiful and spoiled daughter of New York banker and broker John McGinnis. In fin-de-siècle Paris, Adele and her four small-boned, pale-skinned sisters were known as the "McGinnis Beauties." Adele had deep blue eyes and struck a chord in Albert that most other women had not. Bright and easily bored, she was a "modern" woman who smoked cigarettes in public and enjoyed a martini. She was also the first woman who understood Albert's desire to lead a somewhat affected lifestyle dedicated to art. He would adore her for the rest of his life. They married in New York at Saint Thomas Church on April 5, 1893, after which Mary Miles Herter sent her son and new daughter-in-law on a honeymoon to Japan. They lived and painted for six months in the Orient, becoming imbued with the Eastern spirit, and on their return brought with them enough crates of Orientalia to fill a warehouse — or a mansion.

The young couple spent the next summer in a rented house on Georgica Pond (where they managed to scandalize neighbors by using nude young girls as models for nymphs in their nature paintings). That summer Albert and Adele began to covet Sheep Point and the old Dayton farmhouse that stood on it, which local lore held was the oldest farmhouse still standing in New York State. "Before the summer was over," wrote Albert in a reminiscence years later, "we had persuaded my mother to buy the place, crazy as she thought us."

Also with mother's funding, Albert and Adele set out to build a summer cottage in which to put all the Orientalia — not just another summer cottage, but one in the great luxe tradition of the Herter name. For this task they hired New York architect Grosvenor Atterbury, who had spent boyhood summers in Southampton and knew the area well. Atterbury had designed Southampton's Parrish Art Museum and was known for harmonizing color and style by "painting" a house into its background, often using reds, browns, and buff stucco. Building the house with such perfectionists as Albert and Adele as his clients was probably Atterbury's most stressful collaboration; on top of everything, his own house in Southampton burned to the ground. It took a year alone for Albert and Adele to decide the exact spot on which the house would stand, a decision they made by living one summer in a series of canvas tents (again managing to scandalize the local gentry) and tracking the course of a full moon in August or the arc of the solstice sun. It took nearly a decade to complete the house and all its outbuildings, which they first named, appropriately enough, Prés Choisis.

The long, two-story Italianate villa was designed in a gentle U shape to allow maximum light and unobstructed views of the pond. The outside walls of cream-colored stucco had been mixed with sand from the beach to give it texture. The windows, with a mullioned waffle design, were fitted with copper screens to match the copper of the roof, which hung low over the walls, connected by rose-covered arbors and trellises. The main building had five guest bedroom suites, all with ocean views. Adele and Albert had separate bedrooms on opposite ends of the second floor, along with their own discrete staircases. Because the Herters loved the effect of a roaring fire, there was a fireplace in every room, nineteen in all in the main house. It was also one of the first summer cottages to have heat — the ultra-new-sounding "oil vapor" heat. Adele was loathe to see servants about, so beyond the kitchen and pantry, the maids had their own separate kitchen and sitting room, where they would be out of sight.

The building that housed Albert's massive studio was linked to the main house by a trellised arbor of Concord grapes. Because the ugly purple squish marks on the laced-brick path upset Adele, there was a servant whose sole job was to sweep the porte cochere of grapes three times a day. Albert's ivy-covered studio was one of the largest artist's workspaces in the world, fifty-six feet long by thirty-five feet wide, with the north wall full of windows that kept the room bathed in soft light all day. The building also included three more guest bedrooms and a bath. The studio itself doubled as a professionally equipped theater, complete with a hand-carved proscenium arch, scenery flies, dressing rooms, and gaslit handblown footlights. It was in this studio that in the summer of 1929, as Albert and Adele's weekend guest, Isadora Duncan danced in a dramatic presentation that Albert wrote and directed called "The Gift of Eternal Life."

On the opposite side of the main house was another long, low building, a three-car garage (in which the Herters kept a red Phaeton automobile) over which there was a "tower," where there were two more guest bedrooms with views of the pond. Finally, at the farthest end of the property near the highway stood another guest house with its own sitting room, fireplace, bedroom, and bath, plus a small gatekeeper's cottage.

The interior of the main building was like an Oriental jewel box. The moldings were Chinese-red lacquer, and the walls ornately flocked with a 14-karat-gold Chinese-lantern pattern. Every door and wall panel had hand-painted scenes of Eastern life. Herter chairs were mixed with wicker fanbacks, and Chinese-themed rugs covered the floors. In Adele's second-floor studio, the entire entranceway of a Japanese house that the Herters had dismantled and carted back from the Orient was installed as a frame for the huge hearth and festooned with giant peacock feathers.

At the apex of the house, multileveled, basket-weave brick terraces led down to a landscaped glen at the sandy banks of the pond. To the left was a stucco boathouse, where the Herters moored Robert Browning's gondola, which they had purchased in Venice. Adele used the gondola to visit friends who lived on the pond. Harry Easer, the jowly caretaker who worked for the Herters for three decades, was Adele's gondolier. As Harry poled the ornately carved black gondola away from the shore, Adele slowly unfurled a fifty-foot blue tulle scarf into the water behind her, where it floated like a train. This particular blue was Adele's signature color, a faded robin's egg blue that to this day decorators refer to as "Herter blue." When the gondola reached its destination, Adele unwrapped the scarf from her neck with a flourish and abandoned it for Harry to retrieve.

It was Adele's gardens that turned The Creeks, as the property later came to be known, into a legend. Landscaping and horticulture had previously been the exclusive province of the man of the household. "Landscape architect" was a novel profession in America, newly required only because so many mansions were being built, abetted by the cheap brawn of Victorian labor. Women were only just beginning to participate in landscape design as a way to express themselves. In East Hampton it was also a way for rich ladies to compete; extravagant gardens were a sign of status and wealth. Many of the gardens designed in East Hampton at the turn of the century ultimately had some historical value in the annals of landscaping, like the twelve-acre walled Italian gardens of the Frank Wiborg mansion, Dunes; or Emma Woodhouse's seventeen-acre Japanese water gardens at Greycroft, with its pools and streams and lily ponds and Japanese teahouses, designed for her by a horticulturist she imported from the University of Dublin; or Mary Woodhouse's more formal gardens of boxwood topiary she called The Fens.

But there was nothing quite like Adele Herter's gardens. Her gardens were so massive and complex to maintain that every summer she imported thirty gardeners from Japan for the chore, bivouacking them in a small tent city built on a remote corner of the property. Aided by the beautiful natural backdrop of pines, saw grass, and wild flowers, Adele's formal gardens spread out around the house in large geometric shapes, each whimsically themed. Some were solid colors — all white flowers in one, all pink in another; others were labyrinths, with concentric patterns of flowers radiating colors, which she called her "gardens of the sun." Perhaps the most-talked-about garden on the estate was Adele's Herter-blue garden of blue hydrangea and delphiniums, with the blue waters of Georgica Pond just beyond. Adele also had the decorating notion that gardens should be coordinated with the rooms of the house that overlooked them; therefore, outside the windows of the blue-and-white music room, the garden was planted with blue and white foxglove, larkspur, and bachelor's button, and the orange lilies that fringed the walk to the estate's front door echoed the color orange in the house's many awnings.

On occasion, to impress houseguests, Adele would change the entire color of a garden overnight, so guests would wake in the morning to discover a garden of pink flowers where an all-white one had been the night before. To achieve this, Adele's frantic Japanese gardeners uprooted the old garden and planted thousands of water-filled glass vials with cut flowers in them. Because Adele was offended by the sight of the gardeners' toiling in her gardens, her edict was that they had to work only at night. This made their chores rather difficult, especially since the perfection of the gardens was such an obsession with Adele that she decreed they must always look in fresh bloom; so every night the gardeners had to deadhead thousands of fading blooms by lantern or moonlight.

The Herters also planted evergreens, but without much interest — they grew slowly and never seemed to change. There was, however, near the house one extraordinary red cedar that the Herters had turned into living art, much like the bonsai plants they had admired in Japan. Over the years they repeatedly topped the cedar's branches off at ten feet, forcing the branches to spread outward in compensation. When the limbs grew so long that they were in danger of breaking off under their own weight, Adele designed "crutches" of poles to hold up the sprawling, deformed limbs. The Herter children loved the cedar with its odd crutches and called it "the organ tree."

Every Sunday afternoon Albert and Adele had open house at The Creeks for friends, a tradition that would carry on for decades. Albert recalled one of those Sundays when guests arrived for tea. "The late afternoon sunlight slanted through the trees, the water lapped musically on the shore, sails flapped lazily, the tethered horses neighed in the woods, and a feeling of peace and well-being descended upon everyone who had a sense of beauty." Sometimes Albert and Adele wore full Kabuki regalia when they entertained, and when guests went home at night, the two and a half miles of driveway were lit with Japanese lanterns placed every ten feet, as a small army of schoolchildren hid behind the bushes waiting to replace the candles as they burned down.

Adele slept only three or fours hours a night — the rest of the time she read, always biographies and other nonfiction and every morning at dawn Albert would come to her room and over breakfast they would discuss what she had read the night before. Then a set of tennis on the grass courts before going off to their respective studios for a day's work. They would reunite in the late afternoon over a cocktail in the music room and criticize each other's work. Albert gained a reputation as one of the country's best-known muralists, and Adele painted softly muted decorative florals as well as formal portraits of some of the wealthiest women of her time, including Florence Harriman and Laura Spelman Rockefeller. They also carried on in the great tradition of the Herter brothers as decorators, even opening their own looms and furniture shops, importing craftsmen from Aubusson in France to weave their carpets.

For many years Albert and Adele's marriage seemed quite well made. Although Adele could be imperious with servants and outsiders, she was a source of strength for Albert and the beacon of the family. The couple had three children. Their firstborn, Everit Albert Herter, was Adele's favorite. A talented muralist himself, Harvard class of 1914, he was the first doughboy killed in action in World War I at the Battle of Château-Thierry on June 13, 1918. The local Veterans of Foreign Wars hall, which still stands just across the highway from The Creeks, is named after him. Their second child, Christian A. Herter Jr., educated in Paris, was so brilliant that they had to hold him back from going to college at fifteen. He married Mary Pratt, the granddaughter of Charles Pratt (the founder of Standard Oil and the Pratt Institute in New York), and later became a U.S. congressman from Massachusetts and served as secretary of state under President Dwight D. Eisenhower. The third Herter child, a daughter named Lydia, was developmentally disabled and behaved in a way the family characterized as "socially awkward." Lydia spent her entire life with a full-time companion, Miss Ingabrig Praetorious, who lived with her at The Creeks in a specially built guest cottage that the Herters nicknamed "the Happy Hour," in honor of Lydia's perpetual state. It had a bell that rang in the main house when help was needed. She died in Santa Barbara in 1954, Miss Praetorious at her side.

It seemed hardly to cause a ripple in their lives when Albert himself took a companion. His name was Willy Stevens, and their meeting was pure fate. One day in the early 1900s, Albert stood smoking a cigarette on the corner of Fifth Avenue and Fifty-second Street, waiting for the light to change, when he tossed the cigarette down an open manhole. When the light changed, he set out to cross the street, but before he could reach the other side, an electric-company worker scrambled out of the manhole with his hair on fire. He accosted Albert, shouting and screaming at him. Albert surrendered his hat to help smother the fire and invited the chap "up for a drink." Willy Stevens was a poor but handsome young man, with no family or education. He was blond and blue-eyed, and Albert said he would make a good artist's model and offered Willy a permanent job. He became not only Albert's favorite model but his "most constant friend," as Herter described it. Albert never seemed to tire of looking at Willy, who was moved into one of the outbuildings at The Creeks, where he posed as the male in most of Albert's work, including the likeness of Benjamin Franklin in the painting in the Massachusetts State House.

As the decades passed, Adele and Albert began to spend more of the year at El Mirasol, the estate in Santa Barbara Mary Miles Herter had left them, but the cost of operating both The Creeks and El Mirasol became a financial burden. They had spent lavishly over the years, and there was no longer much interest in formal society portraits or the need for Albert's decorating talents. As Albert and Adele's resources began to dwindle, they tried to cut back; caviar was no longer served at parties and flowers were bought at roadside stands instead of at the best florists. Eventually, Adele was distressed to find that she had to make do without a laundress; when she discovered that it took her a full hour to iron her own nightgowns, for the first time in her life she opted to sleep in her bloomers. Finally, the hurricane of 1938 battered them physically and emotionally.

"Mr. and Mrs. Albert Herter," reported the *East Hampton Star*, "isolated on their large estate west of the village, watched the surf breaking on their terrace, washing away their boathouse, and destroying their big oak trees one by one. Within a few hours the place they had loved for forty years was a ruin." They never had the money to repair it. By the 1940s they could afford only one full-time servant at The Creeks, Harry Easer, who performed as gardener, chauffeur, and handyman. They were also forced to turn El Mirasol into a hotel with luxury cottages, all of which they sold off except one that they kept for themselves.

On Tuesday morning in early October 1946, while having her hair done at a beauty parlor in East Hampton, Adele Herter closed her eyes and slid off the chair, dead of a stroke. The frantic beautician called The Creeks trying to find Albert but could reach only Harry Easer. Easer dusted off the red Phaeton and drove to town. When he found his mistress dead on the floor, he became so distraught that he picked her up in his arms and carried her through the streets to the Williams Funeral Parlor. Adele was cremated, and her ashes were spread under "the organ tree."

Albert took Adele's death hard. Already ailing, he drained the water from the pipes at The Creeks, covered the furniture in sheets, and moved with Willy Stevens to the Algonquin Hotel in New York for a year or so. He died in his sleep on February 15, 1950, at the age of seventy-eight, in a small cottage in Santa Barbara. Willy brought Albert's ashes back to The Creeks to be spread under the tortured red cedar along with Adele's. He was never seen again.

The Creeks was left to Christian A. Herter Jr. Christian Jr. had grown into a brilliant but coldly analytical man, with little interest in the creative arts, substantially unlike his extraordinary mother and father. Although he had renewed the family fortune by marrying heiress Mary Pratt, she didn't care much for East Hampton or The Creeks. In any event, Christian's political career prohibited them from taking advantage of the house, and it was put up for sale in 1950. It sat empty, unheated, damp, exposed to the changing seasons. The walls began to rot through in places, and the furniture was soon covered in a diaphanous frosting of spiderwebs. The fabulous gardens, now untended, were overgrown with weeds, fodder for deer. The Creeks remained like that, deserted and forlorn, on the edge of the elegant pond, waiting for an owner worthy of its heritage.

Ossorio

TED DRAGON sold The Creeks to Ron Perelman for $12.5 million. "People ask me, 'What does Ron Perelman look like?'" Dragon said, "and I always say, 'He looked like Christ descending from a cloud to me.' If it wasn't for Ron Perelman buying The Creeks whole, I would have had to sell it off to developers."

Dragon is a youthful-looking man for someone in his seventies, his graying hair cut conservatively short. He has a gentle face and small, fluttering blue-green eyes that practically throw off sparks when Ron Perelman's name is mentioned. Some of the spark is resentment, but most of it is just a wicked kind of mirth. As he served tea and cucumber sandwiches in the oversized living room of his handsome East Hampton house, Dragon was virtually unrecognizable as the bloated man in the famous photograph of him in the 1970s that was printed in so many magazines and newspapers, the one of him in the Bird Room of The Creeks, seated thronelike in a fanbacked wicker chair, glaring imperiously at the camera. In the photo he is surrounded by tall ferns and caged African parrots and is decked out in a brocade caftan worthy of a Pharaoh, open sandals on his feet, a clutter of rings on his fingers, and strands of semiprecious jewels hanging from his neck.

These days, he dresses in navy blue slacks and mohair wool sweaters, like a fashionable country gentleman, and keeps to himself a lot. He delivers meals-on-wheels a few times a week to the needy and goes to church every morning ("What's twenty minutes a day for

God?" he asks), but otherwise, he rarely goes out. His friends worry that he is too reclusive. Although he's a local celebrity and could easily be the toast of the Hamptons cocktail circuit, he's seldom seen in public. "People say, 'Why don't you travel?' " he said, "and 'Why don't you go away for the winter?' But I *like* it in East Hampton. I like being home."

His house on Pantigo Road is a large gray-and-white postmodern, with beautifully tended but modest gardens and a small herb-and-spice patch outside the kitchen door. He calls it "a simple cottage with no upkeep." An interior decorator built the house for himself and his boyfriend, and Dragon got the place for a bargain. "I must have seen one hundred houses before I bought this," he said. He liked most of all the big eat-in kitchen and the spacious "great room" of a living room, where he stores some of the treasures from The Creeks. Standing in the center of the great room is the famous horned loveseat that artist Lee Krasner bequeathed to him — the only object she left to anyone in her will. There is the Chinese opium bed that has been pictured in the hundreds of articles about The Creeks, the snake's skull that once belonged to an Indian raja, the "tramp art" birdcage, and, of course, all the "congregations" by Alfonso Ossorio.

Everywhere is Ossorio. Not just the congregations on the walls, but Ossorio himself, thick in the air, a complement to Dragon. Sitting in his large living room, Dragon seems left behind. They say Ossorio owned The Creeks, but it was Dragon to whom The Creeks belonged. "I can't live in the past," he warned when asked about The Creeks. He put a few logs on the fire, and a black-and-white cat, Annette (whom Dragon saved from Montauk Highway after she was thrown from a car), curled up on a chair with one of Dragon's needlepoint pillows. Dragon scolded her, "I will not have it!" and put her in the kitchen. Then he nestled back into a corner of the sofa, tea in hand.

"Ron Perelman isn't the story of The Creeks," Dragon said, shaking his head. "He's the *irony* of what happened to The Creeks. The Creeks isn't just a place, it's a *time*, about creativity and wonder. For me, The Creeks begins in spring of 1949, when Alfonso Ossorio said to me, 'You will be very surprised by the painting that's going to be delivered today. I don't think you'll like it at all. It's by a painter named Jackson Pollock, and it's all drips.' "

2

IN 1949 Dragon was a twenty-five-year-old ballet dancer with the New York City Ballet. He had never heard of Pollock, but neither had he heard of Giacometti, whose sculpture was standing in the living room downstairs. Dragon and his lover, Alfonso Ossorio, thirty-three, were in the tall, sunny studio of the older man's MacDougal Alley carriage house in Greenwich Village, with its two-story northern skylight, flower-filled balcony, and thick smell of paints and solvents. Ossorio, a tall, courtly man with gentle Eurasian eyes and a lilting British accent, knew about many things that Dragon did not. He had brilliant taste in art and was almost prescient in finding important new talent. He was a polymath with a Harvard degree and spoke eight languages, including ancient Greek; he read and retained a book a night. He was also heir to one of the largest sugar-refining fortunes in the world; Domino and Jack Frost both depended on his family's operation for their processed sugar.

But by vocation Ossorio was an artist, as passionate about his craft as the poorest artisans around the corner on Eighth Street. Surprisingly, in complete contrast to his buttoned-downed personality, his Dalí-esque illustrations of half-human forms, blood-spurting nipples, and screeching faces with sections missing — all heavily laced with Catholic symbolism — were so grotesque and peculiar that they were considered by many to be "outsider art," the work of the estranged or insane. Although beautifully executed and a mesmerizing personal vision, his work was never fully respected, and he was far more appreciated as a wealthy collector than as a painter — a "gilded eccentric fluttering on the edges of postwar American art," as *The New Yorker* once described him. But in his calm, philosophical way, Ossorio didn't care. He was driven to create the images in his work; he had no choice — he believed the urge to create was a gift from God.

For all his optimism and brilliant mind, he was a complicated man with many surprising tastes, including a voracious appetite for pornography, particularly of men of color. In his younger years, when he was in the U.S. Army, he had prided himself on his wildness and the variety of his sex partners. He was also obsessive in everything that held his attention, keeping meticulous notebooks filled with drawings and notations; unfortunately, none of them are autobiographical. He was one of six sons in an unusual union of a Filipino-Spanish-Chinese mother and a Spanish father, and he suffered an almost Dickensian childhood. His cold, selfish parents, obsessed with anglicizing their children, shipped him off to a series of strict Benedictine boarding schools in Europe. During one stretch he didn't see his parents at all for five years. In 1941, at age twenty-five, after graduating from Harvard and attending the Rhode Island School of Design, he married Bridget Hubrecht, a family friend. Hubrecht, a tragic character, was an opium addict, and Ossorio talked himself into thinking he could save her. The troubled union ended in divorce, and Hubrecht died within a year. Ossorio was drafted into the U.S. Army and spent his three-year stint perched on a ladder above an operating table at Camp Ellis, Illinois, making detailed drawings of emergency operations for textbooks. His depiction of entrails and exposed muscle became a leitmotiv in his art and is an odd juxtaposition to his alternative theme of Christian symbolism.

Dragon and Ossorio met in the summer of 1948 in the Berkshire Mountains of Massachusetts, where Ossorio had rented a house in which to paint and Dragon was on a scholarship to Jacob's Pillow, an avant-garde dance troupe. One day Ossorio was sketching at an easel in a meadow brimming with wildflowers when Ted Dragon happened by, in shorts, picking nosegays. Ted Dragon Young (Broadway choreographer Agnes de Mille told him to drop the "Young" at an audition) was the handsome son of a tavern owner from Northampton, Massachusetts. Of French-Canadian extraction, he was handsome and angular, with the body of a dancer. The only formal dance training Dragon had received was at the local YMCA, yet his innate sense of drama and leonine physicality landed him roles in dance companies from the Paris Opera to Jacob's Pillow. Their courtship was peripatetic. After passing the summer together, with a long separation after, the following spring Ossorio asked Dragon to move in with him at his newly purchased Greek Revival carriage house in Greenwich Village. "He wanted to settle down together for good," said Dragon, "but we were so completely different, and I wasn't certain either of us could settle down. But he was willing to try and, I guess, so was I." Two weeks after Dragon moved in, the Jackson Pollock arrived.

Dragon was frankly amazed when the canvas was unpacked. "Alfonso was right," Dragon said, "I couldn't believe it." It was a four-by-eight silver-and-rust-colored field with great gobs of red, yellow, and white aluminum paint splashed across it. "You spent money on *that?*" Dragon asked Ossorio. "I can't believe anybody would pay for that." Ossorio laughed and told him the canvas was called *Number 5* and that at $1,500, it was the only painting Pollock had sold from the show. "I understand why," Dragon said.

What Ossorio wasn't telling Dragon at the moment was that he believed Jackson Pollock might be some sort of a genius, or as Ossorio is famously quoted, "a man who had gone beyond Picasso." Pollock had been one of the Works Progress Administration—supported artists, a drunk and a so-called cowboy from Cody, Wyoming, who was notorious in New York art circles for eating with his hands and pawing women. He had been in and out of psychiatric hospitals for alcoholic cures that never worked, and he could be found almost every night at the Cedar Tavern on University Place, getting drunk and picking fights. Pollock was a disciple of Thomas Hart Benton, but his handsome early paintings — surrealistic, figurative work with a Midwestern bent — never interested Ossorio, who didn't consider them of particular merit.

And now this. In January 1949, at a show at the Betty Parsons Gallery on West Fifty-seventh Street, Ossorio had discovered a reborn Jackson Pollock. The artist had moved out to a farmhouse in East Hampton, where he had miraculously sobered up and started painting these remarkable "drip" canvases — splattering, splashing, dripping paint from his brush like honey from a stick. Ossorio decided that the paintings were not only beautiful but important, and he snatched up the one called *Number 5*.

Alas, "the painting arrived damaged," Dragon said. "When they uncrated it, Ossorio found the paint had been smudged on the left side during shipping, although I told him I didn't see how anybody could possibly tell." Ossorio phoned Pollock personally and asked him if he would repair the painting. Pollock, encouraged by his wife, Lee Krasner, told Ossorio that he would be happy to fix the canvas, but only if Ossorio delivered it personally to East Hampton and spent the weekend.

Ossorio was flattered. He had been all over the world — he was born in the Philippines, educated in Great Britain and Europe, and had lived in Paris — but had never been to East Hampton. "So it was a few weeks later," Dragon said, that in early May 1949 "Alfonso and I loaded *Number 5* into the back of a Ford Woodie station wagon and drove out to East Hampton for the first time."

3

IT TOOK FIVE HOURS to get there in 1949, bucking the endless lights on the Sunrise Highway for 100 miles along a seemingly endless four-lane blacktop that eventually narrowed into Route 27, lined with bait-and-tackle shanties. The small Long Island suburban towns gave way to dense pine forests and fields of produce, fields so tabletop flat that it looked like Kansas. Unexpectedly there were bursts of duck farms — white, foamy fields of feathers, brightly lit even at night to make the ducks fatten faster. Farther east the light seemed to change, the air smelled crisp, and the horizon began to sparkle.

When they finally arrived in the small, sleepy village of East Hampton that May afternoon, it looked just as it had for almost 200 years. No history had really touched it. No wars had been fought there, there hadn't been many local disasters (save a few hurricanes), and there had been little change to the town by way of commerce. Everything from houses to door hinges had been made locally and handed down from father to son for generations. There weren't many places in the world where everything had been kept so intact, from the Yankee stubbornness to Puritan values.

On Main Street there were still hitching posts to tether the occasional horse-drawn wagon. There was a brick police station; one movie theater with hard wooden seats (open only Friday and Saturday nights); a one-room telephone central on the corner of Main and Newtown, where the operator slept on a cot at night; and a pharmacy and soda counter, where a gentleman dared not ask the pharmacist for a box of prophylactics.

Ossorio and Dragon stopped at the Bohack Supermarket on Main Street and bought bags of groceries and a turkey to take to the Pollocks. They found the artist and his wife not south of the highway with the Summer Colony but in a ramshackle farmhouse a few miles north of the town in a place called Springs — population then, 360 — a section literally and figuratively on the other side of the railroad tracks, or "below the bridge," as townsfolk would say. Springs (cognoscenti never use the article) was the backwoods of town, deep country, undisturbed fields, thick woods, gorgeous ponds with green saltwater meadows. It was a closed community, culturally and socially isolated from East Hampton, with bloodlines so intertwined that natives even had their own derisive nickname, Bonackers (after the Accabonac Creek), East Hampton's equivalent of hillbillies. In present-day East Hampton they are known as "Bubs."

Bonackers are mostly descendants of Lion Gardiner's less-well-to-do employees, the Bennets and Kings and Lesters, who unlike Goody Garlick and her husband couldn't afford to build houses in town when they moved to the mainland 400 years ago. They wound up in a patch of rich land about three miles square between Accabonac "Crik" and Louse Point. Fifteen generations of Bonackers had lived on this land, untouched by the good fortune and spoils brought by the Summer Colony. They subsisted as dirt-poor, small-time farmers and fishermen. The most financially productive Springs had ever been was during Prohibition, when the nooks and crannies of its waterfront made it a favorite rumrunners' drop. It had one saloon, Jungle Pete's, and one grocery, Springs General Store.

It didn't even have its own fire department until 1965; when one newcomer asked what to do in case of a fire, the Bubs' solution was "Don't have a fire."

You can still tell true Bonackers in East Hampton because of their distinctive Bonac dialect, an accent and speech pattern whose roots can be traced back to Dorset, England. It's an exaggerated Yankee twang, such as saying "yit" for "yet" and repeating words twice, "Yes, yes," or adding syllables, like "hay-at" for "hat." Bonackers were not apt to be "long in the mouth" with summer strangers, whose presence sometimes turned their little neck of the woods "catty-wumper" instead of "finest-kind," the way they liked things. Strangers were "from away," especially guys like Pollock who they thought didn't work for a living — they were called "drifts" because they appeared for a season or two and then faded from memory.

"We were shocked when we got to where Jackson and Lee were living," Dragon said. "It was squalor." Ossorio called it "lamentable borderline existence." They lived in a 200-year-old house with no heat or hot water and only a coal stove in the kitchen to keep warm. Pollock told them that it got so cold in the winter that the water froze in the toilets, and they still used the outhouse. "Jackson was so poor," Dragon said, "that he held his pants up with a string. They couldn't even afford a car — he rode around on a bicycle." Lee said they lived off the clams Jackson dug himself out of Accabonac Creek and vegetables she grew in the garden. The previous winter the owner of Springs General Store finally took pity on them and accepted a small painting from Pollock to pay off his sixty-dollar bill. The grocer hung the painting in the store and told customers it was an "aerial view of Siberia." Ten years later he sold it for $17,000, and it's likely worth a million today.

"Lee and I unpacked the groceries in the kitchen and cooked dinner," Dragon said. "We were from two different worlds, but somehow we just clicked. Part of it was that we were both hitched to the stars in the family. Also, Ossorio and I didn't want anything from these people, just to like them, and for Lee, anybody who was good for Jackson was like gold." Krasner was forty-one years old, four years older than Jackson and nearly twice the age of the young dancer who sat in her kitchen. Pollock sometimes made fun of how ugly she was. She was the daughter of an orthodox Jew who owned a fruit store in Brooklyn, and was perhaps as unlikely a mate for the alcoholic pseudo-cowboy as Dragon was for Ossorio. Krasner was an important artist in her own right, and her intricately painted abstract forms made her one of the few women respected enough to gain membership in the 1930s WPA art program. But her dedication to her work was easily surpassed by her passion for Pollock. "Of course, I saw right away that she was obsessed with him," Dragon said. "It wasn't just love, she had subjugated herself and her career to his. I didn't think I could ever do that for Ossorio. But the art world was so macho then, and Lee saw that a woman would never achieve acceptance like a male artist, so she became the fire under her man. Her love for him was like a madness. She was his caretaker, blindly."

Out on the small back porch, drinking iced tea, the mandarin, starched Ossorio, with his international education, and the tongue-tied, uncommunicative Pollock, who wasn't particularly fond of homosexuals, were getting to know each other. Pollock, a short, balding man with a cigarette dangling omnipresently from his lips, told Ossorio that he and Lee had come out to East Hampton to visit friends and had liked it so much, they decided to rent a house themselves. It was a pretty common experience, people coming out one time and feeling compelled to return. He said that *Partisan Review* art and literary critic Harold Rosenberg and his wife, writer May Tabak, had moved to East Hampton within the past few years, as had the Dutch painter Willem de Kooning, who moved to Springs from Manhattan. Robert Motherwell was out there too, but he had some family money (he was the son of a doctor) and was able to buy a four-acre plot south of the highway at Georgica and Jericho Roads for a whopping $1,200. He had commissioned a controversial house designed by French modernist architect Pierre Chareau, who had met Motherwell one night at the East Hampton home of Jane Bowles. The house, a celebration of industrial architecture, was built like a vast metal Quonset hut sunk into the ground, with sections of glass-brick walls and roof. It was quite ugly, actually, cold and drafty and in need of constant repair. The house was an object of scorn among the shingled enclaves of the Summer Colony, where it stood out like an icon of its time, daring and challenging, heralding the arrival of the abstract expressionists to the Hamptons. Ludwig Mies van der Rohe visited the house, and in 1964 Samuel Beckett spent a week there.

"When it got to sundown," Dragon said, "Lee and I went out on the back porch, and the four of us watched the waning of the light. Ossorio and I had never seen light like that before." Artists have talked about the sea-distilled "wet light" in the Hamptons for more than 100 years. In the Hamptons, colors can appear more vivid or more muted than anywhere else in the world, yet on days when the sky is clear, the light seems to vibrate, virtually humming. The theory is that because the Hamptons are enveloped by sea and ponds and kettle holes, the luminous, rippling water patterns give off horizontal bands of light reflected by the water molecules, enchanting the ether.

As the two couples watched the sunset on the back porch, the night grew still and the rest of the world seemed very far away. The only sound was crickets, and even the fireflies seemed to be having a hard time moving through the dense air. It was an indelible moment for Dragon. "The next day," he said, "we were miserable to be leaving, and as we headed back to New York, driving through the town,

Ossorio and I decided that we were going to come back and spend the rest of the summer. We just never thought we'd end up there for good."

4

THE ARRIVAL of Motherwell, Pollock, Ossorio, and the hundreds of other artists who migrated to East Hampton in the late forties and early fifties was actually the third colony of artists to claim the town as its own. The first was in the 1870s, when a group of twelve highly spirited young artists called the Tile Club appeared out of nowhere and helped turn a sleepy little outpost into a chic resort. The Tile Club was a nineteenth-century artists' Rat Pack, the up-and-coming art stars of their day, including William Merritt Chase and Stanford White (who would abandon art for architecture). They were brats and libertines, schooled in Paris and recently returned to New York, where they met once a week in a Greenwich Village townhouse to exchange scandalizing gossip about art and women, smoke tobacco, and paint large, square Spanish tiles (which were in vogue at the time), hence the Tile Club name. In the spring of 1877, they cleverly convinced *Scribner's Monthly* to underwrite an expedition of the Tile Club to the eastern tip of Long Island, from which they would return with an illustrated record of their adventures. With *Scribner's* blessings they packed their easels and palettes and, dressed in their brown velveteens, took the Long Island Railroad out to Sayville, where they all bought matching large straw hats. Then by rail to Bridgehampton, where they merrily had matching long red ribbons sewn on their hats at the local milliner's. Then off by carriage to Sag Harbor, and later to Montauk, where they interviewed the dying Montauk chief, Pharaoh. Finally, the Tile Club arrived in East Hampton, where they became infatuated with the town's elegiac beauty and the broad green lawn called Main Street. They lingered, reluctant to leave, staying at Miss Annie Huntting's rambling boardinghouse next to the Presbyterian Church. When the parishioners arrived for services early Sunday morning, the Tilers were still up from the night before, smoking pipes and making a racket, and the Presbyterians dubbed the place Rowdy Hall. The name stuck, and forty years later, in July 1931, when the house was rented for the summer to John Vernou "Black Jack" Bouvier III and his wife, Janet, it was to Rowdy Hall that his daughter Jacqueline, the future first lady, was brought after she was born in Southampton Hospital.

The resulting *Scribner's* article, "The Tile Club at Play," caused a sensation in trendy New York society. The illustrations and descriptions of bucolic life turned East Hampton into the stylish vacation destination of choice. That article, plus two sequels that followed, lured so many aspiring artists to East Hampton that by the turn of the century, the local constable had to clear easels from the fields and orchards so the farmers could do their work. It became, briefly, an American Barbizon, home to some of the best landscape and still-life painters of the day, including Winslow Homer, Thomas Moran, who built a studio across from Town Pond, and Childe Hassam, who loved his house on Egypt Lane so much that when he was seventy-six years old and ill, he took an ambulance out to East Hampton so he could die there. Thomas Moran's daughter, Ruth, wrote that the artists "took away with them on canvas, copper or paper, the essence that was old East Hampton to scatter it over the cities and towns ... everywhere ..."

In time the migration of artists dwindled, and although East Hampton continued to grow as a summer resort for the very rich, the invasion of the art world wasn't revived until the late 1930s by Sara and Gerald Murphy. The Murphys were the real-life models for

Dick and Nicole Diver, the hedonistic couple in F. Scott Fitzgerald's *Tender Is the Night*. Gerald was the heir to the Mark Cross leather-and-luxury-goods fortune and part of the Irish "Golden Clan" of Southampton, where he spent his childhood summers on an estate called The Little Orchard. Sara was the daughter of Frank B. Wiborg of Cincinnati, Ohio, a cofounder of Ault & Wiborg, the largest manufacturer of printing ink in America. At one point Wiborg was the richest man in East Hampton and owned several hundred acres around the Maidstone Club. In 1895 he built his Xanadu, Dunes, a voluptuous eighty-acre estate on Hook Pond, the most famous house of its time, a sensation for its walled gardens and many guest cottages, each with fanciful names like Swan's Cove and Le Petite Hut. The main residence was so large, it required a minimum of six servants and was dubbed the Big House by the Wiborgs.

In 1922 the Maidstone Club's second clubhouse burned to the ground, and the board of directors decided to rebuild a new one closer to the Wiborg mansion. Wiborg threatened to resign from the club if they didn't chose another site; when they built the clubhouse there anyway, he not only quit in a fury but planted a great wall of privet hedge, half a mile long, to block the view, called the Wiborg "spite hedge" by the Maidstoners. Years later, when the club intended to build a new driveway near the entrance to Wiborg's estate, he offered the club $5,000 cash to move the road to the far side of the clubhouse, which they accepted. Old man Wiborg proved that he wasn't always such a spoilsport when in August 1924 he entertained John Drew, Ethel Barrymore, Douglas Fairbanks, and Mary Pickford for lunch at Dunes. Fairbanks turned handstands on the beach and, the *East Hampton Star* was thrilled to report, pronounced East Hampton's drinking water "marvelous" — a huge endorsement — and "went bathing in East Hampton Surf three times Sunday."

Meanwhile, Wiborg's Francophile daughter, the lovely Sara, and her would-be painter husband, Gerald, lived the high life of American expatriates in Paris and the south of France, where they became great chums with Sergey Diaghilev and Sara was rumored to be one of Picasso's plethora of lovers. During the Great Depression the Murphys were summoned to return to America so Gerald could take over the family company, yet every moment they could steal away was spent in East Hampton at Dunes, which Sara eventually inherited. They passed long weekends nursing cocktails on the covered porches in the summer, and in the winter they spent wet, windy evenings playing charades in the glow of one of the huge fireplaces, comforted with hot toddies and houseguests like Dorothy Parker, Robert Benchley, John Dos Passos, Laurette Taylor, and Zelda and Scott Fitzgerald.

Still, the Murphys longed for the stimulation of the artists and writers of European café society and worried too for their friends as the pounding of the Nazis' goosesteps on the streets drowned out Le Jazz Hot in the clubs and cafés. Quietly, with the help of heiress and art patron Peggy Guggenheim, Sara and Gerald began to pay the way to America for many of their European artist friends, forming an escape route first to Manhattan, then to their accommodating home and myriad guest cottages in East Hampton. One of the first artists the Murphys invited to East Hampton was Lucia Christophenetti, who arrived on the arm of her lover, surrealist Fernand Léger. The petite Lebanese-born artist was a mediocre painter but a first-class salonist and cook. At her Paris garret there was always room at her table, or in her bed, for a struggling artist. As she once slyly boasted, "I always have a bed for Marcel Duchamp or André Breton."

Once in East Hampton she soon ditched Léger, and with Sara and Gerald Murphy's largesse, Lucia single-handedly helped lure practically the entire surrealist movement to East Hampton in the early forties, including Roberto Matta, Yves Tanguy, Max Ernst, Marc Chagall, André Masson, Piet Mondrian, Salvador and Gala

Dalí, Wilfredo Lam, Isamu Noguchi, André Breton, Jean Hélion, and David Hare. According to folklore, the Hamptons became so well known as the American base of the European surrealist school that a visitor pulled into a gas station on Montauk Highway and asked the attendant, "Where do we find the surrealists?"

It wasn't hard. They spent their days mostly on Wiborg Beach, also known as Pink Beach, behind Pink House, the pink stucco chauffeur's quarters of Dunes, where the women outraged the local community by making their own bathing suits twisted out of scarves, or just abandoning all pretense and going topless. They were a pretentious, supercilious group — poor but highly mannered intellectuals who mocked the kind of dogged conformity of a place like East Hampton, yet were still drawn to its wealth and beauty. They didn't speak much English, or care to. They played intellectual games on the beach, including chess and charades, as well as a ruthless game of truth or dare called *La Verité*, over which they would get into titanic arguments about one another's emotional honesty, causing scenes that could be heard up and down the beach. Other times they were more placid. Lucia Christophenetti, Maria Motherwell, and Dorothea Tanning dressed as satyrs and nymphs and frolicked in the woods at one party for the artist Max Ernst, much to the distaste of both the Bonackers, who considered them sissys and "drifts," and the Maidstone crowd, who considered them flakes and hoped they would go away.

They did. The war over, the surrealists deserted East Hampton, never to be heard from again. Only Lucia stayed. She married a local man, Roger Wilcox, an inventor who helped design some of the earliest stereo components but who became better known in the art community for his stories about being abducted by extraterrestrials. Lucia and Roger Wilcox moved to a roomy old farmhouse on Abraham's Path in Amagansett, where for years Lucia's kitchen continued to be a hub of the growing artists' community. The Murphys never left East Hampton either, but in 1941 they were forced to sell the Big House, which Gerald now called the Big Bad House because it ate up so much money. It was torn down; a developer bought the property and subdivided it, renaming the once-fabulous Wiborg gardens Dune Meadows; and a series of prosaic homes on five-acre plots were built. The Murphys themselves moved into Pink House, on the beach where the surrealists once frolicked. They spent another twenty summers in East Hampton before they passed away and were buried in East Hampton side by side in their family plot in the South End Burying Ground, behind the large, handsome Hook Windmill that dominates the center of town.

5

THE SUMMER of 1949, Ossorio and Dragon rented a house "not in Springs like the Pollocks," said Dragon, "but a proper summer cottage on Jericho Lane." That July Guild Hall, East Hampton's cultural palace, summer theater, and art gallery, broke with tradition of showing only still lifes and landscapes in its gallery and held an exhibition of what was gingerly referred to as "modern art." Called "17 Artists of Eastern Long Island," it included works by every major abstract expressionist living in East Hampton at the time, including Jackson Pollock, Balcomb Greene, John Little, Lee Krasner, Julian Levy, Ibram Lassaw, and Alfonso Ossorio.

The arts center had recently been criticized for presenting the "communist" show *Finian's Rainbow* in its John Drew Theatre. According to Ossorio, "Guild Hall was so conservative, it didn't show a nude until 1960." Guild Hall was the creation of Maidstone member Mary Woodhouse, "East Hampton's First Lady." The wife of Lorenzo E. Woodhouse, president of the Merchant National Bank of Burlington, Vermont, she was a short woman with a double chin and maintained that a proper lady always wore a hat, day and night, indoors or out. A homebody, she once proudly wrote about herself that "the happiest people are those who have no history, therefore I may be classed in that category." To her great credit, she was a passionate patron of the arts, generous but limited and unadventurous in her taste. Nevertheless, in 1931 she gave the community Guild Hall, which was run for forty years under the rigid doctrine of Woodhouse and her Maidstone friends, many of whom suspected that Pollock stuck cigarette butts to his paintings in an effort to make fools of them. The Maidstone's spokesperson, the *East Hampton Star's* Jeannette Rattray, couldn't wait to mock Pollock and his friends by writing a satirical editorial in which the results of her niece's spilled paint turns out to be just as good as a canvas by Pollock.

"Of course, the artists were impossible," Ossorio said. "They were rude and boring. The old-guard townspeople were polite and boring. They bought the abstract art out of duty but they never learned to love it."

Shortly after the opening of the abstract impressionist exhibition, a group called the East Hampton Protection Society formed and decided that Guild Hall and its gallery and little theater were attracting the "wrong kind" of people and perhaps should be shut down. Anti–Guild Hall petitions were circulated referring to certain "undesirables." A public meeting was called, and the actor and summer resident Robert Montgomery demanded to know who the undesirable people were. When no one at the meeting would tell him, he said, "I'll just say it for you. You're talking about Jews and fairies, it's as simple as that." The Protection Society was disbanded the next day.

The controversy caused by the Guild Hall show was nothing compared with the consequences of *Life* magazine's August 8, 1949, issue, which mockingly ordained Jackson Pollock the crown prince of the abstract expressionist movement, calling him a "phenomenon" but asking, snidely, in a bold, two-page headline, "Jackson Pollock: Is he the greatest living painter in the United States?" The backhanded acclaim made Pollock more paranoid. "The one thing the *Life* article *didn't* do was make Pollock rich," Dragon said. He rarely sold canvases, except to Ossorio, upon whom he became almost totally dependent.

In later years, *The New Yorker* would ungenerously describe Ossorio as being "a rear-wheel on the Pollock-Krasner cart." Living just a few miles apart that summer, the two couples forged an unusual and intense friendship. "Jackson wasn't really social," said Dragon. "He didn't talk too much. He was sullen. He spent most of his time listening to jazz. But he talked to Ossorio, because they had art in common. So they became real friends. Jackson hated to stretch canvas, and Alfonso would go over there to help him. At the same time, Lee and I became close. We were both lonely. Those macho artists weren't interested in me very much, you know, but she showed me around town and introduced me to people. Lee really cared."

She also knew a golden goose when she saw one. Ossorio showered Pollock with money and lavish gifts, including monographs by van Gogh and Goya. He promised Pollock the use of his MacDougal Alley townhouse in the winter, and he pledged a $200-a-month stipend against the purchase of future paintings. By the end of that summer, a grateful Pollock presented the restored *Number 5*. To Ossorio's amazement and horror, it was completely different, no longer the painting he had fallen in love with. "I brought you one painting, but you have given me back another," Ossorio managed to say, while assuring Pollock that he liked the new one just as much.

Although Ossorio talked all that year about buying a house in East Hampton, he never got around to it. He and Dragon didn't return until the weekend after Thanksgiving 1950. They were on their way to Europe, Ossorio to paint and Dragon to dance with the Paris Opera. Friday night they were going to have dinner at the Pollocks' farmhouse in Springs. "Eight were expected for dinner that night," Dragon said. "Everybody was sick of turkey, so I went to the supermarket and bought a huge roast beef, and Lee and I cooked up a feast, with local potatoes and brussels sprouts that had just come into season. I don't know where Ossorio went, he wasn't even there most of the afternoon. Pollock spent all day out back being filmed for a documentary by Hans Namuth, the photographer."

There is much conjecture about what happened that afternoon while Namuth was photographing him that caused Pollock to return to the house and "head straight for the bottle and pour himself a drink," said Dragon. Ossorio had arrived by then, and he remembered seeing Pollock walk in the back door and pour himself "a tumbler full of bourbon. Then he poured it down and Lee went white in the face," Ossorio said.

"The look on Lee's face . . . ," Dragon said. "*God*. So I whispered, 'Why are you so upset? It's only one drink.' She was furious with me. She gave me *some* look. 'You don't know what you're talking about!' she snapped. In the year and half we had known Jackson, we'd never seen him take a drink. But thinking back on it, he wasn't really sober that whole time either. He was on the edge of the trigger. He was what alcoholics called 'dry' — he wasn't drinking, but all of his inner demons were waiting to come out, a walking time bomb. Jackson was one of those drunks who took one little sip and was three sheets to the wind. So ten minutes later we were sitting around the table cutting the roast beef when Jackson shouted, 'Now? Now?' We didn't know what the hell he meant, when suddenly, *bam!* he tossed the table up into the air! He upended it, and everything went all over — the food on the floor, the dishes smashed . . . what a mess! Lee and I got down and cleaned it all up, and everybody went right on to dessert as if nothing had happened. Jackson went out the door and disappeared. We never knew what set him off. I looked at Lee's face, and she was heartbroken. We never saw him sober again. Never. He was a completely different person after that. He also never painted another good drip painting."

Before leaving for Paris that winter, Ossorio bought one more of Pollock's paintings, called *Lavender Mist*, for $3,000. This twelve-by-nine-foot field is considered by many to be Pollock's masterpiece. A gray-toned action painting, it is neither lavender nor misty, and what makes it the more rapturously beautiful than all the rest of Pollock's paintings is hard to say, but even when Ossorio bought it, both he and Pollock knew it was probably the pick of the litter. Ossorio wasn't sure where he was going to hang such an important painting, so for the time being he had it crated and put into storage until he could find the right wall for it.

The main reason Ossorio was off to Paris was that he was eager to meet the French avant-garde painter, Jean Dubuffet, whose work, like Ossorio's, had been mocked for its ugliness. Perhaps Pollock's greatest contribution to Ossorio's art was introducing him to the paintings of Dubuffet, which Pollock liked so much that he kept a picture of one from a magazine article pinned to the inside of his outhouse door. Dubuffet, as it turned out, was assembling a collection of what he called Art Brut, "raw" art made by society's outsiders, the kind of art with which Ossorio's own work had been compared. Ossorio felt that he had found a kindred spirit in Dubuffet and wanted to spend time in Paris working and furthering their friendship.

Neither Ossorio nor Dragon had any thoughts of returning to East Hampton and the drama of Jackson Pollock when in August 1951 Pollock and Krasner wrote to Ossorio in Paris to say that The Creeks was up for sale and that if Ossorio would ever seriously consider buying it, he should come back to the States at once and make an offer. Ted Dragon remembered the events more dramatically. It was a cable, not a letter, he said, and "the cable said that a bunch of nuns wanted to buy the place and that everyone who lived on Georgica Pond was panic-stricken that they were going to have a girls' school run by nuns in their midst and that Ossorio had better come to the rescue."

Ossorio had visited The Creeks the previous summer with Pollock, who had arranged for them to be shown around the old place out of curiosity. It was like visiting Mrs. Havisham's bedroom, the mildew so thick that it made Ossorio gag. The pond side of the bulkhead was rotted away, and termites had all but destroyed the Happy Hour building. But the magnificent studio and small theater was left unscathed; Ossorio was fascinated by the giant rollers for canvas, twelve feet long, one built into the floor and another attached to the ceiling, with huge sheets of canvas on which Herter would paint his giant wall murals before rolling them up and shipping them off to Europe. It was inspiring for Ossorio to think of being able to work in such a studio. He was charmed by the tales of the Herters' wonderfully eccentric world, with their musicales and Sunday teas, but it would cost hundreds of thousands of dollars to save The Creeks, and who in the world could commit financially to running a sixty-acre estate? And yet the huge studio haunted Ossorio, as did the view of the pond and the promise of what The Creeks once was and could be again.

Ossorio obsessed about The Creeks for days. "About a week after the cable," said Dragon, "Alfonso asked me, 'If I buy the Herter estate in East Hampton, will you give up your career in ballet and come live with me there?' Well, I had never really seen The Creeks," although one summer day he had picked flowers on its grounds. "I only heard stories about it, so living there really meant nothing to me. But I loved Alfonso, so I said, 'Buy The Creeks and I'll go there with you. I do not have the "disease" of the ballet. I have a "love" of ballet.' I told him that before we left France, I wanted to dance one last time, a gala with Serge Lifar at the Nice Opera. I danced *La Péri*, by Dukas, a pas de deux, and I danced all done up, in diamonds and chiffon. And that was it. That was the last time I danced professionally."

Ossorio returned to New York and bought The Creeks from Christian Herter for $35,000, "a song," he said, and then immediately flew back to Paris to make arrangements to pack. "A month later we got on the *Ile de France* and came home," Dragon remembered. Dragon got a little taste of what his future would be like when Ossorio spent the entire transatlantic crossing painting at an easel in their state-rooms, emerging to join Dragon only for meals. Dragon passed the days wandering around the boat, chatting with strangers and shopping in the gift store, where he bought his first purchase for The Creeks: an *Ile de France* souvenir ashtray. A week later, when the boat docked on Manhattan's West Side, "Jackson and Lee met us at the pier," Dragon said, "and helped us collect our luggage. Then they drove us out to East Hampton to see our new house for the first time. I was sitting in the back of the car on Sunrise Highway when I showed Lee the ashtray I bought. She looked at it and laughed. 'Oh, Ted,' she said, 'You have *no* idea.' "

Dragon agreed. "I didn't have any idea. None at all, really. I knew it was a nice house, but ... When we drove up that long road through the grounds, acres of flower gardens gone to ruin, the woods, the pines, and then, there in the distance, the ailing Creeks with the pond beyond it and the Atlantic Ocean beyond that, 'My *God*,' I said, 'Holy shit!' "

Krasner turned around in the front seat and said to him, "Dragon, now you're in for it!"

6

"WE STRIPPED the place from top to bottom," Dragon said. "The Herters' fourteen-karat-gold wallpaper, the hand-painted red enamel woodwork, the mandarin scenes on the panels of the doors — all gone, all painted white. We installed wall-to-wall gray carpeting and we put down an occasional area rug — a Bohkara on the polished floor of the music room, and a few palm trees and some rattan furniture." It looked like a modern-art gallery, and indeed it was, as the walls were filled with Ossorio's own work, a place of honor in the west sitting room for *Lavender Mist,* and six entire rooms on the second floor devoted to a display of the entire collection of Dubuffet's remarkable Art Brut, which Ossorio had imported to America to make available to anyone who wanted to see it.

"Ossorio claimed Albert Herter's bedroom, and I moved into Adele's," Dragon said. Albert's studio was returned to working condition. "In the dressing rooms we found old costumes and props, as well as several unfinished paintings that the Herters had left behind," Dragon recalled. "The paintings were already mounted in very valuable ornate frames, and Ossorio loved the frames and kept them, but he gave the paintings to Pollock, who painted over them. It's altogether possible that underneath some of Pollock's paintings there are Herter portraits."

Under Ossorio's aegis The Creeks became a Bloomsbury on the Pond, or as *Newsday* called it, "a Disneyland for esthetes." The house was booked with guests all summer, and there were hundreds of legendary dinner parties given at The Creeks over the years, one every night during the busy summer season. Guests included art critics Selden Rodman, Henry McBride, Clement Greenberg, and Harold Rosenberg; artists Claes Oldenburg, Jasper Johns, Max Ernst, Marcel Duchamp, Grace Hartigan, Elaine and Willem de Kooning, Robert Gwathmey, Robert Motherwell, Roy Lichtenstein, Franz Kline, John Little, Barnett Newman, Mark Rothko, Esteban Vicente, Jimmy Ernst, and Robert Dash. Truman Capote got drunk at The Creeks several times a summer. Jerome Robbins and Dina Merrill came for lunch. Buckminster Fuller was a houseguest and lecturer, and Norman Mailer was so taken with The Creeks that Ossorio loaned it to him as a backdrop for an "underground" movie Mailer directed called *Maidstone.* The controversial philosopher and theologian Paul Tillich was a frequent houseguest, as was Dr. Lewis Thomas, the chancellor of Sloan-Kettering hospital. Juan Carlos, the heir to the Spanish throne, came to see Dubuffet's Art Brut collection, and Mrs. Douglas MacArthur arrived at The Creeks with a police escort after having been pulled over for speeding on the expressway. Louise Nevelson topped that entrance by pulling up the driveway on the back of an eighteen-foot, red hook-and-ladder fire truck, a stunt Ossorio arranged for her sixtieth birthday party, witnessed by 400 guests. Also, always in attendance at The Creeks, at every meal and every party, were Jackson Pollock and Lee Krasner.

To add to the general sense of The Creeks as a nurturing environment for the creative arts, throughout the 1950s each summer Ossorio generously loaned or rented inexpensively the original gatehouse and small barn of the estate to be used as living quarters and studio by up-and-coming artists. These "artists in residence" included painter Grace Hartigan, who one summer changed her name to "George" Hartigan in homage to George Sands and had an affair so torrid with sculptor George Spaventa that Ossorio was summoned from his bed one night by the East Hampton police to moderate their lover's quarrel.

For two summers the painter Clyfford Still, with whom nobody could get along, not even the unflappable Ossorio, was the artist in residence. Midway through Still's second season, some small event sent him into a fury and he packed to leave. On his way out he appeared at the main house and demanded back from Ossorio a painting he had sold him, claiming that it had only been on loan. Ossorio was incredulous at Still's demand and refused to return it. The following month Still appeared unannounced at The Creeks one afternoon along with a lady friend, and while the young woman distracted Ossorio and Dragon in the front hallway, Still sneaked into the sitting room where his painting hung, cut out the inside with a razor blade, and hid the rolled-up canvas under his coat. Then he marched out the front door and into the backseat of a waiting taxi, his lady friend close behind. When Ossorio realized what had transpired, he jumped into his own car and chased the taxi to the train station. But by the time he arrived, the train was pulling down the tracks in the distance, and all that remained of the remarkable incident were flakes of paint on the station floor.

Ossorio obsessively kept notebooks that included not only the names of his guests but which rooms they stayed in, where they sat at the dining room table, the menu and wines that were served, even which china and crystal were used and what the table decorations looked like. Lunch never had fewer than three wines, dinner at least five. ("De Kooning on the wagon!" reads one notebook entry.) Ossorio had the Herters' wine cellar under the studio enlarged and modernized, and he began to amass a collection of 6,000 bottles worthy of the world's greatest sommeliers. After each meal, the labels were soaked from the bottles and pressed into the pages of the daily diary.

The task fell to Dragon to run The Creeks like a five-star hotel. "It was like masterminding a living stage set," said Dragon, who rose at dawn in the summer to direct the show from behind the scenes. "Each day there were three formal meals. At six-thirty in the morning I was out in our own vegetable gardens handpicking the greens and vegetables to give to the cook, Geneva. Ossorio was very particular about his food, and I knew exactly how he liked things." Meals were never simple, not even breakfast, for which guests had a choice of hot and cold cereals, eggs Benedict or Florentine, Bloody Marys or mimosas to drink — served on china and in crystal. The celery was to be stringed and the carrots diced, not sliced. Potatoes were strained, not mashed. "He preferred heavy sauces and the richest of foods, even at breakfast, where his favorite meal was a thick slice of challah bread with a hole in the center, filled with two poached eggs, and a thick slice of pâté on top. Sometimes dinner went to the exotic. It's true that we served stuffed heart, but not human — veal. They're delicious parboiled."

If Ossorio was going to be serving cocktails in the aviary before dinner, Dragon made sure that the ice bucket was filled and that Geneva served almonds — fresh-roasted and still warm — rolled in kosher salt. For each of the many luncheons, cocktail parties, dinner, and concerts, Dragon would prepare dozens of floral displays (which he personally cut from The Creeks' own gardens, fields, and woods) and arrange them in a variety of vases that he placed in every bathroom, sitting room, bedroom, and cranny in the house. He also executed brilliantly conceived table settings worthy of Versailles, including one of antique-lace tablecloths strewn with petits fours and confetti, another of a bed of moss and autumn leaves for the place settings, with a centerpiece of little pears still on the branches.

After the details of the day's social activities were arranged, Dragon began the Sisyphean task of watering the resurrected gardens. The new gardens that Ossorio and Dragon planted were not nearly as complex or fantastic as Adele Herter's indulgences, but they still needed daily attention. Since The Creeks did not have an underground sprinkler system, and outside gardeners were brought in only twice a week to help, Dragon watered the entire sixty-six-acre estate by himself. Every day, following a complicated watering plan, Dragon drove a station wagon around the estate, setting up the hoses and sprinklers, turning them on and off, and rolling them up.

As busy a convocation of artists and intellectuals as The Creeks had become, Ossorio never neglected his own work. "I don't understand the word 'vacation' for people to rest their brains who don't have anything to rest," Ossorio would complain. The Herters' giant studio was an inspiration to him. In the 1950s he completed 300 ink, wax, and watercolor drawings alone. His output was so great, he was able to hold one-man exhibitions at the Betty Parsons Gallery in 1951, 1953, 1956, 1958, and 1959. Unfortunately, the work only seemed to entrench him as what one critic called "the summer stock Dali." In 1956 he sharply increased his role as benefactor to his struggling colleagues by arranging with his East Hampton neighbor, Evan Frankel, to use the lobby of his swank apartment building in Manhattan, the Executive House, as a gallery for emerging Hamptons artists; the unsuspecting tenants were treated to shows of the works of Pollock, Rothko, David Smith, and Richard Pousette-Dart.

In addition, in 1957 Ossorio cofounded, with the artists Elizabeth Parker and John Little, the now legendary Signa Art Gallery on Newtown Lane in East Hampton, the area's first real avant-garde gallery, where he debuted the works of every important artist of the era, including Kline, de Kooning, and Brach — although the Signa might have hit the pinnacle of its accomplishments in the summer of 1957, when Marilyn Monroe, who was honeymooning with playwright Arthur Miller in the Hamptons that idyllic summer, would show up at the Signa Gallery daily to run her hands over the smooth marble curves of a David Slivka sculpture.

7

NIGHT AFTER NIGHT, the troubled artist Jackson Pollock would sit on the brick steps off the back patio of The Creeks and sullenly drink beer, staring at the pond or at *Lavender Mist*, which was visible in the dining room through the open terrace doors. His drinking bouts were more extreme than Dragon had ever seen. "One morning I looked out my window, and there he was sprawled out on the terrace, completely naked, unconscious from drink." He also remembered Pollock doing things to purposely challenge and horrify his friends, like holding his hand over an open flame in the kitchen. On another occasion, "he drove his car into the surf," Dragon said, "and sat there waiting for the tide to come in and cover him up. He passed out behind the wheel and was rescued by some people walking by on the beach."

In one of Pollock's most notorious performances, he appeared at The Creeks in the middle of a black-tie dinner party, stormed into the music room, and began to violently pound the keys of the Steinway piano in a vicious parody of Dragon. "Then he jumped up," said Dragon, "got an ice pick from the kitchen, and chopped up all the ivory keys." It cost Ossorio several thousand dollars to repair.

No matter how mischievous — or downright crazy — Pollock behaved, Ossorio was invariably forgiving. When Pollock binged on booze and had to be carried home from Jungle Pete's, it was Ossorio whom Lee called to rescue him. When Pollock was hauled to the station house for drunken driving or fighting, it was Ossorio whom

the police called to bail him out. When Pollock ran out of canvas, Ossorio not only bought a roll for him but went over to the
farmhouse and helped him stretch it.

At one point, the Pollocks practically moved into The Creeks.
"When Jackson was too drunk to drive home to Springs — and
sometimes Lee was too drunk too," Dragon said, "they slept in the
middle bedroom, the Spanish bedroom, so called because of the
three-tiered Spanish wrought-iron headboard. They were there so
many nights, and so poor, that they asked Ossorio if they could move
into The Creeks with us." Ossorio for the first time in his life looked
as though he was caught off-guard and fumbled for something to
say. "You know I love you both very much . . . ," he managed to say
before shrugging his shoulders hopelessly.

"Then Jackson began having an affair," Dragon said, rolling his
eyes. "It put Alfonso and me in a very difficult position. First of all,
I was Lee's friend, and Jackson's having this affair was a mortal in-
sult to her. Lee put up with a lot from him, but another woman was
too much. It humiliated her." The woman's name was Ruth Kligman,
and Pollock had met her at the Cedar Tavern. "He moved her out to
Sag Harbor for the summer of 1956 for public display, and Lee was
furious," Dragon said. "He used to bring Kligman out to his studio
right under Lee's nose. She called me one day and told me that she
was going to divorce him. She said she told Jackson, 'It's her or me.'
But I told her, 'Don't do it, Lee, don't divorce him. You'd be crazy. If
he keeps up drinking like this, he's going to die anyway.'" But Krasner
did pack her bags and, for the first time in their marriage, went off
without Pollock, to spend the summer with friends in Europe.

With Krasner gone, Pollock went out of control. He had Ruth
Kligman move in with him, "which put us in a very embarrassing
position," said Dragon. "We didn't want to be rude to Jackson,
but we didn't want to be disloyal to Lee." However, Ossorio did
invite Pollock and Kligman, as well as Lucia and Roger Wilcox,

Clement Greenberg, and Wilfrid Zogbaum, among others, on Saturday, August 11, to be among the guests at one of his popular benefit recitals for Guild Hall, candlelit affairs that overflowed onto the terrace, where guests listened to concerts under the stars. But Pollock never showed that night, and about a half hour into the performance, there was the eerie sound of ambulances out on the highway. "It was a very still night," Ossorio remembered. Then the phone rang sharply, and a frisson rippled through the audience. It was the artist Conrad Marca-Relli calling for Ossorio to say that there had been an accident on Springs Fireplace Road and that he better come quick.

Pollock had been in his green Oldsmobile convertible with Ruth Kligman and a friend she had asked to join her for the weekend, Edith Metzger, a beautician from the Bronx who had survived the Holocaust. Pollock intended to show up at The Creeks that night — he had even pulled over to a phone at the side of the road to say he was coming — but he had driven all the way to The Creeks' main entrance when in a drunken rage he spun the car around and sped back toward Springs. The women screamed for him to slow down and stop, but their pleas only made him drive more crazily, and on a curve on Springs Fireplace Road the car skidded and somersaulted into the woods at ninety miles an hour. Ruth Kligman was thrown clear and suffered relatively minor injuries. Edith Metzger broke her neck and was killed on impact. Pollock was propelled out of the car and flew fifty feet through the air, flung headfirst, like a javelin, into a tree trunk. He hit it with such impact that his head was literally cleaved apart. When Ossorio arrived at the scene, Pollock's car horn was still blaring and the headlights were pointing crazily up into the trees. Ossorio agreed to identify Pollock's body for the police and was escorted to the spot in the woods. He wept at seeing his friend and covered Pollock's face with a clean handkerchief monogrammed A O.

By the time Ossorio returned to The Creeks, the concert was over and the guests had left without ever knowing why Pollock hadn't shown up. The next day Dragon and Ossorio had the presence of mind to go to Pollock's house and clear out Ruth Kligman's belongings so that Lee Krasner would not discover them when she returned from Europe. Ossorio was waiting for Krasner when she arrived home at La Guardia Airport later that day, and he took her by limousine directly out to East Hampton to help make Pollock's funeral arrangements.

Pollock was buried, as he wished, in Green River Cemetery out near the end of Accabonac Road. Green River is a bucolic country cemetery, deep in the heart of Springs, with a loose-gravel horseshoe driveway and lichen-covered tombstones, some 300 years old, chiseled with the names of the original Bonackers. Little was known about Green River Cemetery before Pollock was buried there, and even the cemetery trustees aren't sure how it got its name (except that it might be named after a man named Sam Green Miller, who lived nearby). There is certainly no river anywhere. Krasner was able to buy three plots for $300. Pollock is buried on the top of a small knoll, and his friends dragged there, by truck and tractor and dint of will, a fifty-ton boulder called a glacial erratic, to mark his resting place. The boulder is half submerged in the earth, covered in moss and embedded with a modest plaque bearing his signature.

After Pollock died, Lee Krasner had few close friends, save Dragon and Ossorio. She remained a frequent guest at The Creeks. "Lee was afraid to sleep alone," Dragon said, "and so she stayed with us, or I slept at her place. In a couple of years she took an apartment on Madison Avenue, and she asked me to help her with the decorating. She wanted it to look different and yet have the furniture work with her art and Jackson's. One day we were in an antique store on Third Avenue when I saw the horned loveseat. It was such a perfect metaphor — for her life with Jackson, for my life with Ossorio — the twisting shape, the brutality and beauty of the horns, I insisted she buy it on the spot."

Within two decades Pollock's work and life and death became legend — and the subject of a dozen biographies and three movie projects, one developed by Robert De Niro, who wants to play Pollock, and one developed by Barbra Streisand, who wants to play Krasner. Green River Cemetery itself has turned into a mythical burying ground. The price of plots around Pollock's grave began to escalate in value about as much as the price of his paintings. (The year after Pollock died, his *Blue Poles* was sold to pond resident Ben Heller for $32,000, who sold it a few years later to the Australian government for $2.2 million.) Within a decade of Pollock's death, every creative artist of his generation wanted to be buried near him at Green River, and many were, including Ad Reinhardt, Wilfrid Zogbaum, Abraham Rattner, the journalist A. J. Liebling, composer Stefan Wolpe, avant-garde filmmaker Stan Vanderbeek (whose tombstone is a reel of film), Stuart Davis, Fredrick Edouard, the naturalist Merrill Millar Lake, and the poet Frank O'Hara, whose most elegant epitaph says, "Grace to be born and live as variously as possible." When O'Hara, a frequent visitor but not a resident of the East End, was buried at Green River, Lee Krasner was outraged. "He's not even a summer rental!" she cried in protest.

The cemetery sold out in the late seventies, and in the late eighties the trustees were able to obtain an adjacent acre at the price of $50,000, which would allow for 1,500 more grave sites. These are now mostly gone.

Jackson Pollock and the Hamptons have become synonymous. Of all the celebrated figures who have lived in the East End, his fame is the most enduring. The house in Springs that Pollock and Krasner lived in has become a shrine, a national historical landmark, the only one of its kind that belonged to an artist, and is run by the State University of New York at Stony Brook. Tours are given by appointment to the public, who traipse in reverent silence through the house, past the table he overturned that Thanksgiving weekend, the porch where they watched the sunset that first night, and Jackson's studio, where hardened brushes stand in coffee cans just as he left them the day he died. The floor on which he painted his canvases, splattered with layers of dripped paint, is in itself so valuable that visitors are requested to put paper booties on their feet before they are allowed to walk on it.

Lee Krasner spent the rest of her life nurturing the Jackson Pollock legend. Through her crafty manipulations, the price of Pollock's paintings skyrocketed into the millions, and by the time Krasner died thirty-one years after Pollock, in 1987, she had amassed a personal fortune of $26 million. She was buried near Pollock, under a smaller yet still formidable glacial erratic. She left everything to a foundation — not a painting to a friend or a relative, except for one single object: the horned loveseat that she bought with Ted Dragon on Third Avenue three decades before.

Not many artists live in Springs now. It has become middle-class, mostly hardworking families with lots of kids, surrounded by vacation homes in the low six-figure range. It has the highest school tax of any community in the Hamptons. The generation of successful artists, like Brice Marden, Ross Bleckner, and Julian Schnabel, all live south of the highway in million-dollar homes. Robert Motherwell's house, the icon of abstract expressionism in the Hamptons, was sold in 1952 to Grove Press president and First Amendment rights champion Barnet Rosset, who lived in it for thirty years and maintained it as a landmark. Eventually, in 1985, it was purchased by the Peck family, who claimed that the historic Quonset hut had degenerated until it was unsalvageable and had to be destroyed. In response to a public outcry, Stephen Peck offered the house to anyone who could cart it off, but it was impossible to disassemble without destroying it; eventually it was torn down, and the foundation filled in.

Barnet Rosset, for one, was outraged. "It would be fitting," he said, "if all the trees and bushes and flowers that we planted with such great love and nourished from within that house would now wither and die from sorrow."

When the *New York Times* contacted Motherwell in his New York studio to tell him that his unusual house had been bulldozed in favor of a postmodern weekend home by its current owners, he was "stunned." "It reminds me of the title of that great Greek poem," Motherwell sighed, " 'The Barbarians Are Coming.' "

Dragon

I DIDN'T COME to dinner," Ted Dragon said, remembering those heady years at The Creeks. "You see, I'm a Taurian. I loved the idea of tables being set correctly and the menus being perfect, but the people . . . I just couldn't care less." Except for Lee Krasner, "most of the people who passed in and out of the house weren't interested in me in the least." Dragon surmised that they regarded him as "some kept thing." It became a joke among their friends that Dragon and Ossorio were never seen together. "At one point," said Sydney Butchkes, the artist, "Ted Dragon seemed to disappear." Indeed, one acquaintance remembered actually watching Dragon "vanish into the distance as guests arrived for a party, not to be seen again for the entire night."

"I never left the Creeks," Dragon said. "Never. I really *lived* there all those years — summer, winter, and spring. Ossorio continued his exciting life in New York, he would go on trips abroad, but I just stayed at The Creeks. He liked the feeling that I was at home." In the summer he had a few of his own social friends, discreetly gay men who spent the season in the Hamptons, but Ossorio showed no interest in knowing them, and in any event, they left by autumn, when a sense of deep isolation befell The Creeks.

The total population of East Hampton village dwindled to fewer than 2,000 people in the winter. Days ended about 4 P.M., when it got dark, and at night families stayed home. Just one restaurant operated throughout the rugged Northeast winter, and the movie theater was open only on Saturday night, when practically the whole town turned out. To add to the sense of remoteness, after New Year's, the Long Island Railroad cut back its schedule, and on some nights the train ran only as far as Quogue. An hour could go by without even seeing a car on the highway. Weeks at a time Dragon sat alone in the mansion on the pond, the beach forbidding and eerie, the wind howling loudly day and night. "There wasn't one light on Georgica Pond, except for our neighbors, the Larkins," Dragon said, "and every night in the winter we'd flash our lights at six-thirty to let each other know we were okay, like a signal across Georgica Pond."

One practical consideration in Dragon's slavish dedication to The Creeks was security. An invaluable collection of art was on display at the house, including the historic Art Brut collection, more than 100 Dubuffets, and various Pollocks, Stills and Krasners. There was no such thing as home security alarms at the time, and The Creeks' insurer, Lloyd's of London, insisted that the house always be occupied — a demand taken seriously because of the frightening string of burglaries that were taking place in the East End.

Home burglaries were completely unheard of in the Hamptons, maybe one a decade, and even then it was never more than a stolen purse left near an open kitchen door. But from 1955 to 1959, at least twenty of the biggest homes in the Hamptons had been hit, all like The Creeks, standing alone down long driveways or isolated on the dunes. One by one they had been picked off, stripped of priceless art and antiques: Leo Castelli's house on Jericho Road, Robert D. L. Gardiner's mansion on Main Street in East Hampton, the Froelich and Frankau estates, the Condons' and Hemings' homes, and the Findlay estate in Southampton. The booty was museum quality, including Ming vases, Chippendale mirrors, original statuary, sterling candelabra, Kerman Oriental rugs, and a brace of rare antique dueling pistols. At the Lovejoy house in Amagansett, the summer residence of a wealthy physician, the entire contents of furniture was emptied out, a prodigious task, except for a set of china that the thieves had set aside but for some reason left behind.

And so Ted Dragon stood sentry at The Creeks as the police and insurance investigators set out to solve the crimes. People exchanged theories and gossiped at the post office. The combined wisdom of the Southampton and East Hampton police detectives working on the case was that because of the sheer bulk of furniture stolen at each heist — including heavy oak bedroom sets and dining room tables and chairs — the thefts were the work of a team of professional burglars with a small truck. They were more than likely armed and not to be approached. Everyone was on the alert for suspicious-looking vehicles, and the police methodically patrolled the estate areas, hoping to catch the burglars in the act.

The chief of police of East Hampton, Francis Leddy, and Carl Dordelman, a patrolman, were doing just that one wet day in February 1959. It was the second day of a relentless rain made icy by frigid gusts off the Atlantic. Leddy and Dordelman drove out to the windswept tail of West End Road, where it narrows to a slip of sand. At the tip stood Juan Trippe's home, in front of which was parked a familiar-looking 1958 Oldsmobile. The two policemen pulled the patrol car out of sight and waited quietly for someone to appear. Presently, a second-floor bedroom window slowly slid open, and a burglar crawled out onto a sloping roof carrying a chair.

It was Ted Dragon.

Dordelman and Leddy were on him in a moment. He seemed surprised and dazed at first and then was clearly relieved to have been caught. "I knew you would be looking for me at night," Dragon told Leddy, "so I did it in the daytime. Always on rainy days, because I read in Mickey Spillane that the rain would wash the footprints away."

At the Newtown Lane jail, Ted Dragon Young was charged with

grand larceny and put in a holding room. Ossorio was summoned at The Creeks, and the *East Hampton Star* was tipped off. Its editor, Everett Rattray, Jeannette Rattray's son, rushed to the jailhouse to interview Dragon and take his picture even before Ossorio was able to get there to stop it. Dragon was in a pitiful state, terrified of what Ossorio would say. But there was not the slightest trace of reproach in Ossorio's manner. He was dignified and courteous with everyone at the police station. He unfailingly met the gaze of all who greeted him, without a hint of embarrassment; most of all, he was kind to Dragon and solicitous of his comfort.

"He was a rock," Dragon said, "the rock of Gibraltar. He said that I had nothing to worry about, no matter what it took, everything would be taken care of. He said to me, 'I know that you're very upset and that you didn't know what you were doing, and it's fine.' He said that he had called his father to tell him what happened, 'And you know what my father said? "That's *great!* I always thought Ted Dragon was too good to be true!" ' " Then Ossorio arranged for dinner to be brought in from the Maidstone Arms restaurant, and stayed with Dragon until he was allowed to go home.

Dragon has never publicly been able to explain why he took all the furniture, and he's still not sure himself. He didn't do it for gain — he never sold any of it. "I just loved beautiful things so much, and sometimes I was appalled at how badly the furniture was being kept," he said. He felt almost as if he were rescuing mistreated pets. He was also lonely and isolated. It started one day, he said, in late October, the most beautiful month in the Hamptons, when he took long walks with the dogs over the dunes. "I had those standard poodles," Dragon said, "and one day I was walking them and passed Leo Castelli's house." Castelli was an art dealer, and Dragon had been there many times to visit the de Koonings when they had spent a summer with Castelli. A side door to the house had been left wide open, "flapping in the wind," Dragon said. "In those days nobody locked their houses anyway." He walked in with the dogs and sat down. He sat there for a while, looking around and admiring things, listening to the quiet, and then he picked out something he liked, a covered jar, and took it home. When Ossorio saw the jar and asked where it had come from, Dragon told him that a relative in Massachusetts had sent it.

After that, he couldn't stop. He was just so bored — and angry with Ossorio for being left at The Creeks — that it became a pastime. One New Year's Eve, on his way back to The Creeks from a party, he passed Robert Gardiner's huge stone mansion and thought, "I wonder what's in there?" Dragon climbed to the second story, entered through a French door off a balcony, and hunted around the vast house until he chose a mirror and walked off with it. "The reason for the acts of burglary is completely beyond my powers of comprehension," he told the *East Hampton Star* shortly after his arrest. "I just like antiques."

Indeed, Dragon repaired, refinished, and reupholstered the furniture in need. He did such a good job with it that the owners marveled at how handsome their furniture looked when they got it back, and some even wrote him thank-you notes. One pleased dowager from Southampton, upon recovering her chairs from the police, told Dragon, "I never would have thought to put rose and gold on that Empire set." Some of the reupholstered chairs were used at The Creeks; on occasion, Dragon related, they were sat in by their unknowing rightful owners. Most of the stolen goods, however, was stashed in the attic. "That attic — you couldn't move," Dragon said, smiling. When Ossorio began to question where all the furniture stored in the attic kept coming from, Dragon insisted that relatives in Northampton, Massachusetts, were sending it.

As for the police theory that the burglaries were committed by more than one person because of the difficulty in lifting the furniture, Dragon agreed that it took superhuman strength to carry it all.

"God, some of those marble pieces! An entire four poster-bed and an eighteen-by-twenty Oriental rug!" Dragon marveled. But, Dragon said, he had "ballet strength," and anyway, he was committed to the furniture he stole — and that gave him the fortitude to lift even the heaviest pieces. Just one time, though, it got to be too much. "That's why I left the china behind at the Lovejoy house," Dragon said. "I was so tuckered out with the bed, chairs, rug, and so forth, I had no strength for the dishes."

Ted Dragon was treated harshly for his crimes, considering that most of the furniture was returned in better condition than when it was stolen, and that only one of the aggrieved owners pressed charges — Robert D. L. Gardiner. The greatest inconvenience Dragon caused was embarrassment to the victims. The aggregate insurance claims of all the thefts topped $150,000, when the real appraised value of the furniture turned out to be only $35,000. Even Robert D. L. Gardiner dropped his charges when the antique mirror Dragon took was revealed to be not very old — "Brooklyn circa 1941," said Dragon with a wink.

Yet public sentiment against Dragon was scathing, and local authorities were determined that Dragon be punished, perhaps even banished from the town. On the recommendation from Evan Frankel, the so-called Squire of East Hampton, Ossorio hired a noted New York psychoanalyst, Dr. David Abrahamsen, who had a summer home in East Hampton and was the author of the book *The Road to Emotional Maturity*. A criminal attorney in Riverhead that Ossorio also hired recommended that "the defense would be to claim I had a mental disorder," Dragon said. "They said that I had to plead insanity, that it was the only way I could get off without any jail time."

At Suffolk County Court in Riverhead, Dragon was painted by his attorney as an emotionally disturbed man who was seeking psychiatric treatment. The lawyer asked for the court's leniency. Dragon kept his chin up while Ossorio sat in the first row of the spectators' seats, five feet behind him, for moral support. In a plea bargain, Dragon said, it was determined that in exchange for a suspended jail sentence, he would be remanded to West Hill, a private sanitarium in Connecticut. Once released from the hospital, he would continue outpatient therapy with Dr. Abrahamsen in Manhattan, living not in the MacDougal Alley townhouse with Ossorio but with court-approved custodians in an apartment on the Upper East Side until, said Dragon, Dr. Abrahamsen determined when — and if — he was well enough to return to East Hampton. The bill for all, footed by Ossorio.

"I will do everything in my power to be helped," a heartsick Dragon said before he was sent off to the hospital, "and I hope someday to return and live my life here. . . . When this is all over, I'd like to visit those places I burglarized again — if the people would let me in — and see how they're taking care of that furniture."

Dragon made the best of his time at West Hill. He needlepointed and taught the other patients ballet. He also thought a lot about his decision to give up his career to live at The Creeks with Ossorio. Ossorio and his younger brother, Robert, visited Dragon regularly at the clinic, sometimes bringing him bonbons. They sat on benches in the gardens with the other patients and their families, trying to make the best of it. Dragon remembered one of his happiest days at West Hill was when he received a note from the artist Grace Hartigan that said, "Thank God we have a Robin Hood out on Long Island." Another woman whose home Dragon had burglarized felt so guilty that he was sent to a psychiatric hospital, she called him on the phone and asked if he wanted to keep the furniture as a gift. Dragon said no, thank you, but the gesture was worth more to him than any piece of furniture.

Eventually, Dr. Abrahamsen determined that after two years in exile, Dragon was well enough to return to East Hampton. As part of his fee, according to Dragon, Ossorio gave him at least one Dubuffet painting.

Dragon's misadventure was the scandal of the decade in East Hampton. He certainly found out who his friends were. Lee Krasner, for one, thought Dragon's heists were "terrific" and wanted to hear every detail. Others pulled away; some were downright mean. The Guild Hall—Maidstone crowd, whose acceptance and respect Ossorio had painstakingly earned over the years, began to call The Creeks "The Creeps." For a proud man like Ossorio, nothing could have humiliated him more than a public scandal. But he was outraged at the suggestion that he sever his relationship with Dragon or that Dragon should not return to East Hampton. "My dear, nothing human is strange to me," he repeatedly said. "One is *always* sorry at one moment of one's life for *everything* one has done."

What's more, he knew that he was at least partly responsible for what happened. He had asked the young dancer to give up everything for The Creeks and had diminished him in the process. He had taken a young man who loved to dance and turned him into a concierge. He would never think of turning his back on Ted now. He told B. H. Friedman, "Bob, you mustn't ever think it was one of my charities. This was an act of love."

The incident "cemented our relationship," Dragon said. "The sword forged in fire is often the strongest. How could you ever turn away from a person who has stood by you like that?"

It took a measure of even greater bravery for Ted Dragon to return to East Hampton in 1961. But it wasn't as if Dragon was prepared to fade, humiliated, into the woodwork. "I never stopped feeling 'This is who I am, and if you don't like it, you can go away.'" In some odd way his newfound notoriety gave him even more license to express himself, and he began to wear caftans and sarilike robes, accessorized with clunky costume jewelry and headpieces, or to don multicolored wigs, one day blond, one day brunette. No matter what Dragon looked like, Ossorio never uttered a word of criticism. "You're like one of my paintings" was his only comment.

The Summer Colony, and the artist community as well, was unabashedly fascinated with Dragon. Nobody seemed to know how to behave around him, so Dragon decided to show them. Not long after his return, Harry Acton Striebel, a successful fashion designer and a friend of Dragon's, threw a party for several hundred people at the height of the summer. When the party was going full blast, a large hoop with a sheet stretched over it was carried out of the forest and doused in kerosene in front of the curious guests. Then Stravinsky's *Rite of Spring* was put on the loudspeaker system, and the hoop was set on fire with torches. Suddenly, Ted Dragon burst through the flames, leaping through the air in a dramatic costume of gold brocade, greeted by a tumultuous roar of approval from the guests.

2

PERHAPS NOT COINCIDENTALLY, about the time of Dragon's crisis Ossorio experienced a creative breakthrough that dramatically altered the direction of his work. It was almost as if Dragon's *petite fou* had freed him to take a leap of faith in his art. Since falling under the spell of Pollock and Dubuffet ten years earlier, Ossorio's work was mired in abstract, emotional canvases, whorling wax-and-watercolor paintings derivative of the two men he so admired. But when Dragon returned to East Hampton, Ossorio had begun to experiment with the technique of pasting objects onto his paintings, turning them into three-dimensional collages, much the way Dubuffet had used wire and "found" objects on his canvases. Soon Ossorio did away with canvases altogether, using instead pieces of wood as a background — amorphous shapes or slabs of plywood on which he would mount myriad objects and paint them bright colors. These objects consisted of what Ossorio called the "residue of life," or what one critic described as "dead things, remnants and left-overs." Ossorio called them "congregations," and they became his trademark.

In their own way, the congregations were just as peculiar as his drawings of body parts but were even more mesmerizing and phantasmic. Their most recurrent features were brightly colored extrusions of congealed plastic, reminiscent of the entrails of his earlier work. Ossorio made regular visits to industrial factories to hunt for these organlike globs, which he bought by weight. The plastic lumps became a thematic component of the densely filled congregations, which also frequently comprised hat blocks, animal bones ("The house smelled from the dinner bones boiling in ammonia on the stove," said Dragon), human teeth bought by the bucketful from a dental school, doorknobs, garden scythes, rusted rakes, antlers, religious iconography, and most of all, glass eyeballs. Glass eyeballs abounded in all his congregations, peering out from under objects or tucked away as surprises in dark corners. He was so enamored of glass eyeballs that when he heard the eyeball manufacturer was going to switch to plastic, he bought out the entire factory's stock and warehoused it on tables in his studio. It all created a general feeling of Dr. Frankenstein's laboratory. He was in constant need of fresh matériel, and friends and neighbors brought him care packages full of oddities; a local fisherman would turn up with a shark's jaw, or artist Louise Nevelson would drop by with a plastic garbage bag of wooden shoe lasts discarded from her own work.

Once these objects were affixed, they were painted in carnival-like enamels of red, blue, and white. These were the colors of medieval Christian symbolism, Ossorio said — red for charity, blue for hope, and white for faith — and they became his trademark colors.

But the colors looked garish, not symbolic, and the resulting, writhing, overspilling congregations — although in retrospect an extraordinary personal invention — at the time seemed vulgar and cheap. One wag said that they looked as if a pin-ball machine had thrown up. Grace Glueck, the art critic of the *New York Times*, reported they appeared to be "what was left after cannibals feasted on Balkan royalty." Another *New York Times* critic called them "exuberant models of excess and bad taste." *The New Yorker* dismissed them as a pop-art "footnote."

But Ossorio had never been dissuaded by critics. He decided instead to abandon all other methods of work and make congregations exclusively. He began to churn them out at a prolific rate, developing an assembly-line method by making small pieces on individual shingles and storing the components on racks, waiting to be popped into a larger whole. The walls and tabletops of the studio were covered with taxidermied animal heads, bleached bones, plastic blobs, finials, and newel posts. "He made so many congregations," said Dragon, "they began to fill the walls of the house. Quite literally. "Pollocks, de Koonings, Krasners, Dubuffets, wall to wall, floor to ceiling — with barely half an inch of space between them. When we ran out of wall space, we began to hang them inside of closet doors. Next thing, we did the unthinkable — we hired a carpenter and had some of the windows boarded up in the dining room so we could have more hanging space." Finally, in 1970, at Dragon's suggestion, most of the interior walls of The Creeks were painted jet-black, and the dining room, where *Lavender Mist* hung, purple, "so the paintings would stand out," Dragon said, "like diamonds on a jeweler's black velvet tray."

The black walls were part of a process that turned the entire house itself into a congregation. The task of interior decoration had been left to Dragon. He had only one caveat from Ossorio: not to place anything in front of the paintings. Both men were acquisitive;

Dragon had an eye for good antiques, and Ossorio liked the odd-ball trinket. Over the decades The Creeks began to fill with a phantasmagorical collection of objets d'art, thousands of *things*, statues, tchotchkes, hobo art, paintings, junk — all stacked on tables, hung, leaned — the divine intermingled with trash, the precious with the tawdry. Every day more was added, another piece, another doodad, until it went way beyond clutter as a decorative style and into a sort of madness. "A house is never finished until the hearse is at the door," Dragon said. *Architectural Plus* magazine described the interior of the house as a work of art unto itself, like Simon Rodia's Watts Towers, and said it made Salvador Dalí's bizarrely decorated house at Port Lligat "look like a San Diego motel by comparison."

There was also a *motif* of Roman Catholic iconography throughout the house, every imaginable kind of santo and representation of Christ, crucifixes of all sizes and dimensions, so many that one day Lee Krasner, sick of looking at them, told Ted, "Why don't you just put *all* of it in one room and build yourself a damn basilica." Dragon did just that; on the second floor he designed a dramatically decorated chapel by draping the walls and windows in sheets and setting up an altar with a large statue of Christ and pictures of Mary flanked by gold incense burners and a hidden tape recorder that played soft Gregorian chants. It looked like a Gypsy fortune-teller's storefront.

In some ways, more remarkable than the collection of objects was that Ted Dragon moved these things, every day, from room to room, or just to opposite sides of a table. "It wouldn't have been interesting to see them in the same place every day," he said, aghast at the thought. "Many years ago my piano teacher told me that wherever the eye falls in a room, it should find something pretty or unusual or different to look at."

Also integrated into this Dadaesque crush were Dragon's beloved standard poodles, hundreds of plants and flowers, and forty birds, a whole squawking aviary of them — lovebirds, mynahs, and parrots, one of which relentlessly cried out, "Alfonso? Where are you? Stop it, you fool!" Ossorio threatened Dragon, "If I see one more bird, I'm going to wring its neck!" There were so many pets that Dragon consecrated his own pet cemetery on the property, just west of Ossorio's studio, where he installed a small burbling fountain and a statue of the Virgin Mary. Whenever a pet died, Dragon would order a handcrafted little coffin, and the animal would be buried with full Catholic rites and regalia.

3

BEFORE LONG, the interior design of the house began to creep right out the front door, like a trailing vine, one tendril at a time, first covering the outside of the building, then all over the grounds of the estate itself. It began in 1970 when Ossorio built a controversial, 300-foot concrete retaining wall to protect The Creeks from the annual overflowing of the pond. This kind of retaining wall is illegal now, as it denudes the shoreline, but by putting it in when he did, Ossorio saved the foundation of the mansion from certain ruin. Every spring, the swollen waters of the pond turn much of the surrounding land into swamp, filling the basements of the mansions on its shores with water so high that some residents keep rowboats in their cellars. The brackish water also floods the septic tanks, adding an unpleasant urgency to bringing the water down. The simple solution is to "let" the pond into the Atlantic, via a dug channel, every six months, but environmental and wildlife protection laws prohibit disturbing the area's natural ecological balance — health problems and foundations of the mansions be damned. In 1991, in frustration, one of the many millionaires who live around the pond secretly paid to have a trench dug in the dark of night to spare his house from flooding that season. There was a celebration when the other residents awoke in the morning to find the pond let and the waters receding; the police are still looking for the wealthy gentleman in question.

Ossorio might have saved The Creeks by building the huge retaining wall, but he also regretted having to look at 300 feet of unadorned concrete every day. His friends encouraged him to relandscape, but after studying the sweeping gray shape, Ossorio decided instead to accent the wall with an outdoor sculpture. This first outdoor piece was a soaring metal thing, twenty feet tall, triangular, painted the usual red, white, and blue enamel, as if one of the components of his congregations had become supersized and escaped from the house. It was in its own way hideous, as much of his work was, and disturbed everyone so much (it was visible from all over the pond) that Ossorio made dozens more — massive, giant-sized statements planted throughout the grounds of The Creeks. About 200 feet from the main entrance on Montauk Highway, Ossorio installed a stepped red-and-white sculpture so startling that it slowed the traffic with gawkers. Along the driveway at one point were three giant spheres of bright red, white, and blue poured concrete, ten tons' worth, like mammoth billiard balls erupting from the earth. Some of the sculptures were actually put *into* trees, hammered into the branches, or the treetops would be bluntly amputated and crowned with a barbed necklace of wheel rims. "That's to remind you that you don't always get what you want," Ossorio explained of the lopped-off trees. "It's an interplay between the truncated and the successful. Oh, it's a very moralistic landscape."

When Ossorio was included in a group show at Guild Hall one summer, his contribution was a large breastlike cement protrusion that spurted into the air a red liquid from the nipple. "Look, Mommy, blood!" a five-year-old boy shouted at the opening, and a woman in the crowd muttered, "He must be kidding."

It seemed only to follow when in 1974 the entire exterior of the house was painted black, with the trim and landing steps in the signature red, white, and blue enamel of the congregations; the circular swimming pool was also painted black, with a radiating pattern of red and blue petals around it.

It was the outdoor sculptures that first brought the trees to Ossorio's attention. One of the pines got in the way of his sculpture, so he had it pruned, then moved. Later he decided to move two or three more trees, and it occurred to him that it was possible to paint with the trees themselves. "I looked around and realized that most of what I had outdoors was flowers," said Ossorio. "I live here year-round and I wanted color in the winter. I started by putting in a few evergreens by the road, and before you know it, I was hooked."

"Hooked" was the operative word, for like everything else Ossorio took on, conifers became a fetishistic preoccupation. He ordered three textbooks a day on evergreens and forestry and studied them through the night, taking notes and keeping files. He conferred with every landscape designer on the East End, and when his knowledge surpassed theirs, he hired the greatest experts in the field to tutor him, including Dr. Rupert Barneby, the curator of the New York Botanical Gardens in the Bronx. He became so knowledgeable that he invented his own method of planting mature trees without trapping gas in the root ball that is to this day universally used by horticulturists.

Ossorio discovered that it was possible to import odd-looking conifers from all over the globe, in different shapes and colors, weeping or bent or dwarfed. He began to visit nurseries around the world to see specimens, just as he had visited art galleries searching for new talent years before. Over the next decade Ossorio covered more than fifty acres with conifers, a lush forest of more than 100 different species. As the plantings became increasingly complicated, each tree was identified with a brass placard indicating its origin and date of planting.

However, even the gardens had Ossorio's special touch, for he planted these specimens not by genus, but as he would attach objects in a congregation, for their texture or color. Ossorio's forest was a jumble of shapes and colors, a short-cropped golden juniper grew next to long, silvery blue Thomasen spruce, intersected by a wedge of splendid Atlas cedars. He even took to mutilating the trees for effect, forcing them into odd positions. He had a perfect example of what tinkering with nature could produce sitting right outside his window: the extraordinary red cedar "organ tree" that the Herters had planted. Lopped off at ten feet for more than fifty years now, the cedar was still healthy and beautiful, despite its needing crutches to keep the elongated branches from falling.

Through his newfound botanical knowledge, Ossorio discovered that it was possible to alter specimens bizarrely and create Frankenstein-like aberrations. He amused himself by grafting four different species; he mixed and matched different colors and shapes into horticultural anomalies. These creations were anathema to serious horticulturists (not unlike the way many artists felt about his congregations), and one respected botanist from Japan actually fainted when she first saw what Ossorio had done at The Creeks. He loved to show off his landscaping and on occasion would find strangers who had wandered in off the highway thinking The Creeks was a public park, gawking at the trees. A few of these unexpected visitors were invited to lunch and sampled some of his best wines.

Trees were an expensive hobby, it turned out, even more expensive than collecting art. Ossorio didn't have the patience to grow trees from saplings ("I'm not young enough to see things mature," he complained), so he almost always bought adult specimens, sometimes for $15,000–20,000 each. Dragon estimated that with the cost of importing rare specimens from around the globe, Ossorio may have spent as much as $300,000 a month on his trees. He dug into his principal savings so deeply that eventually his trust fund began to run low and he had to sell off paintings to support his tree habit. First he sold some of his Stills, then some of the Dubuffets, and finally, in a move that took away the breath of all those who knew him, in 1976 Ossorio sold Pollock's masterpiece, *Lavender Mist*, for $2 million to the National Gallery. Although a German private collector offered him far more than $2 million for the painting, Ossorio refused to see it leave the United States, where he believed it belonged.

The relationship of the trees to the sculpture, of the sculpture and the trees to the house, of the estate to the pond, all became part of a larger piece. Even the way Dragon looked and dressed was part of it. In some ways, in the tradition of the Herters, Ossorio and Dragon achieved one of the highest aspirations of any artist: almost every aspect of their life was art. As the decades passed, the stories about the odd couple on the pond took on mythological proportions. Some were true. Ossorio did amass one of the largest private collections of pornography in the world: movies, books, and magazines, each one dutifully read or watched and safely stored away. But the cocktail chatter that Dragon and Ossorio kept a black man chained to a wooden support beam in the basement of The Creeks; that young men were drugged and disappeared, never to be seen again; or that small animals were sacrificed in the second-floor chapel is, of course, apocryphal. Dragon giggled deliriously with glee at the thought.

In 1988, at the age of seventy-two, Ossorio was hospitalized for triple-bypass heart surgery. "Years of smoking and rich foods," Dragon sighed. "After that bypass, he was never really well again. By autumn of 1990 he was confined to his bed. We talked a lot about what to do when he passed on." Everything, of course, would be left to Dragon, but Ossorio's family trust-fund money would stop completely when he died since Dragon was not his legal spouse. Ossorio had already sold off the most valuable paintings to support his conifer addiction, and although there was still a handsome art collection left, the cost of keeping up the huge estate and its gardens would deplete the resources within a couple of years. "When I die," Ossorio said to Dragon one afternoon, "there is no choice but to sell it." The two men were silent. "But no matter what happens, don't divide it. Just don't let the developers get it."

"I said I would do my best," remembered Dragon, "but I didn't know what would happen when Alfonso passed on. You must remember, in all those years, I had never even balanced a checkbook."

Ossorio died at the New York University Medical Center on December 5, 1990, at the age of seventy-four, of a ruptured aneurysm. He and Dragon had been together for forty-two years. His body was cremated, and a memorial service was held at The Creeks. One-third of his ashes were strewn into Georgica Pond, another third spread under the tortured red cedar outside the house where they joined Albert and Adele Herter's, and the last third brought to Green River Cemetery, where they were buried just a stone's throw from Jackson Pollock and Lee Krasner. One day, Dragon will be there too.

4

"I COULD HAVE SOLD the Creeks to developers the minute Ossorio died," Dragon said, "but I held out, hoping for a buyer who would want it intact." Dragon formed the Ossorio Foundation, located in Southampton, to protect and maintain Ossorio's extensive personal art legacy and extraordinary archive of historical records, documents, and ephemera of the magic era of The Creeks under his reign. The estate itself was offered to several wealthy institutions, including Harvard University, the State University of New York at Stony Brook, and the South Fork Nature Conservancy, but it was too expensive a chore to take on, maintaining the sixty acres of rare trees. "Streisand came," Dragon said, "and Elizabeth Taylor was interested in turning it into an AIDS center, but that didn't pan out. Anne Bass inquired. Mort Zuckerman was interested, and German princess Gloria von Thurn und Taxis, they all looked at The Creeks." Finally, in desperation, Dragon drew up plans to subdivide the estate into four waterfront lots, with the main house on a seven-acre plot priced at $7.5 million.

It was then that the broker Tina Fredericks brought Ron Perelman to see the estate. At first, he said he wasn't interested because it was right off the highway, but Fredericks persisted. When the billionaire showed up, "Perelman had four security people with him," Dragon said. "North, south, east, and west. They were with him all the time. It was like a compass, and the joke is they looked just like what you see in Dick Tracy. They're in gray suits and you see the bulge [of their guns]. He just walked in the door — he didn't examine the ceiling, the cellar, or the floor — he just walked through the front door and said, 'I'm buying it. The whole thing. I don't know anything about what's going on here. I can't understand the sculpture, I don't know anything, I don't know one damn tree from another. But I was halfway down the road and I said, "This has the look." ' "

The catch was, Perelman was eager to move in right away. The imperiously demanding businessman wanted a country love nest to house his then affair with fashion consultant Elizabeth Saltzman. Perelman told Dragon that he would pay him $12.5 million, but only if Dragon would clear out of the house in two weeks. He would let Dragon live in the gatekeeper's cottage for a while until he found a new home. When Dragon asked how long he could live in the cottage, Perelman said, "When is your birthday?" Dragon said, "April twenty-fourth," and Perelman gave him until April 24, 1993, to move out.

The following days at The Creeks were packed with hurried activity. It was nostalgic and wrenching, "fifty years of things going in and nothing going out," said Dragon. Ossorio's art was moved to the new foundation in Southampton, and the Strand Book Store in Manhattan sent out three trucks and took away most of Ossorio's 8,000-book library. The roomful of pornography was given to Dragon's grateful friends. "I thought to myself, Why not have the greatest yard sale the Hamptons have ever seen?" So, in late May 1992, the residual contents of The Creeks went on sale to the public in a three-day event that the *East Hampton Star* called "the Mother of All Yard Sales." More than 2,000 people attended, and parked cars stretched three miles in either direction down Montauk Highway from the entrance to The Creeks. The first day when the doors opened at 9 A.M., there was practically a buying frenzy, even in 96-degree heat. "The rich are ready to kill each other," said one doctor from Wainscott. Martha Stewart bought all of the estate's Christmas decorations, Kelly Klein tried on Dragon's old Greek sheperd's costumes (which fit her perfectly), and Betty Friedan considered the vicuña lap robe that came from Ossorio's mother's limousine. By the end of the third day, the house was stripped, barren, emptier than it had ever been in eighty years.

The day before the deed to The Creeks actually changed hands, Ted Dragon's attorney called to remind him to bring the front-door key, which had to be turned over at the closing. "The *key?*" Dragon said, amazed. "There is no key. The front door has never been locked. We never went away; we never left the house alone; and anyway, there are so many doors, how can you lock up The Creeks?" Well, said the lawyer, a key would have to be produced at the closing to satisfy the terms of the contract, so Dragon hurriedly called a locksmith and had a brand-new lock installed on the front door. The keys were so shiny, they embarrassed Dragon with their newness, so he fastidiously rubbed them in the dirt by the front door to age them and tied them with an antique ribbon.

The next morning, when Dragon pulled out onto the highway on his way to the closing, he was greeted with a startling sight. "As far as you could see," Dragon said, "on the right and on the left, it was lined up with one truck after another." There were trucks from lumberyards, panel trucks from electricians, heating and air-conditioning trucks, and a small army of craftsmen and construction crews, twelve different contractors in all, sitting on the side of the road waiting for the sale to take place so they could enter the property.

Dragon remembered, "The moment I signed the papers at the lawyer's office and the deal was done, one of Perelman's men spoke a single word into his walkie-talkie, 'Shoot,' I think it was. That was the signal that the property had changed hands and that it was okay to open the gates and move the trucks into The Creeks and begin to tear it apart. By the time I drove back to the gatehouse, every sink, every john, every tub, every lighting fixture, every doorknob, had been removed and thrown into the parking lot. They even tore out the circular pool."

In a hurry to be able to entertain Hamptons society by July 4 weekend, Perelman wanted the legendary mansion stripped, renovated, and put back together again from cellar to attic, including the installation of new floors, walls, bathrooms, plumbing, electrical wiring, and ducts for central air-conditioning — in about six weeks. Perelman insisted that he be in residence on weekends to keep an eye on construction, and during the week all the furniture in the house was carried outdoors, covered with tarps, and then carried back inside for him on the weekends. At one point nearly forty painters worked in tandem on the house, the exterior of which changed color several times over the summer until Perelman settled on light beige.

Perelman dug several new wells and installed a sprinkler system in the vast estate for the first time, tearing out many of Ossorio's sculptures in the process, bulldozed and thrown into a junk heap. Dragon couldn't bear it. "I couldn't live there for long, I felt like I was

suffocating, in a prison. So in a few months I bought this house."
He gestured around his new home on Pantigo Road. "The Creeks
now looks like any expensive estate in Palm Beach or San Francisco
or Michigan or anywhere," he said. "It's just got a look of money, like
any other estate with miles of grass. There's not one bit of originality
in it."

Dragon giggled gleefully when he related that Perelman built a
guest house on top of the pet cemetery. Dragon also claimed that
he never bothered to inform Mr. Perelman that Ossorio's and the
Herters' ashes are sprinkled under the spreading red cedar next to
his house.

It is a bitter irony that since his death, Alfonso Ossorio's work
has been rediscovered and celebrated. Recent biographies of Jackson
Pollock have helped to fix his linchpin importance in the history of
American art, and the *New York Times* belatedly acknowledged him
as the "grandfather of Neo-Expressionism." His outsider art is perhaps more pertinent today than ever, and his once-mocked congregations are now valued at mid–six figures and steadily rising. His
artistic legacy hangs in the Metropolitan Museum of Art, the Museum of Modern Art, the Whitney Museum of American Art, and
the Solomon R. Guggenheim Museum.

But his greatest work is still his collaboration with Ted Dragon:
The Creeks.

The Squire

AT FIRST, she thought she must be dreaming.

Elena Prohaska, twenty-one, was standing in the crowded garden of a Bridgehampton art gallery at sundown, the silvered branches of the trees heavy with leaves. The odd East End light, first orange, then pink, was playing tricks with faces and shadows, when from out of the milling crowd the Magus appeared before her, as beguiling in real life as he was on the pages of the book she had been reading that afternoon.

It was a warm Saturday evening in July 1967, and the beautiful young girl was still a little light-headed from some painkillers she had taken for a recently extracted tooth. She spent the day lazing in bed at her father's house in Sagaponack, drifting in and out of sleep in the cool comfort of the extra bedroom, curled up like a cat. She had been reading *The Magus*, John Fowles's novel about a young man who is the victim of a plot by his ex-girlfriend and a powerful older man with sorcerorlike powers. Just an hour before, her father, Ray Prohaska, a well-known Hamptons artist, had roused her from her solitary day to be his escort at an art opening at the Benson Gallery.

The Benson Gallery is in a renovated Victorian farmhouse, just a few hundred feet off Montauk Highway in Bridgehampton. It had opened just the year before, and already it had become the hub of the booming local art market in the Hamptons. The Pollock legend had taken hold, and hundreds of artists, along with all the people who follow them — writers, psychiatrists, and creative advertising types — were invading the East End, an estimated 5,000 of them. There were so many painters in particular that East Hampton began to be called the "rich man's Provincetown." Jim Dine, Larry Rivers, Adolph Gottlieb, and Roy Lichtenstein were sixties émigrés, "après Jacksons" as they were called. Truman Capote bought a house in Sagaponack, James Jones and George Plimpton moved to Sagaponack, and John Steinbeck and Betty Friedan were encamped in Sag Harbor. New York show business put down roots in the sixties as well. Gwen Verdon and Bob Fosse moved to Amagansett; Eli Wallach and Anne Jackson bought in East Hampton; and Nora Ephron, then a journalist, rented her first house in the Hamptons in 1966, with eleven other singles in Amagansett. Edward Albee bought in Montauk, and Guild Hall even put on *Who's Afraid of Virginia Woolf?* in the sixties, but only because Mary Woodhouse, the mother of Guild Hall, finally died at age ninety-two. There were so many artists and writers in East Hampton that artist Syd Solomon organized a softball game between the two groups that would in two decades become a legendary sporting event.

The gays were arriving in force as well, and not much favored by the locals either. One East Hampton village police chief didn't think twice about bemoaning to the *East Hampton Star* that "on any given weekend afternoon, you can go down to Two Mile Hollow Beach and see three, four hundred head of queer." Late at night newly arriving gays patronized a ramshackle bar called the Elm Tree in Amagansett, where they were forbidden to dance because it was illegal for two people of the same sex to touch each other. The police vigorously ticketed their cars, and all the artists supported the gays.

That July night at the Benson Gallery, it seemed to Elena that every one of the 5,000 après Jacksons was attending the opening. She and her father could hardly see the canvases on the walls for the crowds of people and the cigarette smoke. They stepped onto the nubby lawn in back of the barn for a breath of fresh air and a glass of cold white wine when out of the crowd the Magus materialized before them, or so Elena thought. *I've got to stop reading that book,* she said to herself.

Evan Frankel, the Squire of East Hampton, had the tanned good looks of an aging matinee idol and the mischievous smile of a teen-ager with a dirty mind. He easily managed, even at sixty-three, to be as robust and sexy as a man half his age. It didn't hurt his attractiveness that he was the largest private landowner in all of East Hampton. He held the deed to more than 1,000 acres of developable land — 400 acres of it south of the highway — and owned several prime pieces of property in East Hampton village, including the Old Post Office movie theater and Oddfellows Hall. At one point he owned so much land that it was estimated he paid 50 percent of all the real estate taxes in East Hampton. Not coincidentally, at various times, he held seats on the town planning board, the board of directors of Southampton Hospital, and the advisory board of the East Hampton Free Library.

That night at the gallery, elegantly dressed in pale linen slacks and a summer-weight sport jacket, he was accompanied by an old friend, Joan Cullman, the attractive young wife of Joseph Cullman, chairman of the board of Phillip Morris, the tobacco company. Ray Prohaska had known Frankel for years, had even sold him some art, and he nervously introduced everyone. Frankel's eyes never left the luminous Elena. She was a tall girl, with a voluptuous figure, green eyes, and long black hair parted in the middle and worn down her back in the "hippie" style that was popular that summer. "You know," Frankel told her, "I am the most eligible bachelor in East Hampton."

"That's a shame," Elena responded coolly, "because I date only married men." Everyone laughed, even her father.

Elena was clever and quick, as much fun as she was pretty, but perhaps a bit too sophisticated for her own good. She was a "townie" who didn't belong in the town. She was born in East Hampton in 1946 and grew up on Main Street in Amagansett, but her parents were "from away," and Elena felt that she was too. Her father, Ray Prohaska, had been one of America's premier magazine illustrators before giving up his career and moving to East Hampton to paint watercolors and surf cast; her mother, Carolyn Pierson, was a former John Robert Powers model and actress before she became an East Hampton housewife.

Elena hated the isolation of East Hampton in the winter, and even at the height of the summer season, when the streets were busy with people from New York, it was never crowded enough for her. Ironically, it made her feel just a bit more like an interloper when after her sophomore year in high school, she started dating a boy whose family belonged to the Maidstone Club. When the season was over, he went back to his Ivy League school, and Elena, spurned, was left behind. That's when she convinced her mother and father that at age sixteen, she had learned all she could in East Hampton; they agreed to let her finish high school at Professional Children's School in Manhattan, where she lived with her brother. After graduating, she attended New York University for two years and was working at the Museum of Modern Art and living in a tiny studio apartment on the Upper East Side.

Ray Prohaska — who at sixty-two was only a year younger than Evan Frankel — thought to remind the land baron about the day he bought Brigadoon, his baronial fifteen-acre estate on Hither Lane in East Hampton. They had run into each other on the street. "I bought a house today!" Frankel had announced excitedly, and Prohaska answered, "I did you one better — I had a baby girl today!"

"And here you are all grown up!" Frankel said, smiling. "Twenty years later, almost to the day! Well, then, it was meant to be that we meet this day. It is *bershart*. You must come see the house that I bought on the day you were born. You and your father will be my guests at Brigadoon tomorrow, and we will have lunch under a groaning arbor of bittersweet, and later I shall take you down Temptation Path."

2

BRIGADOON, like the mythical village after which it was named, seemed to half appear in the distance, protected behind a low stone wall with creaky iron gates. The twelve-room carriage house was simple; half-timbered, sand-colored stucco, no doubt the doppelgänger to some country squire's house that existed in eighteenth-century Scotland. Elena and her father came down the long gravel drive just as the noon sun was burning off the remnants of a thin white fog to reveal the undulating green lawns dotted by massive wood and bronze impressionistic sculptures. Nora Bennet, Frankel's housekeeper of twenty-five years, greeted them at the front door and brought them out back to where Frankel was waiting at a glass-topped table set with linen and china. The arbor above, laced with thatches of blooming bittersweet, was as fragrant as promised.

"Can life be sweeter?" Frankel gently asked Elena and her father, gesturing for them to be seated. He waved his hand over the sweeping landscape and the luminescent sky, the few clouds like drawings from a child's picture book. From the distance came the plaintive cry of a peacock. "Can life be more rich and full and giving of its great beauty than this?" he asked.

"Even against the backdrop of his estate," Elena remembered, "Evan managed to be a scene-stealer." Indeed, the *New York Times* described him as "a cross between General Rommel and Laurence Olivier with a touch of Somerset Maugham" thrown in. "He was spectacular company," Elena said. "He could just as easily jump to his feet and launch into a Shakespearean soliloquy" — "If you have tears, prepare to shed them now," the funeral oratory from *Julius Caesar*, was his favorite — "as he could drop an anecdote about having a stein of beer with Hitler, or explain why Jackson Pollock was miffed at him."

"I once owned a Pollock," Frankel said, "but Pollock took it back. The guy who was renting my house one winter didn't like the painting. Nobody knew who the hell Pollock was back then, so I called Pollock from Jamaica and asked him to temporarily store it. He was so angry at me for agreeing to take it down that he went and got it from my house and never gave it back — even though I had paid him for it." Frankel seemed to relish this.

"Do you know why they call me the Squire of East Hampton?" he asked. "Because I wear a houndstooth cape and deerstalker cap in the winter. And I walk, every day, over my property. And many years ago, when the townspeople first spotted me in the distance, they dubbed me 'the Squire of East Hampton,' and I liked the nickname so much, I adopted it myself."

Elena told Frankel about leaving East Hampton for New York, and her part-time job at the Museum of Modern Art, where she had fallen in love with a young security guard. "He's really a talented painter," Elena said, "but he works nights as a guard so he can paint during the day. He's saving up enough money so we can go away together, to live in a commune, where he can paint and I can study." She was concerned, though, because he drank and smoked pot.

Frankel did not try to hide his disappointment. "A commune! Pot! That's a shame you have a boyfriend like that, sweetie," he said. "If you were free, I could show you the world and you could study art in a grand way. You should spurn him for me." Elena, flattered, laughed. "You know I'm right," he told her. "I can make up my own mind in two seconds and someone else's in three."

After a moment Frankel rose and said, "Now, my young lady, let me show you Brigadoon! I will be your tour guide nonpareil." He linked his arm in hers, and they set off down the sweeping lawn together, her father trailing behind. "I named this place Brigadoon not just because I produced the show *Brigadoon* on Broadway but because, like the legendary Brigadoon, this place is enchanted. If you fall in love here and then leave, you can never come back again!"

Down the far end of the lawn they approached a sylvan copse, and Frankel led them to an unexpected break in the foliage, concealed from the undiscerning eye, where they slipped into a hidden world. A few yards beyond, there was a brick path, like a secret passageway from *Alice Through the Looking Glass.* "This is Temptation Path," Frankel said, taking Elena's hand. This part of the estate was more like a maze, a series of hidden glens or meditation nooks, statuary concealed around every corner. A white marble dove, captured in flight, seemed to spring from a bed of sage; farther on, in a shady glade a statue of a young girl reclined in the grass, staring off into the distance, where statues of gladiators stood frozen in combat. Around another turn there was a quiet pergola covered in wisteria, with chairs to sit and think, and then, ahead, or maybe back — she was losing her way by now — was a children's playhouse complete with working fireplace, protected by a platoon of life-size Tin Woodsmen. Off to the left there was a large pen for rare ostriches, who paced and pecked, snow-white and preening. "And here," Frankel said, "is a thicket of bamboo taller than the Great Wall of China." He led them through a passage in the bamboo to the other side, where they skittered across stepping-stones in a pond fed by an overflowing stone bowl.

"There was also," Elena said, "about five hundred feet from the house, hidden from view, the notorious swimming pool." The pool had such éclat that *The New Yorker* even ran a "Talk of the Town" piece about it in 1951, dubbing it "Mr. Frankel's Folly." Frankel himself relished the controversy. "My idea was to build the pool into the charred foundation and basement of the original house, which had burned down fifty years before," he explained. He had the debris of the old house removed, the overgrowth excavated, the sides cemented and waterproofed, but one end was left open and unformed, melding into a glade of canna, mimosa, and tamarisk, with a gushing stream that cascaded over craggy boulders imported from Vermont on the back of a flatbed truck. Set into niches built along the irregularly shaped sides were busts of the Roman emperors, and in the quirkiest stroke, Frankel kept the original fireplace just where it was, imbedded in the side of the pool, complete with logs and andirons. In addition, he pointed out to Elena, the pool had the first "underwater" lights installed in all of East Hampton so guests could swim at night.

But it wasn't the design of the pool that everyone found so provocative, but Frankel's rule that people had to swim nude. The first thing Elena noticed was a large sign in the changing room, NO TOPS, NO BOTTOMS. "A pool is not a Laundromat," Frankel scolded guests who tried to wear swimsuits. "Come on, now, *take off your clothes!*" Noncompliance was met with an icy invitation to leave. Frankel himself was only too happy to set an example, and he darted about in the altogether at every opportunity. An eclectic assortment of people over the years accepted Frankel's invitation to swim naked in his pool, including Marilyn Monroe, Yul Brynner, Jackson Pollock, Ted Dragon, and many of his men and women dancer friends; to be able to announce over cocktails that one swam nude at Brigadoon is a distinction in East Hampton to this day. When Winston Churchill's daughter Sarah first saw the pool, she tore off her clothes, crying, "It would be sacrilege not to swim naked!" and dove in.

However, Frankel's voyeurism was but one of his many pec-
cadilloes. He also loved to shock people with inappropriate behavior. On one occasion he climbed up onto the lower roof of his house
to peek inside the guest bedroom windows, hoping to catch his
houseguests in flagrante delicto. Another time he paraded past his
neighbor's house on Hither Lane and shouted up at the bedroom
windows, "Did you screw your wife last night?" "He also unfailingly referred to the Ladies Village Improvement Society as the
'Ladies Vaginal Insertion Society,' " added Elena.

For many, his behavior went too far. An otherwise suave and gal-
lant companion, Frankel might easily reach out in conversation and
caress the breast of a woman he hardly knew or run his fingers over
her buttocks. When he was rebuked — or his hand slapped away, as
it was countless times (and his face as well) — Frankel would just
smile his dimpled smile and go on about his business. He somehow
couldn't be convinced that his behavior was offensive. "It is the *liking*
of women," Frankel told one reporter who questioned his reputation as a wolf, "it is not lechery." In one famous incident, he gave a
large party at which three generations of women he had bedded from
the same family were his guests, unaware that each one of them had
been a Frankel conquest. "Every girl in East Hampton knew Evan
Frankel's reputation," said Elena with a wry laugh.

It was also rumored that Frankel bedded not only women but
men too. His close friends deny it. "Evan loved the idea that people
were going around saying he was gay," said Joan Cullman, "while he
was secretly screwing all these young girls — and everybody's wife."
Evan seemed to encourage the ambiguity by keeping prominently
displayed in his library a hardcover book with the title *Evan Frankel's
Sex Life*, inside of which all the pages were blank.

Till there was Elena. All the more reason it raised so many eyebrows when the night after the tour of Brigadoon, Evan Frankel
arrived at the crowded opening of a new play at Guild Hall's John

Drew Theatre with twenty-year-old Elena Prohaska on his arm and the self-satisfied look of a cat who just swallowed the canary. "I'm sure it gave everybody a lot to talk about," Elena said. "But I really didn't care. He was fascinating and charming, and not for one moment was he disrespectful of me."

Elena continued to see Frankel intermittently that summer. "He invited me to dinner in the city at his penthouse apartment at One Hundred Riverside Drive. It had views of the skyline and the Hudson River, with art deco glass-brick walls and a wraparound terrace. We had great times. He was immature in a lot of ways and I was mature in some ways, so we sort of balanced things out. Yes, he did have that mischievous side to him. And I had a mischievous side to me. But we weren't mischievous with each other.

"He asked me to travel with him that winter. He wanted me to spend a month or two in Jamaica, where he rented a large estate every year, but I was going back to school at NYU, and anyway, I had a boyfriend. He called me many times from Jamaica that winter, offering to fly me down. He was at the retreat of Rosser Reeves, and it was immense. He said he had five girls staying with him. 'You see,' he said to me, 'it takes five girls to make up for one of you!' "

Nearly an entire year of flirtation passed until "the other man in my life started making ultimatums to me in June of 1968," said Elena. "He was leaving for the Laurentian Hills, where he was going to start a commune with another couple. He wanted me to go, or he was leaving without me. I had a week to make up my mind. One beautiful June day I was sitting in my apartment in New York in a funk, and Evan called me and said, 'Well, sweetie, what are you doing inside on a beautiful day like this? Come hither with me. Spend the weekend at Brigadoon with me, and we'll figure out what to do.' And I realized that he was just what I needed to pull me out of it. He was like a white knight coming to save me."

"It is a *terrible* idea, my sweet, to go to Canada with that man," he told her that weekend. "You know I'm right. It is bound to end in unhappiness. Get rid of him and live here with me. If you lived with me, you would be secure. If you lived with me, when you wanted to go traveling, we could travel together and see the world, not from a knapsack, but in *style*. And you can live in my apartment in the city and continue your education. *That's* what's most important."

"I thought for a moment and said okay," Elena remembered. Evan was so shocked that he was speechless at first. "Then he sort of snorted, 'Oh? Yes? Well, okay!' "

"It started out, for a few minutes," Elena said, "as a sexual relationship. But after that was over, we became good companions for each other. Neither of us was easy. Evan said I was his mother. I'm sure he was my father. We were all these things to each other, but the least of them was sexual. It's still a mystery to me. We had such an unusual relationship. It might have started out as one thing, but it ended up as another. At the root of it, we cared for each other.

"There I was," she said. "I was living in a penthouse apartment in the city. There was an estate in the country, where I had my own room and my own bath. There was a housekeeper and a handyman. I lived a very orderly kind of life. There was a reassuring formality about our days. Every night we went somewhere wonderful for dinner, like Gordon's restaurant in Amagansett, where they greeted him as 'm'lord' and everyone stopped by our table to pay court."

She became known politely as his "ward." Among their friends she was his "no girl" — the only person in a world filled with "yes men" who could say no to m'lord and get away with it. They became a familiar duo at art galleries, where he introduced her to art dealers with a sly wink as his "curator." In winters they went south, usually to Jamaica, and every spring they traveled through Europe. They had dinner with Aldo Gucci in Rome and spent a week at the Villa Medici in Florence. In London they were entertained by Sarah Churchill. At Las Brisas, in Mexico, Elena nearly died of typhoid, and Frankel's friend Jacob Javits, the U.S. senator from New York, who was staying at the same hotel, used his influence to summon a doctor to her hotel suite.

Elena's mother and father were sanguine about the relationship, but not everybody was as generous. "What are you doing with a young girl like that?" Evan's friends demanded of him. "You'll ruin her life. It's not fair. She's wasting all these years," they told him.

Evan would say, "She's wasting *nothing*. I'm giving her one of the greatest educations a young person can get. If it wasn't for me, she'd be off with some drunken boyfriend."

Elena heard it too. "People said, 'You know, he'll never marry you" — as if that was what I wanted." What did Elena want? "What everybody wants, I suppose. To be happy."

"If anybody criticizes you," Frankel told her, "tell them I'm giving you the best years of my life."

3

PERHAPS EVEN MORE unusual than Frankel's penchant for young women or his preoccupation with the human body was his obsession with the earth. Nobody in East Hampton, not even the oldest family or the staunchest preservationist, seemed to care quite as much about the land as Evan Frankel. "His land was his children," Elena said.

"We are in *love* with the land," Frankel would sigh, his eyes misting over. "This place is blessed. These aren't just landscapes, they are living paintings. Some of this land could be a Corot, a Courbet, or a van Gogh. Just as other people collect paintings to hang on the wall, I decided to collect what I call my 'living paintings' — a stretch of grassy dunes, a luxuriant potato field framed by hedgerows, or a weather-beaten barn silhouetted against the sky. I ask you, Who could be so lucky to live in a place such as this?"

Every morning after breakfast, Frankel walked his land the way some men went off to play golf. He set out down sun-dappled Hither Lane at an energetic gait. "Look at this day!" he cried out. "When you look at the fields, when you see the plants reappearing year after year, when you've watched the harvest for twenty-five Octobers — it doesn't seem possible that it's all going to end soon. But all around every field there are more new houses each year, and the land is being nibbled away faster and faster."

Indicating a swath of land between the town and the Maidstone golf course, he said, "I picked up these fifty-four acres back around 1950. I bought most of it from James T. Lee, the grandfather of Jacqueline Kennedy. He was leasing it to a farmer, and I felt that it wouldn't stay in farming very long if I didn't control it. I paid Lee something under two thousand an acre for it. Last week, three men offered me a hundred and fifty thousand an acre for it. They pleaded and begged me to take their money, but I refused. I may sell some soon, and I may not. I don't have to until I feel like it. People call me a land hog, a monopolist, a profiteer, for refusing to sell them land so they can ruin it with their abominations, their cheap tasteless developments, and their ghastly neon lights."

The truth be known, although Frankel was as cutthroat in acquiring land as any real estate speculator, in forty years he had sold off only seventy-five acres, and those only when in dire need of money. For a man who owned so much land, Frankel was unusually cash poor. He held on to his property way beyond good business sense, to prevent it from being developed. At one point in the late 1970s he was so strapped that he was forced to sell off thirty acres of gorgeous farmland on Further Lane. This was the stretch of land abutting Two Mile Hollow (East Hampton's gay beach) that Frankel referred to as his Corot. He found a remarkable buyer who was willing to sign a covenant agreeing to build only one house on the entire thirty-acre property and not to divide the land or sell it off. But at the closing, one of the attorneys remarked, "That property is fine if you don't mind living next to the homosexual beach." The buyer, astonished to learn this, pulled out of the deal on the spot.

Now out many millions of dollars of working capital, Evan reluctantly sold a smaller parcel of the same land to a man who wanted to build a house and didn't give a damn who used the beach. But despite a host of covenants about what the house could look like, the new owner built a "cheesy house," according to Frankel: stark, modern, with a V-shaped wing jutting into the sky. "An eyesore," Frankel moaned when he saw it. "And you can't erase it." Frankel was so distraught, he wanted to punch the man in the nose and had to be dissuaded several times by friends from driving over and ringing the doorbell.

He swore never to allow that to happen again, and not only did he put even more ironclad covenants into all of his land-sale contracts, he began to pay surprise visits to the construction sites to make sure the new houses were going up the way he wanted. He drove a few of the new homebuilders around the bend with his pestering; he even began trespassing on construction sites that had nothing to do with him. Once, he accidentally left his little dog behind in a house under construction, and Frankel received an indignant phone call from the builder the next day when he discovered that the dog, locked in the house all night, had peed all over the floor.

And if Frankel was asked why East Hampton was so important to him, he would reply, astonished that anyone need ask, "The *land* is important. *Menschen are geborgen, land nicht.*" Men are born, land is not. Elena remembered when he showed her around Brigadoon that first day, he whispered it to her reverently, as if he were imparting the secret of life. "This is *all* there is of it," he said, exhaling. "*Menschen are geborgen, land nicht.*"

4

FRANKEL HADN'T BEEN much of a preservationist before he moved to the East End in 1946. His only interest in property had been the "vertical real estate" he owned in Manhattan, the
odd parcels of commercial properties scattered around Midtown,
including half a dozen apartment buildings, a few parking lots, and
the site of the current New York Hilton — all of which he hated.
"Go into the city for a day," Frankel said. "What do you see? Blocks
and blocks of cubicles, narrow streets congested as hell, sirens all
night so you can't sleep, miserable air."

He was born Meshulam Frankel on January 9, 1902, in Laicia, a
Polish-speaking province of Austria, and was brought to America at
the age of three. He was one of ten brothers and sisters raised in a
Lower East Side tenement. His first job was selling chewing gum on
the Staten Island ferry when he was six years old. At thirteen he was
bar mitzvahed in a Lower East Side sweatshop that was converted
into a synagogue on Saturdays. "I was starved for greenery and land,"
he remembered. "I used to sit and wonder what a blade of grass
looked like."

At twenty-one, after studying drafting at Columbia and NYU,
he formed his own company with a master carpenter, Isaac Ross,
to design and install unusual storefronts and office reception areas.
Frankel was a good draftsman and designer but an even better salesman. By the time he was thirty, he had built the first New York
offices of Joseph E. Seagram & Sons and the Fifth Avenue stores
for the Bulova watch company and Doubleday Books. In 1939 he
built the much-photographed fifty-foot marquee for the Distilled
Spirits Industry Exhibit at the World's Fair. Young and prosperous

in wartime, he began to buy up distressed Midtown Manhattan real estate — in particular, apartment buildings and vacant lots.

As he became rich, he shed his Lower East Side background and strove to assimilate into gentile society. He became an Anglophile, dressing in Savile Row tweeds and camel hair overcoats. He rented the terraced penthouse apartment at One Hundred Riverside Drive and had it designed like a movie set. He spent winters in Palm Beach, where he learned to ride horses and play polo. He dined with young beauties at the Copacabana and 21. Winston Churchill's actress daughter, Sarah, became a friend of Frankel's, and they were frequently photographed leaving nightclubs in New York and London, Frankel in black tie. He accompanied her to dinner at Buckingham Palace and was her escort and overnight guest at Windsor Castle. In the 1950s he dabbled in the theater, becoming an angel for the original Broadway productions of *Gentleman Prefer Blondes*, *The Music Man*, and *Brigadoon*, after which he named his East Hampton estate, and he produced the film version of Gian-Carlo Menotti's *The Medium*.

It was World War II that first brought Frankel to the Hamptons, where his company was given a lucrative government contract to build a string of "early warning" radar towers along the South Fork from Westhampton to Montauk. These wooden pyramids housed a small room with a radar device to warn against the Nazi U-boats that lurked off the U.S. coast. In June 1942, through no fault of Frankel's tower design, the system failed to detect a German submarine surfacing 500 yards off Amagansett beach. A band of saboteurs paddled ashore in a rubber boat with cases of explosives with which they intended to blow up buildings crucial to the war effort, including the Pennsylvania Railroad terminal in Newark. The German spies were arrested two weeks later without doing any damage, but the incident went down in history as the only time Nazis ever invaded U.S. shores, and it rankled Frankel's pride to the day he died.

It was while his company was building the radar towers that Frankel first lived full-time in East Hampton, renting a suite of rooms at an old hotel on Main Beach called the Sea Spray Inn. "As I toured around working at my job," Frankel remembered, "I simply fell in love with the land. It had an ineffable quality. I wanted to preserve that quality. This land was more than mere countryside. It was beauty, it was poetry, it was art." By then, Frankel had accumulated a personal fortune of more than $2 million, at the time a considerable sum, and was anxious to change the direction of his life.

When Frankel decided to buy his first piece of property, he went not to a real estate broker but to the barber shop. In his travels he had discovered that the best local news was to be had at the barber's. It was there that he heard about a rubble of a house at 150 Hither Lane, the old McCord mansion. D. W. McCord, who made his money in grain markets, had built the large shingled house as a summer retreat in the early 1900s. One scorching July day in 1920 his daughter, Janet, was sneaking a forbidden cigarette in an upstairs room and tossed the lit butt out the window, where it landed in old dry vines and started a fire. By the time the fire truck was summoned, the entire third floor of the west wing was already ablaze. In any event, the water pressure was so low that only a dribble came out of the hoses; all anybody could do was watch. The younger men from the town and the Summer Colony banded together and raced in and out of the house, rescuing belongings, silverware, even managing to drag the grand piano outside. Within four hours the entire house was burned to the ground, at a loss estimated at $60,000 in 1920 dollars. All that was left were the foundation and the charred fireplace that had been in the living room. McCord was so disheartened, he never rebuilt.

However, a few hundred yards away, still unscathed, stood a charming yet modest wood carriage house, with a hand-crank elevator. Twenty-six years after the fire, the carriage house was overgrown with vines and weeds — "Wuthering Heights when I first saw it," Frankel said. He paid $21,000 for it, a king's ransom in 1946. It was around the carriage house that Frankel decided to build and amend and enlarge what eventually turned into a twelve-room, Sussex-style country estate behind a long cement wall, its diamond-paned leaded windows sparkling in the sun.

Soon after Evan moved in came the stories of what he was doing to the grounds — not only his display of indecent nude statuary but the construction of a swimming pool that sounded alarmingly bacchanalian for the demure Hamptons. On top of that, Frankel had a series of girlfriends barely of legal age, some of them quite beautiful, including, back in 1937, a ravishing Lucille Ball, then an unknown actress who was introduced to Frankel by mutual friends. There are pictures of them together, stiffly posed, Lucille Ball perched on the edge of a chair with Frankel lounging on the arm behind her. When Lucille Ball first went to Hollywood, she sent him a letter that was tantamount to a marriage proposal, but the idea of marriage suffocated Frankel, and he ended the relationship.

He came to a similar end with a young beauty named Peggy Goldsmith. In 1942, when he was forty and she was twenty, he spotted her standing at a bus stop in Long Beach, Long Island. He pulled over in his "mile-long" Packard convertible and offered to give her a lift. That night they went to Radio City Music Hall and later to the Stork Club. She was a stunning young girl, perhaps even more beautiful than Lucille Ball; when Frankel discovered that their twenty-year age difference left her unfazed, he asked her to move in with him.

By all accounts, they had an extraordinary ten years together. However, the question of marriage always hung in the air. "One day," Frankel told Elena, "I found myself engaged to Peggy. I don't know how it happened. I had a friend who was in the diamond business and I had some loose diamonds in my pocket and I showed them to

Peggy." The next thing he knew, Frankel claimed, he saw his forth-coming marriage announced in the newspapers. Of course, Frankel knew exactly what he was doing; he not only showed Peggy loose stones but gave her an engagement ring. Yet the thought of marrying anyone made Frankel so sick that he took to bed for several weeks after the engagement was announced. A month later, in 1952, Peggy moved out.

For the next fifteen years there were dozens of beautiful women in and out of Frankel's life, but not one struck his fancy until the night he met Elena.

Gates of the Grove

BEFORE ADOPTING East Hampton as his hometown, Evan Frankel never really embraced his Jewishness. In fact, most of his life was about WASP assimilation, learning the dress, sports, and manners of the gentile rich. Ironically, though, in East Hampton society, he was not only primarily a Jew but the most prominent Jew of all. "The King of the Jews," as one nasty nickname had him; "Evan Bagel," another.

"Evan knew that people in East Hampton called him names," Elena said, "and it infuriated him." Frankel always recounted the shock he felt when he first came to East Hampton in the 1940s and discovered that anti-Semitic materials were prominently displayed on the wicker furniture in the lobby of the Sea Spray Inn or that up until the 1950s, Gurney's Inn and the Montauk Manor were known not to accept Jewish guests. He was mortified at the unembarrassed way first-generation Polish farmers openly called Jews "Bejid" and blamed the "Jew swimming pools" when they were forced to stop using insecticides that polluted the fragile aquifer.

"This is a town," Frankel said, "where some of the deeds to houses and land still contain a covenant prohibiting the transfer to 'Jews, Negroes, and entertainers.' " Even in the 1980s pop star Billy Joel had to form a corporation to buy his Further Lane house because of such a covenant, and back in 1946, when Frankel bought the McCord estate, it was unheard-of for a Jew to be living in the triumverate of Further, Middle, and Hither Lanes. Owners simply wouldn't sell to Jews. "What is the name of your client?" they would demand of brokers, slamming down the phone at the sound of a Semitic name like Cohen or Frankel.

Frankel had to resort to obfuscation to buy the McCord house. He asked his gentile friend Emerson Thors, who was a partner in Kuhn, Loeb, to buy the house in secret partnership and later transfer ownership of the deed to him. Having to buy the house through this deception chagrined Frankel no end, and with great bitterness did he put the Thors name on a sign at the entrance to the driveway for the first three months he owned the house, to complete the deception. It didn't make the Maidstone Club very happy with Thors either when they found out; he was never extended membership, lest he bring his friend Frankel around.

"It is the Maidstone Club that is at the root of all this, that *perpetuates* this," Frankel insisted to visitors at Brigadoon. He marched his guests upstairs to the master bedroom and pulled aside the window curtains with a flourish. "There!" he said, pointing to the west. "A bastion of bigotry!"

Off in the distance, like a grand dowager high on the dunes of Wiborg Beach, stood the ivy-covered Maidstone Club, its gambreled roofs silhouetted against the ocean sky. The club's twenty-seven holes of manicured, verdant golf links — 180 acres of the most exclusive seaside golf course in the world — spread out like a floating green gown. The large, handsome clubhouse, with its behemoth ballroom on the second floor, straddled a sturdy dune; below, down long staircases, was a sprawling beach club complex, rows of rustic wood cabanas, painted tan and gray, the awnings comfortably faded in the WASP style. There was also a seaside restaurant for lunch, and an Olympic-sized saltwater swimming pool that had its water changed every Sunday night.

It certainly didn't look like a bastion of bigotry. In fact, it looked quite bewitching. But no matter how much Frankel assimilated or dressed like an Englishman or spoke like a WASP, he would never be welcome there. Nor would people of color. Or what they called "single men." "And if they told the truth," Frankel said, "they wouldn't have let the Irish in either if so many of the WASPs didn't jump out of windows during the crash of 1929." Frankel was so rankled by the club, he planted a thick stand of pines to block the view from his bedroom window, and every morning he would dramatically exhort to them, "Grow, trees, grow! I wish you'd grow tall and fast so I wouldn't have to see that place!"

2

IT WAS IRONIC that the club Frankel hated so bitterly also defined many of the wonderful things about the town. More than just a country club, the Maidstone Club was the dominant influence in East Hampton life for over half a century. It determined the entire character of the village, its social graces, even its look. Every significant institution was founded, donated, or controlled by Maidstone Club members, from Guild Hall to the East Hampton Free Library. Maidstoners supported the volunteer fire department, the Ladies Village Improvement Society, and the Garden Club. They put in the sidewalks and the streetlights and helped saved the town in crises. After the devastating 1938 hurricane, during which 524 of the town's famous elm trees were uprooted and destroyed, it was Maidstone members who raised $65,000 to replant them. During World War II they gamely donated their lawn ornaments to be melted down for scrap iron. They also kept forever safe from development the magnificent rolling grounds on which they — and only they — could play golf, and even Evan Frankel begrudgingly had to be grateful for that.

The Maidstone Club was founded in 1891 in the living room of Dr. Everitt Herrick, the man Evan Frankel referred to as the "chief anti-Semite." Herrick wasn't so much an anti-Semite as he was a tyrant. His authority over the early Summer Colony was practically absolute. He was not only the Summer Colony's social arbiter, he was also the physician to most of them. Herrick was also a pompous ass who never doubted the correctness of his own opinion. Perhaps some of his authority came from his being a tree trunk of a fellow, six feet three inches tall, with a bald pate from which sprang bushy muttonchops, conjoining an untamed mustache worthy of Buffalo Bill. Herrick was a flinty New Englander, born in New London, New Hampshire. He formed the Maidstone Club initially as a place to play tennis and golf with a tight-knit group of twelve other summer visitors, who appropriated the name "Old East Hampton" — much to the consternation of the real Old East Hampton, locals who had lived there for generations.

Dr. Herrick's Old East Hampton was composed of wealthy and refined families of bankers, industrialists, and prominent clergy who had been lured to East Hampton by the talk in chic publications of playing tennis in dappled orchards. They were the flower of Northeastern society in their age, what one turn-of-the-century writer called "a society based on intellectual tastes rather than a feverish craving for display and excitement."

Another journalist in the *New York Herald* wrote that East Hampton "excluded the vulgar parvenus that so often make life wretched at the conventional summer resort [because] six miles to the nearest railroad at Bridgehampton keeps off the rabble." When Dr. Herrick and the first hundred or so summer visitors arrived in East Hampton, that extra six miles from Bridgehampton was managed by a stagecoach ride over a long dusty road, so dusty that each wagon fought to be first loaded and away from the train station so as not to eat the dust of the wagon ahead. During dry spells the dust got so thick that the drivers blew bugles like foghorns to avoid collisions. Once the visitors arrived in the village, they found a sleepy town completely unprepared for guests. Main Street was a wide green lawn, like a meadow, with grazing cattle and geese. It was lined with plain farmhouses and at the far end, a working windmill. The village was so bucolic that the town's only justice of the peace, Henry B. Tuthill, had been blind since childhood.

Since there were no hotels, Herrick and his crowd had to convince the wary locals to rent them rooms. At first suspicious of the tourists, the local families soon realized that summer visitors were a dependable source of income — and the Boardinghouse Era was born. These boardinghouses were elegant and formally run, not fleabags. Their guests were often celebrated, people like John A. Roebling and his family, who spent a summer on Main Street while he designed and built the Brooklyn Bridge. Rooms went for seven dollars a week, payable sixty days in advance by post, and hearty Yankee-style breakfasts were served at dawn, with a main meal, or "supper," served at noon.

Within a few years the boarders began to rent entire houses for the summer for about $200, and two of the local stagecoach drivers, B. M. Osborne and C. E. C. Homans, reinvented themselves as real estate men, waiting at the Bridgehampton train station in their horse and carriages for prospective clients to disembark. The train was finally extended to East Hampton and Montauk in 1895, and visitors began to build their houses. Sommarvaria, the very first summer "cottage" in East Hampton, was built in 1873 by Philadelphian Charles P. B. Jeffreys, a civil engineer who helped plan the Pennsylvania Railroad and was also president of Old East Hampton.

Dr. Herrick built a house too. He married, for the first time at age fifty-one, Harriet Ford, the daughter of John R. Ford, a prominent

East Hampton summer visitor; together they built Pudding Hill, the dark-shingle house that still stands at the entrance to town, on the site of the farmhouse where Mrs. John Osborne rolled a "pudding" down a dirt hill rather than turn it over to marauding British soldiers.

Herrick walked about town every day in his spats and cutaway with a wheezing little Pug, Bessie, harnessed to a tether, and he passed judgment on just about everything that he laid eyes on. His authority was as complete as it was arbitrary. He banned women wearing white gloves as being "too citified" and disapproved of "afternoon tea" as a barbaric interruption of the day. At 6 P.M., an hour he regarded as the end of the day's pursuit of pleasure, he personally stopped summer visitors from playing tennis by dropping the nets. He further insisted that parched tennis players abstain from drinking water for ten minutes after playing, and then only from a jug of "oatmeal" water he had concocted himself and hung from the branch of a tree next to the grass court.

Perhaps Herrick's most trying ordinance was that no matter how sweltering the weather, not a single member of Old East Hampton was allowed to swim in the ocean until he deemed the water warm enough. Toward the end of May every year, in what became a breathless ritual, Herrick would go down to the beach, covered from neck to ankle in a dark flannel bathing suit with white braid, carrying a huge wooden thermometer. Half the town would follow him, standing expectantly on the shore as Herrick waded into the water and dipped in the thermometer, soon raising it into the air to read. When the temperature finally met his approval, a cheer went up from the crowd, and Old East Hampton plunged into the surf — but only after Herrick deemed every bathing suit appropriate.

As it turned out, Dr. Herrick's most unpopular mandate was

that there be no golf on Sunday, the day of the Lord. Since Herrick leased some of the land under the golf course, there was little arguing with him. Eventually, in 1906, the disgruntled golf-loving membership summoned the courage to challenge him and took up a petition, signed even by members of the clergy. In the face of insurrection, Herrick relented and allowed Sunday golf — but not until after 12:30, when church was finished.

He also wouldn't have a telephone at the club until 1904, and only then just to be able to call the fire department (the building had twice burned down). The club's hallmark was always stoicism and strength in the face of adversity; when the original club burned to the ground on Friday, August 9, 1901, the members built a temporary shed, eighty feet long, and Dr. Herrick ordered tea served for 200 members while the ruins were still smoldering.

Dr. Herrick died at the age of eighty-four on April 11, 1914, with his hands still on the controls of the Maidstone Club, and it took years to pry them off. He left $7,500 to the club under the conditions that it could never serve liquor, that it must maintain its "present character," and that its tennis matches must be decided three sets out of five, not two out of three. Otherwise, the club had to donate the money to the library. Alas, on June 11, 1934, when the club applied for its first liquor license, one of the members gladly ponied up the $7,500 for the library.

As the years passed, the club became the center of social life in East Hampton. Membership was considered such a dire necessity that applicants who were rejected often moved. Traditionally, the club's membership consists not of names from social columns but of those more familiar to readers of the financial pages, men like Julian S. Myrick, "Mr. Life Insurance," who started Mutual of New York; John Hamlin, president of Douglas Elliman, the real estate company; Juan Terry Trippe, who founded Pan American Airlines; William Clay Ford of the motor company family; John A. Dix, president of the Union Pacific Railroad; and John Deere Velie, the tractor trailer manufacturer. The revered sportswriter Grantland Rice was a member too, and his locker and original nameplate are kept as a shrine in the clubhouse, last offered to Vice President Dan Quayle when he came to play golf.

Despite the club's distinguished membership list and its contributions to the community, its ultimate reputation has always been about its restricted membership policy. The membership committee made no secret or apology about keeping the club exclusive. "I don't understand why it matters to people," snapped one Maidstone matron. "Why would people want to go where they're not wanted, anyway?" It wasn't just Jews who weren't wanted but also people of color, and even entertainers. Although one of its original founders, John Drew, was the most popular matinee idol of his day, the only show business figures who belonged to the club became members through family or marriage, like actor Cliff Robertson, who married Maidstone member Dina Merrill (the daughter of Marjorie Merriweather Post), the actress and Post cereal heiress, or Sonja Henie, who became a Maidstone member when she married polo-playing Winthrop Gardiner. When singer Diana Ross married Maidstone member Arne Naess Jr., the Norwegian shipping magnate, in 1985, the president of the club was asked by a reporter if Diana Ross was going to become the first black member. "I have absolutely no idea who Diana Ross is," the president, an investment banker, snapped. Arne Naess subsequently resigned from the club.

The Maidstone Club is also famously touchy about who plays on its premises. Legend has it that in the 1960s, when through some unavoidable circumstance Senator Jacob Javits played on the golf course, the grass turned brown wherever he stepped. Once, when a South American housekeeper swimming off the public beach was swept down the shore by the strong currents and managed to drag herself out of the ocean and collapse on Maidstone sands, the members promptly complained to the management. The Bouviers knew to bring servants for a swim in the club's pool only on Sunday nights, just before the pool was going to be drained; even years later, in the early 1980s, a teenage member of the Bridgehampton Racquet and Surf Club intramural swim team was called a "dirty Jew" when she arrived for an ill-conceived swim meet. (Founded in 1961, the Bridgehampton Racquet and Surf Club's membership requirements amounted to a driver's license and a MasterCard.)

Maidstone members are relieved that the Jews aren't knocking on their club's door anymore, wanting to play on their links. Jews now have their own course, the swank Atlantic Golf Club in Bridgehampton, which Maidstoners refer to as the "Hebrew National." The Atlantic opened on May 1, 1992, on $6 million worth of farmland sold to the founders through the Allan Schneider Agency. It was the first golf club built on the South Fork since 1963, and the only one that encourages a Jewish membership. Its founding members include financier Henry Kravis, Seagram's Edgar Bronfman Jr., Blackstone Group partner Stephen Schwarzman, and Loews Hotels CEO Jonathan Tisch, who each paid a $125,000 initiation fee (which has now soared to $250,000). So democratic is the Atlantic that Lawrence Taylor, the football player, was asked to apply (but did not).

The first Jew in the Maidstone Club was Theodore Kheel, a labor lawyer, in 1977. Recently, because of newly passed anti-discrimination laws, the Maidstone has admitted three (nonobservant) Jewish members, whose greatest ambition in life is to be mistaken for WASPs. Not surprisingly, the newest generation of real blue-blooded WASP Hamptonites do not care for the club's rigid formality, nor do they need its tennis courts — they all have their own. They also don't want to dine at the club with the same people every Saturday night; they want to be seen at a celebrity hot spot like Nick & Toni's. Still, a few Maidstone members cling to the notion that although the Hamptons may be changing all around them, within the walls of their hallowed club, everything will remain safe.

Evan Frankel never lived long enough to see the club accept its half a dozen or so Jewish members. In his lifetime, he took the Maidstone Club as a personal affront. And he wasn't alone. He didn't have a way to bring it down, but he would find a way to checkmate it. He didn't know exactly what that way would be, until one day, serendipitously, it presented itself to him.

3

FOR ALL of Evan Frankel's bluster about anti-Semitism, he rarely went to synagogue in the Hamptons. If he went at all, he preferred the elegance of Temple Emanu-El on Fifth Avenue in New York City. All the years he lived in the Hamptons, the only indication he saw that Jewish life existed was an untidy Jewish cemetery on Route 114, hardly even noticeable when driving by, and a damp, Orthodox schul called Adas Israel, in the unlikely Jewish outpost of Sag Harbor, the historic whaling village.

Adas Israel was the oldest Jewish temple on Long Island. It had hardwood benches with room enough for fifty men, and a small, bowed balcony where, in the Orthodox tradition, the women were segregated behind a lacy curtain. Also for women, much to Frankel's astonishment, was a *mikvah* in the basement, an Orthodox ritual bath the size of a hot tub where women could come for a monthly hygienic blessing. The synagogue's Torah was one of Adas Israel's greatest distinctions, in that it was a gift from Theodore Roosevelt. In 1898 Roosevelt and 1,200 of his Rough Riders were briefly quarantined for malaria in Montauk after the Spanish-American War;

when the troops departed, Roosevelt left behind the Torah, used by his handful of Jewish soldiers, as a gift to the schul.

The Jews first came to Sag Harbor in the 1880s, when it was a fading honky-tonk town, formerly the sixth-busiest shipping port in the world, whose economy was totally dependent on whale oil. The last whaling ship had set sail in 1871; ten years later Sag Harbor was on the brink of financial insolvency. An unlikely hero by the name of Joseph Fahys came to the rescue. He was a tall, barrel-chested man who owned one of the largest watch-case manufacturing plants in the world in Carlstadt, New Jersey. After marrying a young woman from Sag Harbor, Fahys moved his operation to a Dickensian-looking, four-story redbrick factory on Division Street. The plant would employ 400 watch-case makers, which would be a huge percentage of Sag Harbor's workforce. The townsfolk rejoiced, but instead of needing to hire local people, Fahys's business depended almost entirely on watch-case engravers from Eastern Europe, where engraving had been turned into an art.

Fahys made monthly trips from Sag Harbor to Ellis Island, where he solicited immigrants just off the boat looking for a steady job and a place to settle other than the confines of the Lower East Side of New York. Almost every single one of these immigrants was Jewish, and within a few years, Fahys was responsible for bringing more than 100 Hungarian and Polish Jewish families to Sag Harbor, almost 15 percent of the population.

Although through the years there had been an odd Jew in the East End, this was the first time they had arrived in force. Simon Bonan, a jeweler who appraised Captain Kidd's stolen jewelry, was a Jew, as was Aaron Isaacs, an Ashkenazic Jew and merchant who owned property in East Hampton, Montauk, and Sag Harbor. Isaacs married a Christian woman descended from one of the original settlers, Mary Hedges, and embraced her religion. One of their eleven daughters, Sarah, became the mother of John Howard Payne, who composed the song "Home Sweet Home" about his Jewish grandfather's house. He's the only person of Jewish birth buried in the town cemetery, where his small tombstone reads, "an Israelite in whom there was no guile."

With Fahys's workforce, a whole Jewish subculture began to flourish in Sag Harbor, including peddlers, *mohels*, and even a *shochet*, Schmere Heller, whose profession was to slaughter fowl and beef in the kosher manner. At one point there were so many Jewish peddlers in the Hamptons that Heller turned his home into a kosher boardinghouse. Many of the peddlers stayed to open shops along Sag Harbor's Main Street; first a clothing store, then a confectionery, a crockery shop, a fruit seller, a shoemaker, and seamstress shop opened. By the turn of the century, the *Brooklyn Daily Eagle* noted that "in business, the Jews have pushed rapidly to the fore in Sag Harbor. They control the clothing and fruit trade, and upon the main business thoroughfares 15 large stores testify to their industry. This does not include the number of wagon and pack peddlers who work the surrounding country, making the village their headquarters."

From the start, a cultural rift developed between the aristocratic Hungarian Jews and the bumpkin Polish and Russian Jews from the provinces. The Hungarians so despised Eastern Europeans that they called them "orientals." In 1890, when the Russian and Polish Jews bought for $50 a patch of land for a cemetery on what is now Route 114 between Sag Harbor and East Hampton, the Hungarian Jews immediately bought the adjoining property and consecrated their own duplicate cemetery with their own gate — separated from the Eastern European Jews by a two-foot-tall rusted iron "spite" fence. Eventually, in 1898, the Eastern European Jews scraped together $2,500 to build a synagogue on the corner of Elizabeth and Atlantic Avenues, a self-consciously churchlike structure with Gothic stained-glass windows that was later named Adas Israel; years later the Hungarians Jews joined them there to worship.

But the Jews never flourished as a tribe in Sag Harbor. In 1925 a fire destroyed most of the Fahys watch-case factory, and the Jews stopped coming. The Bulova watch company later purchased the plant and operated it for a few years before closing it for good after World War II. In time the parishioners at Adas Israel became so elderly that they had to be carried up the steps of the synagogue in chairs.

When Evan Frankel moved to the Hamptons, Adas Israel was so poor that it had to "rent" a rabbi from a congregation in Riverhead to drive to Sag Harbor on Wednesday nights, when he would preside over "pretend" Sabbath services. The membership had dwindled to only thirty-five members, although, as Irving Markowitz, an Adas Israel member and CPA who moved to East Hampton in 1946, remembered, "There were a lot of Jews hiding under rocks."

Agreed his business partner, Bernard Zeldin, "Clearly, Adas Israel wasn't growing as a synagogue. If a synagogue had a chance to make it, it would be in East Hampton," where it could attract the newly arriving Jewish weekend homeowners, or "summer Jews," as they were called.

In 1951 Zeldin, Markowitz, and five other families, determined to build their own synagogue in East Hampton, broke away from the Adas Israel congregation and started holding Reformed services wherever they could find a place each week — in rented or borrowed halls, in their own living rooms. For seven years they made do, all the while fund-raising to build their own synagogue. At one point they approached Alfonso Ossorio and Ted Dragon about having a benefit for them at The Creeks. Dragon personally called Evan Frankel to suggest that it would be more appropriate for him to hold the benefit at Brigadoon. "Are you out of your mind?" Frankel snapped at Dragon. "Why would I want those peasants to rip up my estate?"

However, Frankel occasionally worshipped with "those peasants" because they began to hold their High Holidays services just a mile from his house, in the Parish Hall of the East Hampton Presbyterian Church on Main Street. In a gesture worthy of a Norman Rockwell painting, the Parish Hall was loaned to the Reformed Jewish congregation by the sympathetic church elders. In return for their generosity, Zeldin held the Yom Kippur appeal on behalf of the Presbyterians and presented the congregation with a check for $1,300 toward the purchase of a new organ.

In 1959 ten members of the wandering sect borrowed $15,000 to purchase two acres of a scrub oak forest north of Montauk Highway in East Hampton, on which they hoped to build a synagogue. The ten families cosigned a loan from Osborne Trust, each promising to pay off $150 a year for ten years. "We immediately put up a sign at the side of the road," said Zeldin, "lit up with spotlights at night, that said, 'On This Site Will Be Built the Jewish Center of the Hamptons.'"

Zeldin was shocked at the negative reaction from summer Jews. It seemed that they left their Judaism in the city on Friday afternoons. "What the hell are you trying to do?" one of the weekend crowd demanded of Zeldin. "We come out here to avoid all that crap. This is a vacation spot, not a religious retreat."

But Zeldin and Markowitz found unexpected support from Jacob Merrill Kaplan, who called them one day with a $10,000 contribution to their building fund along with a challenge to Evan Frankel to match it. Jake Kaplan, then sixty-seven, shunned publicity but got plenty of it. He was the only Jew in town richer, and in some ways more controversial, than Evan Frankel. The president of the Welch's Grape Juice Company, among other businesses, he was a tiny old man with a warm, wrinkled face and a white halo of hair. In 1956 he stunned the business world by selling Welch's to a grape-growers cooperative in upstate New York; in the rabidly anticommunist fifties, this was perceived as a very suspicious thing to do. He also controlled half the export of blackstrap molasses in

Cuba and, it turned out, was a major backer of Fidel Castro's munitions factories. It caused no less than a national scandal when in 1964 a congressional investigative panel claimed that the CIA was using Kaplan's J. M. Kaplan Fund as a pipeline for $1.25 million in funding for a Costa Rican CIA training center.

The Kaplan Fund continued to contribute to such liberal causes as Planned Parenthood and the National Association for the Advancement of Colored People — charities unfamiliar to most folks in East Hampton, where Kaplan and his family summered on a huge family compound unfashionably north of the highway on Route 114. Kaplan kept mainly to himself over the years, quietly becoming one of East Hampton's greatest private benefactors. He was moved by an article in the local newspaper about the wandering Jewish congregation, and he suggested that perhaps Evan Frankel would match his pledge of $10,000.

Frankel was incensed to learn that Kaplan was daring him into coughing up $10,000 and was in a pompous mood when Markowitz and Zeldin arrived at Brigadoon with a drawing of a one-story brick synagogue, modest and unassuming. Frankel examined the plans for a minute before dismissing them with a shake of his head. "It's not *balabatish* enough," he said. "If this is going to be the only temple in all of East Hampton, then it must be important."

Markowitz and Zeldin left Brigadoon disappointed, certain they would never hear from Frankel again, but first thing the next morning he was on the phone. "Meet me at the Borden house on Woods Lane," he said, "Do you know where that is?" The two men knew well where the Borden house was. Woods Lane, with its arbor of giant oaks and gracious homes, was the curtain-raiser to the whole town of East Hampton. The last house on the right was the Herricks' famed Pudding Hill. The house at which Frankel had asked Markowitz and Zeldin to meet him, just down the lane, was known throughout town as the "house that mooed" — the

1899 estate of Gail Borden, the grandson of the man who invented condensed milk. The Borden family and descendents had lived in the beautiful house with its expansive entrance foyer for fifty years, Maidstone Club members in every generation.

Frankel purchased the twenty-two-room, four-acre property for $21,000 from Gilbert Smith, a local businessman who owned a fish-processing plant in Amagansett. Frankel had heard for years that Borden was an anti-Semite, and upon taking title, sure enough, he found stacks of anti-Semitic materials stored in the upstairs closets. Frankel had hoped to resell the property at a large profit, but something happened the night before that changed his mind, he told the two accountants when they met him on the lawn of the old estate.

"I went to sleep last night thinking about the services that I went to as a young boy," Frankel told them, unlocking the front door and leading them inside. "They were held in a sweatshop — all we could afford to rent. My bar mitzvah was held in that sweatshop, at seven in the morning on a Saturday before the weekend workers came in. I can still remember the stench of it." He fell into an uneasy sleep and in a dream his late, dear, departed sister, Annie, came to him. " 'Evan,' she said to me, 'I will not rest until there's a synagogue in East Hampton.' " Evan stopped and looked at them with a pleased look on his face. "So, I will lease this house to you for a dollar a year. How's that? What will the Maidstone Club think of that, huh! A synagogue at the entrance to town!"

"It's a generous offer," Markowitz said, "but probably an imprudent idea. Jews running around in yarmulkes and prayer shawls right on the highway as you come into town? Who needs to look for trouble, Evan?"

"What is more," Zeldin added, "how can fifteen families pay the upkeep of this big house and grounds? Where would we get the money?"

"I'll tell you what. You go tell Jake Kaplan with his ten thousand dollars that I'm leasing you this building for a dollar a year and that if he's such a big shot, he should give you an endowment that would cover the yearly maintenance cost."

When Kaplan heard this challenge, he wasn't impressed. "Lease it to you for a dollar?" he demanded. "If he's such a big shot, why doesn't he *give* it you? Then I'll endow its upkeep." Within a few days the deal was done. Frankel signed over the deed to the house, and Kaplan established a six-figure endowment to support the synagogue. Since then the synagogue has never held a mortgage or been in debt. Shortly before the opening ceremonies of the newly named East Hampton Jewish Center, Frankel was outraged to learn that Jacob Kaplan wanted a plaque in the lobby attesting to his generosity. "What a vainglorious man!" Frankel said, insisting that if Kaplan got a plaque, his own would hang right next to it.

Beaches of Mammon

BY THE 1970s Evan Frankel was a celebrity in East Hampton, a familiar presence in photographs in the local papers or darting up and down the village streets in his Jeep, waving hellos with the back of his hand like a royal figure. Journalists considered him an authority on everything from East Hampton history to politics in Israel, and he gave numerous interviews to newspapers and magazines, portraying himself as the "the fair-haired boy" whose outspoken voice on the town planning board had made him the "savior of East Hampton," a credit that he knew would rankle many. Yet the septuagenarian land baron seemed to relish the controversy, and only half-jokingly told a reporter from the *New York Times* that "I am the only man alive who not only wears a crown of laurel but grows it himself." In the great tradition of the Roman emperors, he had not one but two busts of himself commissioned, one for his house and one for his pool.

Frankel consolidated his status by becoming a public companion and "walker" to none other than Jeannette Rattray of the *East Hampton Star*, in whose honor he raised a considerable sum of money for an addition to the local library named after her. "When Jeannette's husband died," Elena remembered, "she became Evan's very good buddy. She used to come over quite frequently for dinner. Sometimes I was not asked to join them. They would be a 'date,' the two of them, and they were very regal. They'd both get dressed to the nines and go out to Guild Hall or to dinner at Spring Close House or Gordon's, and they became quite the item, the nearest thing that East Hampton ever had to lord and lady."

At the same time, he was also becoming a curmudgeon. Years before, when he was at the top of his game, his pointed comments could be bracing or witty; now they were downright rude. Even Robert D. L. Gardiner complained that Frankel was "unnecessarily mean." "God, I didn't recognize you," Frankel told a neighbor he met walking down the street. "You've gotten so fat!" The woman lost twenty pounds after the encounter, but she stopped talking to Frankel.

Yet much of his pompous behavior and braggadocio hid an increasingly vulnerable man, one gripped with a helplessness about impending old age. "I am not one to believe my days get sweeter as I get older," he said. "I shall *not* go quietly into that good night." He clung to Elena as if she were youth itself. He wanted her with him always, and yet he did not make himself easy company. In 1970, much to Frankel's dismay, Elena went off to graduate school for two years at the University of Virginia in Charlottesville. "You'll probably take up with the first guy you meet at school," Frankel worried, and Elena said that was nonsense. But it wasn't nonsense. She did have an affair at graduate school, possibly with the first guy she met, she admitted, suddenly out from under Frankel's hawklike eye. "I made it my policy not to tell Evan about my affairs," Elena said, "and he put me on a pedestal." To Elena's mind, she and Frankel had a discreet agreement: "We went out with other people but still came home to each other." Whether Frankel understood this agreement remains in some dispute, but she pointed to an article in Long Island *Newsday* headlined THE OUTRAGES OF M'LORD, in which Frankel is quoted as saying, "I have a lovely girl, but I'll make every girl feel that she's the most desired creature on earth."

When she returned from graduate school, in an effort to keep her around, Frankel financed an art gallery for her on Newtown Lane in East Hampton, the Upstairs Gallery. The smart-looking, sunny gallery, with its many windows, was located on the second floor of Oddfellows Hall, a historical village meetinghouse that Frankel had bought years before and had turned into retail property. Larry Rivers taped the gallery's opening party, to which Frankel escorted Jeannette Rattray. Given that Elena had access to the works of John Little, James Brooks, and pieces from Frankel's own collection (as well as being the paramour of one of the town's richest men), the Upstairs Gallery had instant cachet and success. Elena worked hard at it for a few summers, changing the shows every three weeks through the season and building a trade, but she was drawn back to Manhattan, as always, in the winter.

In early 1972 Frankel moved to a rented villa in Freeport, the Grand Bahamas, and insisted that Elena come down and spend time with him and his friends. Elena demurred, saying that she was feeling depressed and was considering going into therapy. "Well, come down here," Frankel said, "you'll have your own room, you can walk the beaches and think, and my new doctor, Ray, will be here. You can talk to him about finding a good therapist." Elena flew down sometime in February and met Frankel's new young doctor. He had just returned from scuba diving and was wearing a bathing suit. The handsome doctor was married, but his wife was back in New York. "That trip to Freeport," said Elena, "was the beginning of an intense, four-year relationship with Evan's doctor, without Evan's knowing, because he didn't need to know."

2

"I THINK EVAN was bitter because he was disillusioned," Elena said. "I think it made him unhappy that he couldn't save the whole place and that he couldn't save himself. It made him angry that he couldn't make people think the way he did. He began to believe that he was responsible for the fate of the town, and he was scared."

There was certainly reason to be scared. By the mid-seventies East Hampton was experiencing the highest growth rate on Long Island. More than a third of the developable 43,000 acres (an estimated $100 million worth) had already fallen into the hands of speculators and builders, while men like Allan Schneider were expanding their factories of destruction — multiple real estate offices to help chop up the land and sell it away. The woeful zoning plan that East Hampton had adopted in the late sixties allowed for a year-round population cap of 64,000 people — nearly 40,000 more residents than were already there. On a summer weekend the number might easily swell to 100,000. The thought was unimaginable to Frankel. With the town of Southampton's growth plan capping its year-round population at 127,000, sometime in the new millennium it was possible that 300,000 people might try to squeeze onto the South Fork at any given time.

To see what lax planning had wrought, one needed to look no further than right next door, in Amagansett's Beach Hampton. Once a primeval landscape of untouched dunes and cranberry bogs, Beach Hampton had been divided into half-acre lots of tacky summer houses in which shares were allowed. The adjoining beach became so crowded with singles standing around, trying to pick up one another, it was nicknamed "Asparagus Beach." In 1972, much to Frankel's relief, East Hampton passed a "grouper" law prohibiting four or more adults from sharing a rental house.

In his frustration, Frankel became a Bible-thumping evangelist. His battle cry was "upzoning." He stunned the community in the early seventies by voluntarily upzoning the most expensive parcels of his own land south of the highway. He donated tracts to the Nature

Conservancy as well. Through the pure Herculean strength of personality and persuasion, he managed to get all his neighbors along Further Lane, from East Hampton to Amagansett, to pledge not to build south of the second line of dunes for the next fifty years. He helped crusade to ban convenience stores, motels, and fast-food franchises. He was crucial in drafting a master plan for the village outlawing buildings taller than two stories. He made impassioned public speeches against a Gristede's food store on Newtown Lane, even though the extra traffic would benefit his own properties across the street. But he lost his quest to ban a huge parking lot at Two Mile Hollow Beach, which he predicted would become a "shimmering mass of molten cars" (which it did).

His greatest tool was his bully pulpit on the town planning board. The board was created in 1952 by the town fathers, but Frankel considered the group too pro–real estate and development. The board was composed of five members — two town trustees and three local citizens — whom Frankel lectured and berated without mercy for years. "What do we have here on this board?" he would demand of them. "People who are concerned with their owwwwwwwn little bailiwick?" He pointed to a local mortician who sat on the board, saying, "You're pro-development because you want more people to move here, because the more people who move here, the more people will die and the more business you'll get." He turned to the owner of a local shoe store. "Here we have a shoe salesman; more feet mean more shoes." Charles J. Osborne, a real estate broker and Maidstone member, from an old esteemed family, was another of Frankel's favorite targets. But no one infuriated Frankel more than Clayton Morey, a local architect. Frankel didn't think Morey, another Maidstone member, "knew a fig" about architecture. It galled Frankel that Morey, who didn't even move to East Hampton until 1964, had more sway over how the town looked than any other person. Over the years Morey was chairman of the village planning board, chairman of the town planning board, chairman of the design review board, and a member of the town housing authority. His every utterance drove Frankel mad with frustration, and he took to calling the powerful official "Mr. Moron" in public.

This kind of discourse and name-calling soon became tiresome, no matter how righteous Frankel's position was, and the elderly man faced several moments of public humiliation at town meetings. One night he was railing against a proposal to build a 7-Eleven in Amagansett and threatened, "If that thing happens, I move out of here!" The audience spontaneously broke into applause of approval. "Evan almost had a heart attack at that meeting," Elena remembered. "He was really sick after that." On another occasion, Frankel was lecturing a crowded town meeting about upzoning when a dog wandered into the building, moseyed up to where Frankel was standing at a podium and barked loudly at him. It caused peals of laughter from the audience.

One day it came to the attention of the village trustees that a New York State law forbade town trustees, like real estate broker Charles J. Osborne or George B. Hand, from sitting on the town planning board. But instead of Osborne and Hand simply resigning, very quietly one Friday night in autumn, the board was dissolved and then reformed — without Evan Frankel on it.

Frankel was in a rage when he discovered what had happened. "Of course they got rid of me, those bastards!" he ranted in his living room the day after the news appeared in the *East Hampton Star*. "I was the voice of reason! But they have made a very grave mistake, very grave, because they have made me a martyr."

When the members of the town planning board were asked by a reporter if there was some specific reason why Frankel wasn't reappointed, not one of them could explain it. They said to ask the town trustees, who said to ask the mayor, Ronald P. Rioux, who could only shrug and say, "I can't answer that question." Maybe Mrs.

Charles Osborne herself answered it when the following week she wrote a letter to the *East Hampton Star* quoting Chekhov: "The most intolerable people are provincial celebrities."

3

"BY 1975," Elena said, "I was in full Freudian analysis, seeing a psychiatrist four times a week, paying for it myself. I was trying to figure it all out." In retrospect, Elena was hard-pressed to explain why she would do anything as capricious as having a torrid affair with Frankel's own physician, except that it was an overpowering physical infatuation and that she was the pursued, not the pursuer.

"It wasn't fair," Joan Cullman, Frankel's longtime friend said. "Even the doormen in Evan's building knew she was having an affair with the doctor." Cullman sat Elena down and had a talk with her. " 'Look,' I said to her, 'We've all had affairs, but there is such a thing as discretion. Don't have an affair in the man's own apartment.' But Elena just didn't get it."

Elena couldn't bring herself to end the relationship with Frankel either. "Evan and I had exhausted our repertoire," Elena said, "yet he wanted me to be there all the time, and when I was there, we argued. He was restless and wanted me to travel with him or come out to East Hampton, and I just couldn't. Not only was I in therapy but I was teaching art at a private school, the Towne School, twenty-two classes a week, and I was also in training as a docent at the Guggenheim.

"The winter of 1975 he wanted me to drop everything and go to Saint Moritz with him. It was very important to him, his friends were going, the Bigars and the Cullmans, and so I finally said I would join them. It was a long, tiresome journey, and as soon as we got there, Evan didn't like the place. It was too snooty, and the altitude didn't agree with him or me. Since we couldn't ski, there was nothing to do except bundle up and walk through the streets in a blowing snowstorm. One day we got back to the hotel and Evan discovered that one side of his face was paralyzed, as if he had had a stroke." The paralysis was eventually diagnosed as Bell's palsy, a virus of the muscle that often disappears by itself, but at the time "he was scared of having a stroke," Elena said, "and anxious to get back to East Hampton right away."

Later that winter, Frankel went to Manhattan on business without alerting Elena and arrived at his apartment to discover her having a drink with his physician. Frankel was stunned to see his doctor in his apartment with Elena, but he behaved like a gentleman. "Is this anything I should be jealous about?" he asked them.

Elena and the doctor both said no, and Frankel, wanting it to be true, believed them.

Elena's deception continued for a few more months, until a bizarre denouement. Frankel was godfather to one of his sister's children, Seymour, who had been born deaf and dumb. Frankel had a special relationship with his nephew and helped support and send him through school. Seymour had his own key to Frankel's penthouse, and one night he went to his uncle's apartment unannounced to pick up some books Frankel had left for him. To his great distress, he stumbled in on Elena and the doctor in a compromising situation.

Knowing how much his uncle cared for Elena, Seymour burst into tears and ran from the apartment in anger. Unable to call his uncle on the telephone to tell him what he had seen, loyal Seymour got on the last train for East Hampton that night. He arrived in the small hours of the morning and took a taxi to Brigadoon, where he woke his uncle and tearfully wrote down for him exactly what he had seen.

Frankel was devastated. "He was crushed," Elena admitted. "Really crushed. It was awful. He was very hurt, very quiet. Of course, he fired the doctor. We were very adult about the way we handled it from there. I continued to live in his apartment and go out to his house for weekends, but it was decidedly different." One gloomy weekend when Elena was at Brigadoon with Frankel, the doctor appeared at the estate uninvited, and a boisterous screaming match ensued between Elena's two suitors. Frankel's friend Frank Farrell was also present and escorted the doctor to his car, with Elena sobbing in her room.

Coincidentally, in October 1976, Frankel's New York apartment building was going cooperative; instead of buying the apartment and giving it to Elena, he declined the offer and moved out, forcing Elena to find her own place. He was gentle about it and even helped Elena buy furniture. Now completely on her own, Elena broke up with the doctor. "We decided we had hurt enough people," she said.

Evan's friends never forgave her, and they never forgave Frankel for loving her the best. Elena held a place in Frankel's heart that none of his other adoring friends could reach. They remained connected. When she decided to get married to a young investment banker, Evan gallantly paid for the wedding reception at 21. When the marriage didn't work out, Evan was there to support her. In 1982 she came to Evan and told him that she was going to marry Burt Glinn, a respected photographer and partner in Magnum, the international photo agency. Elena wanted Frankel to meet Glinn and give the wedding his blessing. Evan prepared for the meeting for days. It was late fall and he had his raccoon coat taken out of storage and wore his best Squire of East Hampton half-belted tweed sport jacket and hunting cap. He met Glinn and Elena in his study for a drink, and then the two men left Elena behind to have a man-to-man talk during one of Frankel's tours around Brigadoon. After about half an hour of conversation, Frankel said to Glinn, "I don't know if you're the right man for my girl."

Glinn was indignant at Frankel's gall but held his tongue. Moments later, as they passed the side of the peacock shed, Frankel unzipped his fly and peed on the side of the peacock house in full view of Glinn. "What you do think you are doing?" Glinn demanded, appalled.

"See," Frankel said proudly, full of mischief, pointing to his penis and the birds, "pee-cock."

Later, driving back to Manhattan, Glinn repeated the story to Elena and asked, "What kind of thing was that?"

Elena couldn't help but laugh. "Oh, he was just showing you his colors," she said.

5

AT AGE EIGHTY, Frankel turned his prodigious energy to what he knew would be his last great contribution to the town of East Hampton, a new sanctuary for the Jewish Center. Just as he had hoped, the East Hampton Jewish Center had become the core of Jewish life in the Hamptons. On High Holidays, easily 1,200 people would overflow the small original sanctuary into a white tent erected on the lawn. A large new building was needed, one big enough for everyone, and Frankel set out to find $1 million to build it, mortgage-free.

For a man eighty years old, Frankel's quest for money was formidable and unrelenting. To be cornered by him was sometimes a costly thing. In one of his most bravura feats of fund-raising, he ran into an old business acquaintance in the elevator at the Carlyle Hotel in Manhattan and extracted a $50,000 donation from the man between the twenty-fourth and twenty-seventh floors. When Frank

Farrell gave him a check for $10,000, Frankel held onto it for months before depositing it, waving it in everybody's face. "Now here's a friend," he would say, unfolding the check. "Ten thousand dollars! He's a black Irishman, and yet he gave me ten thousand dollars!"

There was one other, unexpected contributor to the new sanctuary: Evan Frankel himself. It is not known exactly how much money he donated, but it is likely to have been many hundreds of thousands of dollars, since Frankel intended to have control over the project. It would not be just a sanctuary, of course, but an Evan Frankel production, from the man who brought you the Distilled Spirits Industry Exhibit at the 1939 World's Fair, from the man who saved East Hampton. It would be the most prominent building along the approach to the village. Evan even chose the site and axis of the new building before he chose the architect.

Or, more appropriately, the architect chose him. Norman Jaffe, a lanky, handsome man in his early fifties, was already an architectural legend. Although he had proved his mettle in Manhattan with a prize-winning, shimmering skyscraper at 565 Fifth Avenue, and a capacious waterfront office complex called Seven Hanover Square, it was Jaffe's houses in the Hamptons that made him famous. Nothing else looked like them, at peace with the land, each one a sculpture, sweeping angles and low, low, overhangs, half walls of quarried stone and slate, the landscaping built against the house like a verdant cushion.

By the mid 1980s Norman Jaffe's houses were so exalted, they had become a status chip. Jaffe found himself becoming a brand name, like Mercedes. The next step was a line of sheets, and Jaffe hated it. He hated that kind of notoriety; he disliked, in particular, the kind of people it drew to him. "Weary from earning and spending," Jaffe said contemptuously, "my clients make a long perilous journey each weekend to escape the city." Jaffe was so disapproving of the motives of most of his prospective clients, desperate to write him a check for

Elena Prohaska as she looked around the
time of her breakup with Evan Frankel.
(Property of Elena Prohaska)

Evan Frankel and Elena Prohaska in Jamaica in the
bloom of their romance. (Property of Elena Prohaska)

At an opening at Elena Prohaska's Upstairs Gallery, artist Larry Rivers is behind the video camera
while Evan Frankel and his escort, Jeannette Rattray, are interviewed. (Property of Elena Prohaska)

Evan Frankel's last birthday party, at age eighty-nine, flanked by Elena Prohaska and Joan Cullman. (Credit Burt Glinn/property of Elena Prohaska)

East Hampton's Town Pond at the turn of the century, when it was known as Goose Pond. (J. G. Thorp, courtesy of the East Hampton Library)

Fourth of July, 1915, actor and Maidstone Club member John Drew next to his automobile festooned for the big parade. (F. B. Eldredge, courtesy of the East Hampton Library)

Sabbath services in the Norman Jaffe–designed sanctuary of the East Hampton Jewish Center. The arches are in the shape of the tenth letter of the Hebrew alphabet, *yod*. (© 1997 Gordon M. Grant)

The Maidstone Club as viewed across its immaculately kept golf links and sand traps. (© 1997 Gordon M. Grant)

On the campaign trail, from left, candidates Kevin Guidera and Charlotte Harris with the campaign manager, Harry Marmion. (Property of Kevin Guidera)

Chestertown House, the home of Henry F. du Pont,
before the Trupins got their hands on it. (© P. Boody)

Barry and Renee Trupin's half-finished Dragon's Head
in Southampton, a "hideosity" as seen from the beach.
(Courtesy of the *Southampton Press*)

Barry Trupin proudly stands with his creation behind him. (© 1986 *Newsday*)

Barry Trupin hoists his wife, Renee, jubilantly in their indoor lagoon.
(© 1984 Harry Benson)

Handcuffed Jerry Della Femina and his partner David Silver are led to a waiting police car as Jerry bites his lip to stop from laughing. (© Jack Otter)

Judy Licht, Jerry Della Femina, and their son J. T. at the polls for the big election of 1996. (© 1997 Gordon M. Grant)

his $500,000 fee so they could tell their friends, "We live in a Norman Jaffe house," that he turned down nine out of ten commissions. The tenth, lucky client who passed his scrutiny wound up with a brilliant house, an ulcer, and sometimes a lawsuit, like the prolonged litigation Jaffe got into with actor Alan Alda and his wife, Arlene, over his fee. Jaffe became so famous for being difficult that the *New York Times* architecture critic, Paul Goldberger, said Jaffe had "raised the alienation of clients to an art form."

Unhappy with building houses for people, Jaffe decided that his talents were more worthy of building a house for God. He just didn't expect Evan Frankel to be the client. When Jaffe offered his architectural services, completely gratis, to the Jewish Center, he found a cool reception from Frankel. "I don't see why a builder of skyscrapers and modern houses would know anything about building a house of God," Frankel said. Jaffe set out to show him. For the next nine months the architect submitted eight sets of plans to Frankel, all of which were dismissed. Frankel seemed almost frightened to make a decision. It had to be something special, he kept saying, "East Hampton isn't just anyplace."

One night the elderly man and the architect were having dinner, trying to find common ground over the design, when Frankel told him the story of his childhood, of selling chewing gum on the Staten Island ferry when he was six years old and of being bar mitzvahed in a sweatshop. "I saw in Evan then," said Jaffe, "something I hadn't seen before. I saw for the first time the struggling Yiddish-speaking child lost in a gentile world." Inspired by this thought, Jaffe turned for inspiration to an old book of photographs of synagogues in rural Poland, which he had found at the Jewish Center. They were mostly shingled buildings in the woods, not very different from the setting in East Hampton. All of them had been destroyed by the Nazis.

The next plan that Jaffe drew up is the one that stands today on Woods Lane. The resulting collaboration took nearly three years of titanic egos vying for their own perception of perfectionism, and the building that resulted is for many transcendent. The theme of the building is ten, the minimum number to complete a *minyan*, or prayer group. The exterior is set off by a series of multileveled, rectangular arches, between which tall, narrow windows let in the warmth of ambient light. The spacious interior is made completely of smooth, blond Alaskan cedar, with beams in a series of ten staggered, angled shapes, derived from the tenth letter of the Hebrew alphabet, *yod*. The south wall is penetrated by ten floor-to-ceiling windows, and the soaring arches seem to pull the congregation upward. All the lighting is diffuse, and the only direct sunlight falls on the ark, which contains the Torah.

The Gates of the Grove has in some ways become a monument to Norman Jaffe's work, as well as to Frankel's. On the morning of August 19, 1993, Jaffe drove out to the end of Ocean Road in Bridgehampton and went for a morning swim on the beach, never to be seen again. Mysterious rumors circulated that he had faked his own death, sick of his life in the Hamptons. A month later, his pelvic bone washed up on shore a quarter of a mile from where he had been swimming and was identified by the medical examiner's office.

The placement of the Jewish Center so prominently at the entrance to the town gave Frankel great satisfaction over the years and had its desired effect, particularly during the Jewish High Holidays, when Woods Lane was lined end to end with the luxury cars of those attending the services. One year, a local man was provoked to count the number of German-made cars parked in front of the synagogue and remark in an indignant letter to the *East Hampton Star* that the Jews must have forgotten the Germans' war crimes. The following week another letter writer suggested counting the number of Japanese cars in front of church on Sunday, to determine if the Christians had apparently forgiven the Japanese for Pearl Harbor.

The contretemps eventually died away, but the synagogue remains an indisputable reminder of Evan Frankel's legacy.

In October 1987, on Yom Kippur, Frankel collapsed coming out of the Jewish Center. He was never completely well again. He lingered in bed at home for a year, tended to by nurses and friends, shouting out, "The lord of the manor is not dead yet!" He was right. He lived another four years, and when he turned eighty-nine years old, all the women he had loved in his lifetime, save Peggy Goldsmith, held a symbolic "ninetieth" birthday party for him at Brigadoon because he wanted to live to be ninety years old. "Evan's girls" gathered around him for one last ensemble photograph. Frankel lived long enough to see the changing of one more season in the living paintings he so loved, until one spring morning in April 1991 he passed away in his bedroom at Brigadoon. His memorial service was held at the Gates of the Grove, and when the service let out, Woods Lane was closed to traffic in his honor.

Toward the end of his life Frankel had liquidated much of his property and left a large amount of cash to establish a philanthropic foundation, the Evan M. Frankel Foundation, for the enrichment of life on the East End. It is one of the largest endowments of its kind on the South Fork. He also left thirty-seven separate bequests to friends and relatives, totaling nearly $3 million. One of the largest personal bequests was a $200,000 trust fund established for Sam Glinn, Elena Prohaska's son with Burt Glinn.

The family that bought Brigadoon from Frankel's estate built a new, modern house on the property that Frankel would have loathed, all his friends agree. The new owners gave the old house to the local fire department to use for practice in putting out fires, and it was slowly burned down. The wandering maze of paths with their surprises, the pool built in the foundation are gone now — but after all, the legend of Brigadoon is that it appears only one day every 100 years.

Philistines at the Hedgerow

THERE WAS CONSTERNATION in the wicker-filled sunrooms of Southampton. They fretted about it on the grass courts of the Meadow Club. On warm afternoons at the Southampton Bathing Corporation, the members nibbled away at the details of what "those Trupin people" were doing to Henry F. du Pont's famed Chestertown House the way they munched on cold, crisp cucumber sandwiches as the ocean crashed onto the clean sand at their feet.

By spring of 1983 everyone in Southampton had heard *some* morsel. The indoor barrier reef with underwater grottoes and a twenty-foot waterfall. A freshwater aquarium large enough to swim in, with underwater oxygen jets. An entire sixteenth-century Normandy pub imported from France and reassembled inside Mr. du Pont's former library. A private zoo for burros. A heating system that could run on gas, coal, or oil at the flip of a switch. And not just one Rolls-Royce — which in Southampton would have been considered gauche enough — but seven, one a wicker-and-ivory model that belonged to a maharaja.

But perhaps the worst part: The first thing the Trupins did when they bought the house was to Scotch-tape a 24-karat gold mezuzah to the front door.

"Hank" du Pont must have been spinning in his grave.

"Mr. Trupin has insulted the memory of my family's old friend, Henry du Pont," said socialite Henry Mortimer, who was married to the granddaughter of Lord Curzon.

"Here I am," sputtered John Randolph Hearst, Trupin's exasperated neighbor, "with a grandfather who built San Simeon — *but he didn't build it in someone else's backyard!*"

Yet nowhere in Southampton was Barry and Renee Trupin's assault on Chestertown House more decried than at the Squabble Lane residence of Charlotte McDonnell Harris, sixty-two, the former sister-in-law of Henry Ford II. Harris was a small woman of aristocratic bearing, her hair gone gray, at her ears diamond clip-ons. Her deeply lined face and whiskey-throated voice attested to the cigarettes that seemed to drip, always, from the long, bony fingers of her right hand. She took deep, Tallulah Bankhead drags on her Parliaments, talking sharply as she exhaled through her nostrils, dragon-style. She talked mostly about Barry Trupin and how Southampton was "going to hell in a handbasket."

Harris knew all about going to hell in a handbasket. She had been there herself and back. After her son Richard Jr. was born in 1945, she became agoraphobic and was subject to panic attacks — afraid to go out of the house, afraid of crowds, afraid of people in general. It became a struggle for her to play bridge at home with friends. "I spent the next thirty-five years with a psychiatrist," she said, "back when only crazy people went to psychiatrists." To make matters more difficult, Richard, her tall, handsome husband, cheated on her from almost the start of the marriage. She would have divorced him, but she was a devout Catholic, and "nobody is closer to God than the Irish," she deadpanned. To deal with it, she began taking tranquilizers and drinking, and before long she was a full-fledged alcoholic and drug addict. "There wasn't a rehab center on every corner in those days," Harris said, and she underwent a series of "cures" for her drinking and pills, all of which failed.

Harris hit a low in 1974 when her daughter, Laurie, took an overdose of pills at age twenty-four and lapsed into a coma before dying in New York Hospital weeks later. Asked whether Laurie committed suicide or if it was an accident, Harris would only say, "Debatable," and let out a long plume of smoke. After Laurie's death, she kept herself in a drunken stupor, and the following year, on a holiday in Russia with her family, she was too drunk one night to attend a party at the American embassy. "That's the night I knew I was an alcoholic," she said. Eventually, she signed herself into Silver Hill, a private hospital in Connecticut. "Quite enjoyed it" she was fond of telling people. "Very attractive. Very nice people. It's low-key, and I've never had a drink since."

Instead, after mass each morning, Harris went to AA meetings, where she appeared in Gucci loafers and simple sleeveless summer dresses with pockets, or little cardigans, and when she smiled her gap-toothed smile — a warm, real smile that crinkled her already very lined face — it was still easy to see all these years later why John F. Kennedy was once so smitten with her that he proposed marriage before he met Jacqueline Bouvier. But the McDonnells wouldn't hear of Charlotte marrying Jack: The Kennedys weren't good enough. The McDonnells considered Joe and Rose nouveau riche — riding around in those big black limousines, looking like dowdy Boston Irish made good. The McDonnells had every bit as much money but they drove station wagons. And they played tennis and hunted, not chased women. They were the famous Golden Clan, the Brahmins of Irish society, descendants of the chief pooh-bah Irishman of them all, Thomas E. Murray. Their money was old — old compared to the Kennedys, when twenty years meant a lot to Irish immigrants. And Charlotte married well anyway, to Richard Harris, whose father owned the U.S. Lines shipping company.

The McDonnells and their in-laws, the Murrays, hadn't just summered in the village for the past seventy-five years, they were *of* the village, some of its fiercest protectors. Harris was vice president of the Southampton Association, a tax-exampt, nonpartisan group of concerned estate owners formed in 1962 to "preserve the character and environment of the village." She knew damn well that this Trupin thing would signal the beginning of the end if they didn't put their foot down. The philistines were upon them. Not just across the Shinnecock Canal in Westhampton (not really a "Hampton" anyway, but a tacked-on invention), where the divorced dentists bought homes for their second wives, or in Sagaponack, where the screwy or alcoholic writers like James Jones and Truman Capote lived, or in East Hampton, where the artist community paved the way for the show business crowd and the Jews, but close by, just outside the hedgerow, on Meadow Lane.

Harris was sitting in command central, her favorite chair in her favorite room in the house, the sunroom. It had double-paned glass — on the rare winter's day in the East End when there was sunshine, the room stayed just as toasty warm as it remained cool in the summer from the ocean breeze blowing beyond the privet. A corgi, the breed favored by the queen of England, panted silently in a chair next to her. On the chintz-upholstered sofa was a pillow needlepointed with the words "I Love the Irish." The house was roomy yet somehow plain and quiet on an otherwise remarkable street; Squabble was a private lane with a dozen magnificent houses, carved out of her family's own private compound.

What irked Harris about Trupin and Chestertown House, what irked everyone, was the arrogance of it all — not just to tamper with a famous old house, but to tamper with it so badly. "The house is a horror, a *hideosity!*" Harris said. It was her favorite expression for it, "a hideosity." The house was indeed a grotesque creation, part faux–Normandy castle, part Disneyland on LSD. It was the largest private renovation project ever undertaken in New York State. It stood ominously on Meadow Lane, ringed in barbed wire and laced with scaffolding, while hundreds of workmen swarmed over it daily like bees tending a hive. The handsome Georgian facade had disappeared behind walls of steel and mortar, with cathedral-like windows, fanciful spires, and pinnacles worthy of a fairy castle.

Darius Toraby, of Manhattan, was the architect of record, but according to the gossip, the construction was proceeding at Mr. Trupin's own caprice. Chimneys were built and knocked down at whim; a newly installed kitchen was destroyed so it could be moved six feet to the right; and one day architectural columns were covered in malachite, the next day in onyx. Trupin even renamed the house Dragon's Head. That really galled Harris. "Dragon's Head," she grumbled. "With any luck, and given cyclical hurricanes, the whole thing will be blown away by Christmas.

"And don't be misled about what you read in the press about anti-Semitism. This isn't about anti-Semitism, this is about *bad taste.*" Harris sparked a controversy when in one of her many outspoken interviews, she admitted, "If Mr. Trupin is involved in drugs or gambling, we don't want him. What if he's just a smart Jew who made a lot of money? In that case, we don't want him either." Harris later claimed not to have said it. "I thought he was Italian," she said, or because Trupin's company used the name Rothschild Reserve International, "we thought some Rothschilds fleeing France were fixing up the old place. After all, we've gotten a lot of those Euro-types out here recently." She had also heard rumors that he was a front man for Imelda Marcos or a big-time drug dealer, so who knew what to think?

"I didn't say, 'We don't want him, he's Jewish,'" she pointed out, and launched into her "wives of Jews list," a litany of Charlotte's Southampton friends who were married to prominent Jewish men and who were accepted in her circle: "Carroll, Ginny, Carolyne, Allison, Judy . . ." Carroll was the wife of drugstore tycoon Milton Petrie; Ginny was the wife of William Salomon, the founder of the brokerage firm; Carolyne was Carolyne Roehm, the designer, who was married to millionaire takeover king Henry Kravis; Allison was the wife of Hartz Group chairman and *Village Voice* publisher Leonard Stern; Judy Taubman was married to root-beer mogul and Sotheby's chairman A. Alfred Taubman.

"But these people are *names*," said Harris, borrowing a sentiment from the movie *Sunset Boulevard*. This man Trupin — this stranger who appeared out of nowhere, in his gold chains, with his "cute, hip number" of a wife who wore black leather minis or tight white pants with ankle boots with hats that teetered on the outlandish — "is a complete mystery." Not even the name of his company was real — Rothschild Reserve International. It was reported that the Rothschilds of the French banking dynasty demanded that Trupin stop using the name, a request he satisfied by occasionally removing the middle *s*. When *New York* magazine asked the Trupins if they were related to the French Rothschilds, Renee Trupin answered, "Please don't compare us to them — we see them socially."

"Socially?" Charlotte Harris chortled. The Trupins didn't seem very social to her. They didn't give to charities or try to ingratiate themselves, the way people did when they first moved there. After all, this was a small place, Southampton. Of all the stories told around the village about the Trupins, one in particular rankled Harris in a way that some friends thought was a tad obsessive. Ginny Salomon had stopped by Chestertown House on a neighborly stroll with Robin Duke, the wife of Angier Biddle Duke, to take a better look at the saltwater pool that everybody was talking about, when they were told by a member of Mr. Trupin's security force to "move along."

As Mrs. Duke was led off by the guard, she cried out in indignation, "Southampton is a friendly place!"

"Southampton is a friendly place," Harris repeated solemnly, stubbing out a cigarette and lighting another. The thought of it, Ginny Salomon and Robin Duke being told to move along! The incident so haunted her that she was spurred to do the kind of thing she used to do when she was drinking. She got in her car and drove the two miles to Ocean Castle, the mansion where the Trupins were temporarily living while Chestertown House was being renovated. On the pretense of asking the Trupins to sign a petition to stop the village from assessing beachfront homeowners for road repairs, she rang the front doorbell. Renee Trupin appeared on her doorstep and said, "I am a very big property owner out here, and I have no intention of paying for the repairs." Renee later denied saying it, but Harris insisted that before she could speak, the door was shut in her face.

"Imagine!" Harris said.

After that it was war.

2

IT WASN'T as if Charlotte Harris didn't know what it was like to be on the outside. God knows, there was no welcoming committee on hand when *her* tribe arrived in Southampton in 1927. The only reason the Irish showed up in Southampton in the first place was that they weren't wanted by the WASPs in Newport. They weren't wanted in Southampton either, but they overran the place. Southampton was "founded" as a summer resort in 1875 by a rich Presbyterian dry-goods merchant from Manhattan named Depeyre De Bost, who was the grandson of one of the ministers of the Southampton Presbyterian Church. The wealthy retailer spent most of his youth in Southampton before he left to find fortune in Manhattan. For years he longed to return to the idyll of his youth; when the Long Island Railroad finally extended tracks that far in 1870, De Bost built a house there. (Railroads were built coast to coast, crisscrossing the United States for twenty years, before one ever made it to Southampton.)

There wasn't much to do in Southampton back then, unless you liked to hunt or fish. The isolation helped retain the town's antique charm of being the oldest English settlement in New York State, started in 1640 by the same group of Kentish Puritans, via Massachusetts and Connecticut, that later moved on to East Hampton. De Bost's house was the genealogical grandfather of all summer houses, and it was remarkable to the local gentry because it was the first house built to be used for just the summer. It had never occurred to the farmers and fishermen of the 1870s that an individual could afford to build a three-story, unheated house to be used for only one season of the year. So remarkable was this white wood house that it became the village's preoccupation to watch it being built. It was erected on a naked field on the east side of Main Street, with nary a tree or hedge in sight. It had a wide veranda surrounded by railings and a sunporch shielded by a canvas awning. Out front on the semicircular driveway stood De Bost's surrey with fringe on top.

De Bost was a consummate sportsman who appreciated the East End for its game bird hunting, and he highly recommended it to his wife's gynecologist, Dr. Theodore Gaillard Thomas, as a place for a visit. Legend has it that Dr. Thomas fell so completely in love at first sight with the East End that he walked seven and a half miles along the beach, from Southampton to Water Mill, in an ecstatic trance. The charismatic Dr. Thomas was the most celebrated gynecologist of his age. He was responsible for the invention of dozens of lifesaving gynecological instruments and surgical techniques, including the first surgery for ovarian cancer. His fame brought him an international following as a healer, seats on the boards of half a dozen prestigious metropolitan hospitals, a handsome house at 600 Madison Avenue in Manhattan, and in 1877, what was to become Southampton's second summer cottage, The Birdhouse.

The Birdhouse was a silly-looking house, encased by two stories of wraparound porches with closely spaced picket railings, which made the house look like an ornate canary cage. This time the villagers thought Dr. Thomas just plain dumb when he built this enormous house out on the dunes, unprotected from damp and hurricanes. "It is difficult to understand," sniffed *Long Island Magazine,* "why anyone should wish to imitate the inconveniences that plagued our ancestors, and which they endured because they could not avoid them." The writer was correct. The Birdhouse was soon lost to a hurricane, and Dr. Thomas rebuilt farther inland, closer to Lake Agawam, on what had once been the cattle enclosure of early settlers.

Dr. Thomas almost single-handedly midwifed Southampton into being as a summer resort. He began by encouraging his wealthy Park Avenue clients to visit its shores for the recuperative effects. In short time the area gained such a salubrious reputation that another issue of *Long Island Magazine* claimed, "Southampton water is of the purest quality . . . the prevailing winds being from the ocean, the air comes laden with no germs or disease, and malaria, with its attendant evils, is utterly unknown. It is for these reasons that physicians, with the greatest unanimity, recommend the place as a most desirable resort for invalids and especially as a summer home for children."

By 1890 there were more than 200 houses, giant cottages with rooms for thirty servants. The new owners came from Pittsburgh, Cleveland, and Chicago: financiers, businessmen, judges, and clergy. Some were notables of their time, like Robert I. Lincoln, the son of the president; W. K. Vanderbilt, of the railroad fortune; and Harry Payne Whitney, who made millions manufacturing streetcars. One of them, Judge Henry H. Howland, was such an important social leader at the turn of the century that "not to know him," wrote one commentator, "argues oneself unknown in Southampton." As popular as the resort had become, in 1897 there were still only five telephones in Southampton, and the only way for the outside world to keep in contact with the wealthy men who owned the mansions was through Western Union. All summer long, under the hot sun, the exhausted delivery boys bicycled up and down the sandy paths from the telegraph office in the center of the village to the houses that dotted the shores of Lake Agawam.

The cottages had in common a fresh, bald look, without any shade or privacy, and the first thing the new homeowners did was to disguise the flatness by planting impenetrable walls of fast-growing privet hedge. Privet had made a brief appearance in the South Fork 150 years before, until a mysterious epidemic of something they called "lung disease" killed more than 100 people. The medical experts of the day suspected that the illness was caused by some poison given off by all the hedges, which were subsequently hacked down and destroyed. When they returned to fashion years later, the privet was of a new, heartier variety imported from California, *Ligustrum ovodifolium*, which grew as high as fifteen feet. While in East Hampton friendly picket fences and primrose were common dividers, in Southampton canyon walls of privet in a Minotaur-like maze became the symbol of its intolerance. (In the early sixties, Frank Sinatra once rented a house in Southampton on Meadow Lane. He arrived to discover that the owners had cut back the privet, hoping to please him, but it so exposed the house to prying eyes that he refused to move in.)

With the growing need for an Episcopalian church, Dr. Thomas purchased an old lifesaving station from the government and moved it to a site on the dunes not far from his own house. Saint Andrews on the Dune stands there today, with four oak corbels supporting the belfry roof, representing an abbot, an angel, a friar, and a devil. It was almost wrecked in the hurricane of 1938, when floods carried the church organ out the door and onto the road.

The only Irish in Southampton were servants, and their spiritual needs were tended every four to six weeks by a visiting priest, Father Joseph Bruneman, who journeyed east from up island. In 1881 Mrs. Fredric H. Betts, who worshiped with the Summer Colony at Saint

Andrews on the Dune, worried that her Irish help would leave without a place to worship weekly, so she instigated the building of the first Roman Catholic church in Southampton.

The Golden Clan didn't show up until the 1927 arrival of Charlotte Harris's grandfather, the legendary Thomas E. Murray, a businessman and inventor who held more than 1,100 patents, second only to Thomas Edison. He shunned the Presbyterians by building his own very big house, with both freshwater and saltwater swimming pools, on the other side of the village, near Wickapogue Beach. Legend has it that Murray fell so in love with Southampton that in early 1929, he sold off most of his stock to buy up 160 acres of Southampton, narrowly avoiding being wiped out in the stock market crash. This 160 acres became the Murray family compound, where the rapidly expanding clan all built houses to join the patriarch. The Murrays intermarried with a few Cuddihys and many McDonnells, and soon dozens of houses sprang up on the landscape on the Golden Clan compound, many of them by the staid architectural firm of McKim, Mead and White. There were so many Murrays and McDonnells in Southampton that the priest, Father Killeen, would click off the sixty or so first cousins with a hand counter as they arrived for church every Sunday morning.

The Golden Clan was ignored by the rest of the Summer Colony, and probably would never have cracked into Southampton society if it hadn't been for the pool filter Thomas Murray invented, which removed sand from seawater. The Bathing Corporation, which had only a freshwater pool, was so covetous of Murray's invention that they invited him and his family to join. Charlotte Harris remembered that in the beginning "we used to sit by ourselves [at the beach club] ... all in a row. People called us the Irish group. I don't know why we sat alone. Then we sat by ourselves because we wanted to. By God, we were going to show *them*."

Eventually, the line blurred between the Catholics and the

Protestants. All good Christians had to band together. They had a common interest in keeping out the real riffraff. In the summer of 1929, a writer who profiled Southampton for the *New York Times Magazine* noted, "All of social Southampton stands firm against one dreaded danger. This is the invasion of the quiet town by swarms of New Yorkers who do not even know what the Social Register is. Good roads have brought motorists to the eastern end of Long Island. Make the village of Southampton too amusing for these outsiders and its exclusiveness would vanish overnight. The Summer Colony, functioning as human nature normally functions under such circumstances, will fight such a development to the last ditch."

3

"ASSHOLES," Renee Trupin said when she heard that the village was going to make a fuss over her turrets. If they carried on about it, Renee told the press, she just might cut the turrets down and use them as planters on her front lawn.

Barry Trupin had a different approach. "Moses was accepted because of Ziporah," he said, "and when these people in Southampton meet Renee, they'll see how fine she is." For Barry Trupin, who grew up in a three-room apartment in Brownsville, Brooklyn, this house would be his legacy. This house would be a testament to what a shrewd boy who had been smiled on by God could do. Not long ago he had had seventy-six dollars in his pocket, and his idea of a big night on the town was to drive to Coney Island and buy a hot dog at Nathan's. Now he owned a house with 100-foot-long hallways. "For a kid from Brooklyn," he said, "you gotta live grand when you make it."

Burton Howard Trupin was short and pear-shaped, with a wide

grin, dark woolly hair, and a boyish face. A man of considerable charm and warmth, he had a glibness that all great hucksters share. The son of a silver craftsman, he had a colorful past. After attending Hofstra University in New York and running a short-lived night-club in Manhattan called the Charlie Bates Saloon, Trupin worked in the nuclear power industry with a top-secret "Q" clearance. His specialty was a "mobile combat reactor for tanks." He also had a significant role in developing the first handheld pocket computer.

But what made Trupin really rich was his 1976 discovery of a tax loophole from which he would spin a personal fortune of $300 million, a "money machine," he called it. Trupin found that a company could earn huge tax deductions by leasing computers instead of buy-ing them. Almost every aspect of the transaction was deductible: the devaluation of the computers, the money paid to lease — all of it. Then in a year or two, the company could lease all new computers and get brand-new tax advantages. He was able to demonstrate to Wall Street the financial advantage of leasing by securing an IBM mainframe computer for Mattel and a fleet of trucks for UPS, saving both companies millions of dollars, so he said. Trupin began to sell limited partnerships in the leasing companies, so the little guy could buy in, perhaps with his life savings, for as little as $16,500 a share. Within a few years Trupin's Rothschild Reserve International had nearly 200 leasing companies in operation, with hundreds of inves-tors. Although perfectly legal, the dodge was a little cloudy. He began to proudly proclaim himself the "master of the corporate veil." The structure of his RRI umbrella corporation was so complicated that he hired one employee solely to keep a loose-leaf "bible," as it was called, to help unscramble the maze.

His wife, the former Renee Cornelius, thirty-seven, was work-ing for one of Trupin's companies when she met her husband at the Xerox machine. She told the local papers that she was from a promi-nent Midwestern steel family, although others reported she was the daughter of an air force man who moved a lot when she was a kid. "She was goyim" was the way Trupin's father, Benett, put it, before she converted to Judaism for Trupin. Renee eventually became vice president of RRI. She was noted for tooling around Southampton village in a Rolls-Royce with the license plate TRUP, and she dressed in eye-catching costumes — color-coordinated show-stoppers complete with fanciful matching hats.

The Trupins wanted to enjoy their money and didn't care who knew it. They were in love, they had money to burn, and they spent for pleasure. They bought the former Cartier mansion at Ninety-sixth Street near Fifth Avenue and a 150-foot yacht (which they docked next to Malcolm Forbes's yacht) with its own Chagall painting, *Le Petit Concert*, that Trupin kept safe from salt water behind a hand-carved wooden cabinet. And when they bought a piano, it wasn't just a Steinway, but a $500,000 museum piece, the Alma Tedema, which they loaned to the Museum of Fine Arts in Boston.

Trupin also liked to collect unusual things. He owned one of the largest private collections of Judaica in America, as well as a world-renowned collection of medieval artifacts and suits of armor. His pride and joy was a suit of armor from Hever Castle in England that had belonged to Henry II. Trupin wanted to own the armor so passionately that he paid $3.2 million for it at auction, outbidding both the Tower of London and the Louvre. ("The Louvre!" he shouted in recounting the story to a reporter.) Even Prince Charles was impressed with Trupin's armor collection and invited him to dine at Kensington Palace. During dinner Trupin was bragging to Lady Lindsay that he had bought Henry F. du Pont's home in Southampton, New York, when she interjected, "Henry to you, but Harry to me."

It was the same kind of thing with the renovations on Chestertown House. Trupin was the first to agree that they had gone beyond their original scope. At first, they thought they'd just "throw up some chintz curtains and redo the bathroom," Renee said, but when they tried to paint the walls, the plaster came off with the brush. So after putting in new walls, they decided to fix up one of the kitchens (for $15,000) so Renee could cook a decent meal. But they soon realized that the kitchen was too small for catering — after all, what's the use of having such a big house unless you're going to throw parties? So they built a second kitchen, this one as big as a kitchen in a catering hall. But where would all those cooks and waiters and bartenders and kitchen staff change? So the Trupins decided to build locker facilities near the kitchen to accommodate the staff.

And if everybody in the East End had an outdoor pool, why not then an indoor pool? Perhaps an indoor saltwater pool? No, better yet — an indoor barrier reef. So then began the construction of a vast sunken aquarium, sixty by forty feet, with a twenty-foot waterfall cascading down chunks of rock imported from Vermont, into a pool in which guests could not only swim but skin-dive, with hidden underwater air nozzles. The reef was stocked with 500 species, including lobster, parrot fish, sea anemones, grouper, and octopus. The creation and maintenance of such an ecosystem, dubbed TIME (for Trupin Indoor Marine Environment), was so scientifically challenging that Trupin was obliged to hire a full-time marine biologist.

Up a tight corkscrew staircase from the reef was du Pont's old bedroom, which the Trupins discovered to be "a *fahrkukte* mess" when they moved in, with flaking walls and warped floors. So they built a "real" master bedroom in its place, thirty-five by thirty-five feet, with its own sitting room and a green soapstone fireplace, adjoined by his-and-her exercise rooms, nine-by-twelve walk-in closets, and a Jacuzzi complete with underwater "love benches" from which one could watch the stars over the black ocean in a glass-walled tower.

And if there could be a marine environment, why not an animal one? So plans were filed to build a private zoo that included burros, goats, and miniature Arabian horses. And since the traffic out to the Hamptons was such a nightmare, why not build a helicopter landing pad on the roof? (The village saw this one coming and had passed an ordinance banning them before the Trupins even applied.) And everybody on the East End had fireplaces, but what about a hand-carved jade hearth imported from Bolton Castle? And not just a sunporch, but a wide promenade on which to stroll in the sun named Muhammed's Alley because it was decorated in tents and pillows. And a paneled, two-story library with a hidden door. And out over the sea grass, a maze of wooden boardwalks with benches, so his parents could sit and rest as they walked to the beach. "It's really just a simple three-bedroom country French design," Renee Trupin said.

And so it grew, by leaps and bounds, concrete and steel, from 36,000 square feet to 42,000, then 55,000. They hired a "fast track" engineer who had experience in building hotels and skyscrapers and who could work around the constantly changing design. Foundations were poured and walls erected without plans. Every time Barry and Renee changed their mind, instead of suspending construction until new permits were granted, the Trupins went along pell-mell, changing and fixing, figuring they'd get the variances later. Between 1981 and 1984 Barry Trupin poured an estimated $10 million into Dragon's Head without almost one thing being legal.

4

PERHAPS if Barry Trupin had fooled around with another house, he would have gotten away with it, but Chestertown House, with its 535 feet of beachfront property, was one of the proudest summer homes in town, at least as famous as William Paley's Four Fountains or Jay Rutherfurd's Malaprop. Not only was this the "sister" summer cottage to du Pont's famed Winterthur mansion/museum in Delaware, but du Pont's wife, Ruth Wales du Pont, was a direct descendent of Phoebe Halsey, whose husband, Thomas, built the very first house in Southampton, in 1648. And for all the scandal that had befallen it in recent years, Chestertown House had somehow managed to retain its physical grace, even when it was deserted and forlorn.

Built of whitewashed brick in a formal Georgian style in 1925 by the architectural firm of Cross and Cross, the street facade was the most modest aspect of the 30,000-square-foot, H-shaped house. The estate comprised three large buildings: a main house, with an upstairs hallway one hundred feet long and fifteen feet wide, a separate servants' building (which would later become someone else's entire mansion) in addition to the servants' quarters in the wing behind the kitchen, and a separate two-and-a-half-story, ten-car garage with five apartments above. The house was built with walls thick enough to withstand the fiercest nor'easter, and in the basement, in a pit two stories deep, stood one of the world's largest furnaces ever installed in a private home, large enough to heat a Manhattan apartment building (although all two dozen bedrooms had their own fireplaces). To protect the house from the encroaching ocean, du Pont virtually erected a cement factory at Chestertown House and had a seawall built. Alas, even cement was no match for a good nor'easter, and it was gone in six months.

The rooms of the main building contained the third-largest collection of early American furniture in the world. Du Pont had entire rooms of early American homesteads dismantled and reassembled inside the house. Each and every door hinge and cabinet knob was museum quality. The living room, a thirty-nine-foot wainscotted room facing the ocean, with brick fireplaces at either end, was one of the most famous rooms in Southampton for its elegant paneling. Despite the enormity of the estate, du Pont had few guests and was a shy man who partook little of the Southampton social life. The long oak table in his paneled dining room seated three dozen, and behind the high-backed chair of each guest stood a servant in full livery with white gloves. Du Pont was so particular about his food that even though the East End was known for its produce, he had his own flown in from family vegetable farms in Wilmington, Delaware.

The du Ponts lived quietly ten weeks out of the year in Southampton, from 1925 until Henry's death in 1969, when the house and its contents were inherited by his daughters, Pauline Louise and Ruth Foster du Pont. The early American furniture was tagged by appraisers, and what wasn't given to the museum in Winterthur was sold off. The house was on the market for years. It was a hopeless sale, a house so huge, so impractical; the buyer needed to be someone either very rich or with a madcap sense of the absurd, and the house found them both in Leonard and "Baby Jane" Holzer.

Lenny Holzer and his blond, lion-maned wife, Jane, were the toast of Manhattan's Swinging Sixties demimonde. Baby Jane, a nickname she now understandably abhors, was discovered at a party by Diana Vreeland, who explained, "She just happened to have the greatest head of hair. And a tiny face like a narcissus." Tom Wolfe named her "girl of the year" in 1964. She was in reality a Jewish, Park Avenue housewife born in Palm Beach who at the moment had no greater ambition than to catapult herself to fame on the pages of *Women's Wear Daily* and to appear in half a dozen Andy Warhol movies.

Jane was funded in her endeavors by her husband, Leonard, a Princeton graduate who built apartment buildings in Manhattan. Along with the Holzers came bubble furniture with speakers inside, Warhols on the walls, and wild parties — a mixture of tanned young girls from the Topping Ranch and decadent New Yorkers — along with so many drugs that Lenny Holzer says he hardly remembers living in the house. Baby Jane Holzer told *New York* magazine that the house was a mélange of "jet setters, rock and rollers, every producer in Hollywood, degenerates, whatever. You name it, we did it all." One Southampton resident complained to the local papers at the time, "She has a lot of parties with a lot of weirdos."

In August 1974, two months after Baby Jane attended Sly Stone's all-gold wedding at Madison Square Garden, Lenny Holzer defaulted on $22,000 in taxes due the town of Southampton, as well as $12,000 in back mortgage payments to the du Pont sisters. When the sisters went to visit the house, they discovered that it had been stripped of everything worth salvaging, including every last early American door handle and brass hinge from the hundreds of cabinets. On a bleak and cold April morning in 1975, a sparse crowd assembled around the steps of Town Hall to watch as the town of Southampton auctioned off Chestertown House to the highest bidder, a mysterious and romantic figure named John Samuels III.

Samuels was a handsome man in his forties, with inestimable wealth and well-realized pretensions to a Gatsbyesque lifestyle. So dedicated was he to his literary doppelgänger that he actually purchased Salutation, the forty-five-room, Glen Cove mansion upon which F. Scott Fitzgerald fashioned the fictional West Egg home of Jay Gatsby. However, Samuels's background was less mysterious than that of his alter ego. He was the son of a postman from Galveston, Texas, and the numerical appendage to his name was as much of an acquired accessory as his Savile Row suits and vaguely British accent. A shrewd man whose mother worked as a secretary to send him through Harvard, Samuels made his money almost overnight in a brilliantly staged international coal-mine deal that netted him more than $500 million, thanks to the Arab oil embargo of the seventies.

He also made a smart marriage to a woman who gave him four beautiful children. They bought UN ambassador Marietta

Tree's double-width Manhattan mansion on East Seventy-ninth Street, where they gave elegant dinner parties. He also purchased Chestertown House in Southampton as his growing family's summer retreat. Southampton liked Mr. John Samuels III, no matter how new his money was. He did the right things with it. He became a supporter of the arts and turned himself almost overnight into the most powerful culture baron in New York. He became, in breathtaking succession, chairman of the board of directors of Manhattan's City Center, the New York City Opera, the New York City Ballet, and the Vivian Beaumont Theater at Lincoln Center, upon all of which he began imposing his personal tastes. For a time, he was the toast of Manhattan.

And then things began to go differently for Mr. Samuels. At the end of the seventies, he surprised very few of his intimates, except perhaps for his wife, by declaring his sexual preference for men. A quiet divorce followed. While the Southampton Summer Colony feigned shocked disapproval, in Manhattan this soupçon of scandal only increased his cachet, and he began to chum around with Andy Warhol, for whom he helped back a Broadway show called *Man in the Moon*, and was regularly seen with an entourage at Studio 54. Chestertown House, which he never much decorated, stood empty as the years passed, unheated, and he occasionally loaned it to friends who camped out there on weekends and kept themselves warm against the ocean winds with the heat of the fireplaces.

In the 1980s one of Samuels's partners in his coal ventures sued him, claiming that $5.8 million had been diverted from the business to buy Salutation and Chestertown House. The suit was settled out of court. In the early eighties the price of coal began to plummet, and Samuels's clever business deal lay shattered. He was forced to sell off pieces of his holdings to meet the payment on his business loans, and possession by possession he lost his kingdom, including,

eventually, Chestertown House. In the late eighties, his life in a quag-
mire of debt, Samuels left America to start his life over again, this
time, improbably, in an oil deal in Bahrain, an oil boomtown. But
within two years he was accused of criminal fraud in a business deal
and summarily thrown in a Bahrainian jail, which could have meant
the most unpleasant end of Mr. John Samuels III had he not been
freed by his attorneys and allowed to return to New York City, from
where he continues to do business.

The great house stood empty again, until one day in 1979, on
a lark, Renee Trupin dragged her husband out in their 1932 Rolls-
Royce to Southampton for the first time. Trupin was reluctant to
take so long a ride. "I thought that's where the secretaries went," he
said. But succumbing like his predecessors, within just a few hours of
arriving on the blessed shores, Barry Trupin plunked down $700,000
to buy Chestertown House.

Ocean Castle

IN WHAT SEEMED to everyone in the village like a delirious act of *Beverly Hillbillys* indulgence, Barry Trupin bought yet another landmark mansion just down the road from Chestertown House, an extraordinary, 25,000-square-foot citadel known as Ocean Castle, easily the most notorious house in the Hamptons. Trupin bought it, he said modestly, "really, so we could keep an eye on construction at Dragon's Head just down the block."

The Castle, as locals refer to it, was a fairy-tale relic of a bygone era, a rambling complex of tile-roofed buildings and cobblestone courtyards that looked like a fishing village had been plucked from northern France and nestled into a spit of sand between the Atlantic Ocean and the great Shinnecock Bay. It had been commissioned in 1929 by stockbroker William F. Ladd, a dashing character from Galveston, Texas, who made a great fortune advising the rich on how to invest. He built two other formidable mansions, one in Cedarhurst, Long Island, and one in Palm Beach. Even by Southampton standards, the Castle was immense. The single longest house on Long Island, it has seventy-two rooms, three turreted towers, stables, garages, and five kitchens. To prevent their bowing, each massive interior support beam was milled from oak that had been buried in the Shinnecock Bay for two years to season. The house was also a marvel of engineering, built in a huge excavated hole in which stilts and pylons were shunted two stories deep and sand pumped in around them to anchor the foundation. Later the dunes around the house were contoured to varying heights and shapes and planted with sea grass and beach pines so the Castle would look as if it had been there forever.

Although the construction of the Castle was completed in the year of the stock market crash, and most brokers were jumping out windows and not building mansions, Ladd's financial status seemed strangely unaffected by the ensuing Great Depression. This was most likely because Ladd's finances were in part aided by a boot-legging operation that he ran out of the Castle. The harbor and coves of the irregular coastline made safe haven for ships carrying liquor up from Cuba or down from Canada, so the Hamptons be-came a major distribution center during Prohibition. Speakeasys, some with dancing girls, abounded in the village, and once or twice a week thirty or forty young men, looking to make a few extra bucks, would form a human chain from ship to shore, unloading cases of liquor in the moonlight. (Even years later the Southampton Chamber of Commerce boasted that the village was "the Queen of America's Drinking Spots.")

After Ladd's death a secret suite of six rooms were discovered in the Castle, a warehouse to accommodate contraband booze, as well as a secret room above the dining room that was kept full of hooch, accessible only by standing on the top of the dumbwaiter. The good townsfolk of Southampton probably knew about the operation, but a case of Scotch now and then helped them turn a blind eye.

Ladd married three times, the last in September 1948 at the age of sixty-three in a quiet ceremony at the Castle. Alas, less than six months after taking a new bride, he was diagnosed with virulent cancer and given only a few weeks to live. After writing a tearful note of apology to his wife, he went into the bathroom of his Palm Beach estate and shot himself in the mouth. Unfortunately, the bullet didn't do the trick, and Ladd was brought back to his New York apartment, where he lingered for three months before mercifully passing away.

Yet it wasn't bootlegging or suicide that first made Ocean Castle famous, but a society coming-out party on Labor Day weekend of 1963. On August 31, Fernanda Wanamaker Wetherill, the most celebrated debutante since Brenda Frazier, was being feted at a party for 800 guests at Westerly, her stepfather's thirty-five-acre estate on Ox Pasture Road, not far inland from Ocean Castle. Fernanda, the great-granddaughter of Captain John Wanamaker Jr., the Philadelphia department-store founder, wasn't just the "deb of the year," she was the essence of her breed and the envy of millions of young girls across America: pretty, blond, rich, surrounded by boys with perfect teeth and good addresses, a girl whose nightclubbing and dinner parties were chronicled in the pages of *Women's Wear Daily*. So many fine young men of the Social Register were expected in Southampton on Labor Day weekend for Fernanda's introduction to society that her stepfather rented Ocean Castle from its then owner Robert Mallory Harriss, a wealthy cotton broker, to be used as a "dormitory."

Westerly was booked solid that weekend. It was a redbrick Georgian Colonial mansion, with a putty-colored slate roof, built in 1929 by the Chicago millionaire Henry Kaiser. Set at the end of a long, tree-lined white-gravel driveway, the formal house had rows of dormer windows trimmed in white wood. It was one of the few estates in Southampton to still have its own ballroom, which was put to good use by Fernanda's heiress mother, also called Fernanda, and her stepfather, Donald Steward Leas Jr. Favorites of the Southampton social set, the Leases were famous for their extravagant parties, like their 1955 "Night in Baghdad" celebration, at which a 734-pound elephant mingled with 250 guests under a silk tent, or their "Gone With the Wind" evening, where the estate was turned into Tara and one of the guests dressed as a Ku Klux Klansman. They were also known for their teeny eccentricities, like being tipsy half the day and keeping three chimpanzees as permanent houseguests. ("We used to take them to El Morocco," Mrs. Leas explained of the chimps, "but naturally we dressed them.")

Not since Anne McDonnell married Henry Ford II in 1940 on the Murray compound had Southampton seen such a party as Fernanda's coming-out. It had been in the society columns for weeks that pink was the color scheme; pink invitations and floral arrangements and pink champagne, Fernanda's pink evening dress, and the pink, three-pole tent — one of the largest tents ever erected in Southampton — that billowed over the vast green lawn of Westerly that splendid night. Fernanda took to the dance floor with her handsome escort, Sheldon Prentice, of Westbury, New York, a Yale student, who also delivered the toast. The actress Joan Fontaine and cartoonist Charles Addams joined them on the dance floor, as did Fernanda's mother, and Roy Chapin, the vice president of American Motors. The Twist was the popular dance of the moment — everyone in Southampton knew that Jackie Kennedy had recently been to the Peppermint Lounge in New York, and the crowd was thrilled to swivel to a "twist band," the first all-black rhythm-and-blues band ever to play in Southampton to anyone's knowledge.

The party thinned out about 2 A.M., but the younger crowd, fueled on what one of them called a "liquid diet," continued to dance and drink until the first light of dawn. When the band tried to pack up and leave, a group of well-heeled young men chipped in a few hundred dollars and hired them to play an additional three hours at Ocean Castle. Just as the sun rose, more than 100 of the young guests, the boys with their evening clothes in disarray, Fernanda Wanamaker Wetherill barefoot in her party dress, marched through the quiet Southampton streets to Ocean Castle and proceeded to destroy it in a drunken rampage.

It seemed at first like harmless fun. They began by dancing on the polished antique tables and doing the Charleston across the marble mantelpieces. A cheer went up as twenty-one-year-old Eaton Brooks, a student at the University of North Carolina from Darien, Connecticut, swung Errol Flynn—style from a huge chandelier and brought it crashing to the floor. Roving packs of young men ransacked the bedrooms, jumping up and down on the antique beds until the springs gave way and the wood frames cracked. One lad from Boston amused himself by shattering every piece of china and glass in the house with an air gun.

But all hell didn't *really* break loose until Granville Toogood, twenty-one, of Chestnut Hill in Philadelphia, while dancing on a tabletop, was "checked" by another boy and went sailing through the glass panes of the French windows out onto the terrace, where he emerged miraculously unharmed. At that point another reveler threw a rock through one of the exquisitely mullioned windows, and then another, until the crowd was stoning the house in a frenzy, the sound of crashing glass filling the early-morning air as every one of the estate's 1,600 panes was smashed.

It wasn't until late the next afternoon, alerted that there had been a disaster at the house, that Fernanda's stepfather went to investigate. He discovered dozens of young men passed out on the beach in their evening clothes, sprawled on mattresses they had dragged from the house. The beach was littered with broken glass from bottles and the windows of the house, so much broken glass that the town of Southampton had to sift the sand for it, and decades later shards still emerge around the mansion. Inside the house another dozen or so revelers continued to party; when the stragglers defied Leas's order to leave, he summoned the Southampton police. The small police force, so baffled by such a well-bred bunch of ruffians and incapable of dealing with them en masse, for identification purposes, insisted that all of them pose for a group photograph on the front steps of the beautiful stucco mansion. There they stood — handsome, unsmiling and unrepentant, looking very much like a Ralph Lauren ad in their Brooks Brothers slacks and blazers, surrounded by sturdy urns of Chinese-red geraniums.

That photograph became part of a six-page spread in *Life* magazine, and the rampage at Ocean Castle made headlines across the country. It became one of the most widely reported news stories of its day, filling not only the tabloids but the front page of the *New York Times*. Robert Mallory Harriss refused to press charges, and some money quietly changed hands to pay for the damages, assessed at $3,202 — curiously low. Harriss wanted to put an end to the matter by saying, "I'm appalled that these youths who are meant to head up their generation could stoop so low." He encouraged them to "return to God and their religion."

But interest in the incident would not go away. The public and the press were strangely fascinated by the dissolute behavior of the children of the rich. Didn't they have to pay a price like the rest of us? Or were they spoiled so rotten that they could rip apart a famous old mansion and get away with it? DO THE RICH HAVE IMMUNITY? asked a front-page article in the *New York Times*. Finally, in late September, after intense public pressure, the Suffolk County District Attorney's Office convened a grand jury in Riverhead and indicted thirteen young men and one woman to stand trial for the destruction of Ocean Castle. Five of the defendants were in the Social Register, and the one girl, Mimi Russell, age seventeen, who lived at One Sutton Place, was the granddaughter of the duke of Marlborough and the daughter of Lady Sarah Churchill. (Charges against her were later dropped.)

The defendants each stood to get six months in jail and a $250 fine, and the trial in Riverhead turned into a media sideshow. Photographers and reporters camped out on the front steps of the courthouse to crowd round the glamorous young accused. They arrived in expensive sedans with high-priced attorneys who protested that the attendant publicity was "punishment enough" for their clients.

Inside the courtroom a partylike atmosphere prevailed as the defiant youngsters took the stand. When James Curtis 3d, of Glen Head, Long Island, was asked if he slept in the house, he said, "Only when I passed out." When Eaton Brooks, the one who had swung from the chandelier, was asked by the assistant district attorney how he had been invited, he snapped, "There is a social secretary. If you'd like to have me explain it, I will." Samuel Shipley 3d accused the police of "ruthlessness" in even indicting them, saying that the authorities used "innocent people's lives as instruments of publicity." To which the assistant district attorney responded, "He's just a snotty kid."

In the end, the judge reluctantly acquitted all involved, saying that it was unfair to punish a few for the deeds of many. As for Fernanda Wanamaker Wetherill, who was not charged, she was "tired of the whole thing," she told the *New York Times,* which described her as "blonde, tanned, golden brown by a Bahamas vacation" upon her arrival in court to testify. Fernanda lost most of her enthusiasm for debutante parties after her own. A supper dance scheduled for later that year in Philadelphia was canceled to avoid "another unfortunate incident," explained the family. Fernanda said that she intended to get on with life by signing a contract to appear in the next James Bond movie, but her career as an actress never took flight. In 1967 she married James Niven, the son of actor David Niven, and settled down to become a solid citizen and philanthropist, later working as head of special projects for Manhattan's Center for Alcohol and Substance Abuse and for the New York Parks Conservation Program. She remains a vital part of Southampton society.

Her mother was not as lucky. One night in September 1974, after unsuccessfully undergoing treatment for alcoholism for more than seven years, Fernanda Sr. fell or jumped from the window of her fifth-floor apartment on the Upper East Side and broke almost every bone in her body. She died two months later at Lenox Hill Hospital.

Back in 1963, the columnists and pundits tried to figure out what the destruction of Ocean Castle meant. They dissected and examined it, predicting that "affluent delinquency" would become a growing menace. For its analysis, *Life* hired the same psychiatrist who had treated Ted Dragon, Dr. David Abrahamsen. In explaining the malaise of the children of the rich, Abrahamsen called the rampage "an expression of mass psychosis — mass madness . . . the irrational actions of people temporarily unbalanced." An essayist for the *New York Times* surmised that the wanton behavior was a product of too much time on affluent hands. "In modern society," posited the *Times* writer, "teenagers are given fewer useful outlets than their predecessors in rural society."

It turned out that it meant nothing.

That fall John Kennedy was murdered in Dallas, and the nagging question of what was wrong with the rich kids didn't matter anymore. As it turned out, the leaders of the next generation of the country weren't a bunch of towheaded aristocrats, who were, in fact, on their way to extinction, dinosaurs of a gilded age and debutante balls. The leaders of the next generation were wearing hippie beads, smoking pot, and making love, not war or money. For the moment, the party was over for the Southampton swells, only they didn't know it yet.

2

BARRY TRUPIN bought Ocean Castle from the darkest homeowner in the history of Southampton, Roy Radin, a six-foot, three-inch, 300-pound cocaine addict who made a fortune producing traveling vaudeville shows for Police Benevolent Associations across the country. "The Roy Radin Review," as it was called, headlined the likes of George Jessel and Tiny Tim, backed by opening acts of Elvis impersonators, singing dwarves, and fire-eaters. It brought millions of dollars into the coffers of police fraternal organizations and widows' funds, and even more money into the hands of Roy Radin, who sometimes took 75 percent of the proceeds and was able to pay $300,000 cash for Ocean Castle in 1978.

Everything about Radin was smarmy, including his impeccably trimmed black beard and his hucksterish smile. Helicopters flew him and his guests in and out of town, and it was said that movie stars visited him in the dead of night. It made the goings-on at Ocean Castle all the more curious when it was discovered that everyone who worked for Radin was required to live with him, including Mickey Deans, Judy Garland's widower. In the summer of 1979 Radin was asked to leave the Parrish Art Museum Ball when his female companions bared their breasts. There were also rumors that Radin and his entourage frequented local Southampton bars, where they sent drinks to attractive customers and invited them back to Ocean Castle for late-night parties at which drugs were used.

But nothing seemed more freakish than Radin's gluttony. Several nights a week, ensconced at his favorite table at Herb McCarthy's restaurant, Radin would order "one of everything" on the menu as his dinner. At Herbert's, the town's old-fashioned grocery, Radin's minions would roam the aisles, one day purchasing every kind of yogurt in the shop, the next day every kind of bread. Eventually he got so fat that he needed first a cane to waddle down Jobs Lane, and later a wheelchair.

Then came the Friday afternoon in April 1980, when twenty-two-year-old Melonie Haller and Robert B. McKeage IV, forty-two, both of Manhattan, appeared at a drugstore in Southampton Village and bought several dog collars and leashes before disappearing into Ocean Castle for the weekend. Haller was a show-stopping blonde with a long torso and slim hips who had been that May's *Playboy* magazine's playmate of the month. The next time Haller was seen in public was Sunday morning, when she was discovered by a Long Island Railroad motorman — unconscious on the 8:42 A.M. train to Penn Station.

According to Haller, there were seven guests staying at Ocean Castle that weekend, two men and five women, some dressed in leather gear and dog collars. Haller contended that after consuming a great deal of alcohol and cocaine, the other guests entered her bedroom and held her down, biting her breasts, while Radin raped her. Later Radin had his minions drive the dazed Playboy bunny to the Long Island Railroad station and deposit her on a train, where she was found and taken to a hospital.

Radin scoffed at the story, saying that Haller was asked to leave the house because she drunkenly broke things. Sure, they had spent part of the weekend in "suggestive and exotic leather uniforms," Radin blithely admitted, but that didn't mean he raped her. In any event, he was too busy to pay much attention to what Haller did that weekend because in a bizarre sidebar to the story, Mickey Deans tried to commit suicide that Saturday by overdosing on the antidepressant Elavil, and Radin spent most of the day at Southampton Hospital with him. Eventually, the police searched the castle, and Radin was arrested for the possession of an unloaded gun and released on $250 bail but was never charged with rape.

The publicity destroyed Radin's vaudeville review. No police fraternal organization would touch him, and within the year he fled to Los Angeles, where he expected the kinky, drug-ridden movie industry to embrace him. Radin listed Ocean Castle with Allan Schneider, and the moment it went on the market, in 1983, Barry Trupin jumped at the chance to buy it for a little more than $8 million. In an article published in the *Southampton Whale*, a well-read giveaway weekly paper, it was coyly noted that "[no] connection was found between Radin and Trupin except the property transaction."

In California Radin descended into a byzantine world of petty L.A. gangsters and coke dealers. He tried to use cocaine money to help bankroll the movie *The Cotton Club*, but before the movie was made, his body was found in a creek bed outside Los Angeles, one side of his head blown off by a stick of dynamite that had been stuck in his mouth after he was shot eighteen times. What was left of him was shipped out to Southampton, where he was buried in Southampton Cemetery, in a plot just next to busy Montauk Highway.

Now Barry Trupin was the master of Ocean Castle, where he moved his medieval armor and twelve-foot-tall taxidermic bears, a brown kodiak and a white polar in attack position. It was at Ocean Castle one balmy summer night in 1984 that he gave a lavish, medieval-themed banquet in the flickering light of burning torches. While Charlotte Harris quietly fumed in the Murray compound two miles away, Trupin's guests — most of them "outsiders," people imported for the weekend — were dressed as if they had just stepped out of Robin Hood's Sherwood Forest, in tights and brocade jackets, the women in ornate gowns and veiled tricornered headgear. The smell of seared meat cooking over an open pit wafted through the night air as a thirteen-course dinner was served, including roast suckling pig prepared on a spit and delivered to the table supine on a litter, with an apple in its mouth. Later guests watched displays of jousting in the courtyard and were entertained by jesters and lute players. The party went on deep into the night, while just down the block, Chestertown House stood dark and unfinished, its turrets and peaks the lightning rod for a brewing storm.

Dragon's Head

NOTHING STAYS the same," Charlotte Harris conceded in a soft, raspy voice. She was sitting in the sunroom of her Squabble Lane house in a cloud of cigarette smoke, her corgis curled up next to her. One opened pack and a backup were squared off on the table, along with a pad and a telephone. "The only thing that's stayed the same here is the ocean," she said. "Sure, it would be ideal to be able to look out over farmland for the rest of your life, but that's not realistic."

The thing about Southampton that very few outsiders understood was that Southampton never pretended to be anything but a close-knit enclave. It didn't have a summer theater or art galleries or a welcoming reputation for writers and artists. It didn't want all that. What Southampton wanted most of all was *to be left alone*. That's why the village was so unprepared for the sudden and drastic development explosion in the early eighties. Unlike East Hampton, Southampton had been notoriously lax about zoning and land preservation — it wasn't until 1957 that a simple town zoning ordinance was adopted. Subsequent plans hadn't saved it from the developers, who were flocking to Southampton from up and down Long Island, parceling it off. Even Fordune, the former 215-acre estate of Henry Ford II, was being developed into forty-eight lots.

"The village is disappearing overnight," Harris said. "Quite literally. Now you see it, now you don't." It struck terror in the hearts of the Summer Colony in the winter of 1983 when the von Stade house on South Main Street vanished. Leveled to the ground without a demolition permit. It had been a legend in the village, a Tudor mansion set on six and a half acres fronting Lake Agawam. It had twenty-two bedrooms and servants' quarters for fifteen; the floor of its ballroom was inlaid in a herringbone pattern. But it was useless, unheated, a relic of a bygone era. It passed through the hands of the von Stade family for five generations until it was quietly bought by a developer from Palm Beach. One night between Christmas and New Year the house disappeared, so quickly that locals drove by the empty lot several times in disbelief. "Symbolically, it seemed sinister," Harris said.

Or if not destroyed, great mansions were being transmogrified into condominiums. The Orchard — the James L. Breese mansion, with its music conservatories and hand-carved ceilings and eighteen-foot gilded columns and wall-sized tapestries, the last house designed by Stanford White before he was shot — was chopped up into two-bedroom apartments. There were already four condominium complexes — the Canterbury Mews, Farrington Close, The Colony, and Southampton Meadows — and no matter that they allowed the elderly and retirees safe housing close to the village or that the great ballet master Balanchine had bought an apartment there.

They should have seen it coming in the sixties and seventies. Oh, the people who showed up! Singles. Democrats. Divorcées. Liberals. "The litter of humanity," said one Southampton dowager. Betty Friedan was touting women's lib, and George Plimpton was hosting cocktail parties for the prisoners of Attica. Elizabeth Taylor and Richard Burton rented in Quogue. Larry Rivers made videotapes of Lee Radziwill's masseur massaging Truman Capote. Andy Warhol, attending Chessy Rayner and Mica Ertegun's benefit for the Southampton Parrish Art Museum, said he would "rather go over to Jane Holzer's and sit on the floor and drink champagne." Even Ethel

Scull, the eccentric art collector and wife of the Scull's Angels taxi fleet baron, had had enough. "A lot of people are talking about leaving the Hamptons for Pound Ridge . . . ," she told a society reporter at the time. "We've just bought a hundred and seventy-five acres in Connecticut, and the best thing about it is it's an unchic area. Thank God. Look what happened here when things got chic." Finally, in 1981 *New York* magazine ran an article titled "Forget the Hamptons, Now It's Country Chic," saying that the Hamptons were over and that Connecticut was in.

The small business district of the village itself became unrecognizable. At one time forty of Manhattan's better shops had summer annexes in Southampton, including Saks, Abercrombie and Fitch, Lily Pulitzer, and Elizabeth Arden. Now trendy boutiques lined Jobs Lane, including four Christmas tree ornament shops and a shop that sold a T-shirt that said, GRANDPA WENT TO SOUTHAMPTON AND ALL I GOT WAS THIS LOUSY T-SHIRT. Not so very long before, on a Saturday morning before going to the beach club, a smart young couple could stroll down Jobs Lane and see everyone they knew, the women in cotton dresses that never wilted in the heat, the men and boys in their blue linen blazers and summer chinos. At the Irving Hotel the wealthy old people sat on the porch facing Hill Street and watched as the Summer Colony strolled up from the beach to buy locally grown, fresh-cut flowers from a horse and wagon on the front lawn. But the Irving was a condo now.

The straw that broke the camel's back for Harris was Mayor Roy Wines's approval of a plan to extend Nugent Street in a route that would funnel all the bumper-to-bumper summertime traffic onto First Neck Lane, a street that was laid out in 1644 and was one of the wealthiest in America. This was a betrayal. It was Mayor Wines's job to protect the estate area, not to endanger it. For more than 100 years a symbiosis had existed between the Summer Colony and the year-round community. Because of the quirky way Southampton was laid out, almost the entire estate section — all the important houses — fell within the jurisdiction of the small "village," and the Summer Colony wound up paying 65 percent of the village property taxes. The estate dwellers entrusted the village to the local people to keep it safe for them. "Mayor Wines has a real debt of honor to the Summer Colony," Harris said, "not to develop the village out of greed and make a Hicksville out of it."

Fifty-six-year-old Mayor Roy Wines Jr., in his trademark aviator glasses and cardigan sweaters, was so popular with his constituency that he was known as "Mr. Southampton." He was the perfect small-village mayor, a good guy, low-key and so accessible that if your neighbor's dog barked too much, you could call Wines and he'd put in a word with the neighbor for you. Public service was in Wines's blood: In 1894 his grandfather became the first elected trustee of the newly incorporated town of Southampton. Wines had unsurpassed experience. He was deputy mayor of Southampton from 1971 to 1979; a past trustee and chairman of the police committee; past president of the Suffolk County Village Officials; a member of the New York State Conference of Mayors; a former chairman of the Southampton Town Planning Board; a trustee of the United Methodist Church; a member of the Southampton Volunteer Fire Department; past president of the Rotary Club; and a trustee of the Southampton Hospital and the local library. In 1974 he became a hero when as a member of the Southampton Fire Department he saved a family of three from their burning upstairs bedroom.

"He was also," Harris said, "a terrible businessman who was infamous for not paying his bills." He was rumored to have gone through a substantial fortune that his father, who founded the family plumbing business, had left him; he was notorious for owing people money. He probably bounced more checks than any single person in the history of the village. Southampton was certainly the only village in the United States where there was a sign up at the local post office warning clerks not to take checks from the mayor. Yet somehow his constituency just didn't seem to mind that the mayor bounced checks. He was one of them.

But Charlotte Harris minded. And she minded the unchecked development. And there was something else about Wines, something bad, but she couldn't put her finger on it. So one day in April 1983, tired of complaining and in a "fit of pique," Harris shocked the community by resigning from her position as vice president of the Southampton Association and announcing that she was forming her own political party, the Tradition Party, and that she intended to run for one of the two open village trustee seats. Her doctors were against it, and her friends thought she was crazy. She went to see Roy Wines himself to tell him, and he tried to talk her out of it, but she was determined. To fill out her ticket, she enlisted as her running mate a respected Southampton high school teacher and longtime president of the local teachers union, Kevin Guidera, forty-eight.

Harris didn't as much run for trustee as run against Roy Wines for mayor. Although her slogan was "Trust Me for Trustee," it might as well have been "Wines Is a Wimp," she repeated that phrase so many times. She said it everywhere she went. Wines was a wimp for not standing up to the special interests of the construction trade, and Wines was a wimp for selling out the village to "condocrats." Harris took her campaign much more seriously than Wines did, who was so securely entrenched that he hardly lifted a finger. He held only one fund-raiser, at the Polish Hall, pulling in $6,000 in campaign contributions, most of which he didn't even bother to use. Harris raised money daily, bringing $15,000 into her campaign coffers — a whopping amount considering that only 200 voters had turned out for the previous election. She used the money to bombard the local radio airwaves with commercials, 160 a week, and to take ads in the *Southampton Press*, ads not with political endorsements but with a reproduction of quotes from an article written in *W* magazine, a fashion publication that doted on the Summer Colony crowd, about how the "BP" (beautiful people) were fighting to save Southampton from the "veritable freak show" of "merchants, strollers in cheap tee-shirts, daytrippers ... condominiums spread[ing] like a disease."

Despite her poor health and fear of crowds, she seemed dauntless. She screwed up her courage and marched up and down the streets of the village, from the Sip N' Soda on Hampton Road to Shep Miller's haberdashery on Jobs Lane, where her husband bought those velvet slippers with a pheasant embroidered on the vamp, handing out pamphlets. She pressed the flesh in the curtained cubicles at Elizabeth Arden and at the perfume counter at Saks Fifth Avenue. On Sundays she drove her red Cougar with its corgi hood ornament over to the black churches and spoke passionately about upgrading property to two-acre minimums to parishioners who cleaned her house and cut her hedges during the week.

She also despaired. Two or three days before the election, she sat in her house with her head in her hands and said, "Why? What in God's name am I doing?" Sometimes she thought of drinking again, but instead, she fixed herself an iced tea and lit a cigarette and thought about how much she hated Roy Wines and what a hideosity the du Pont house had become.

That June Harris at least captured the imagination of the electorate; the election brought out 1,437 voters, the second-biggest turnout in village history. But alas, the Guidera-Harris ticket came in third, with Harris losing to incumbent trustee Orson Munn, 771–700, and Guidera losing to Mayor Roy Wines Jr., 799–619. On election night, while the Wines campaign machine was celebrating at Herb McCarthy's Bowden Square restaurant, Charlotte Harris was smoking cigarettes in her sunroom on Squabble Lane, good and angry. In a conciliatory gesture, the other side offered her a seat on the architectural review board, but "I refused," she said, "because I have no intention of being buried. . . . Show me a good loser, and I'll show you a loser." She drank black coffee into the small hours of the night.

On the morrow she would call for public "sanctions" against Wines and his administration. It would be a real shocker, these sanctions, a call to arms. In protest of Wines's reelection, she was asking that all her supporters who gave so generously throughout the year to local charities cut their contributions by 50 percent — except to the hospital and fire department — to punish the Wines administration. That would wake them up. "The Summer Colony has power and rights too," she said. "Sanctions may be the only language they understand."

Then she discovered something else they might understand.

2

HARRIS DISCOVERED — probably through an attorney hired by the Southampton Association — that Barry Trupin had never received building permits for most of the construction at Dragon's Head. He had poured $10 million into the place with permission only to renovate a kitchen for $15,000. "Imagine!" Harris said. "In Southampton you need a permit to put up a new gate, let alone renovate a mansion!" (This was a law Harris knew well; years before she was roundly criticized herself for not applying for a building permit to add a second story to her home until after the construction began.)

Harris also learned that she had been right all along about the height of the turrets; Trupin's hideous cupolas violated the thirty-five-foot height limitation in thirty-three different places. One, the southwest cupola in the master bedroom — the one with the vulgar Jacuzzi and "love benches" — reached an arrogant 65.3 feet.

As if that wasn't enough, Harris was also tipped off that many of the construction crews were being paid "under the table" in cash and that thick rolls of hundred-dollar bills were being flashed around at Dragon's Head. The project had become a favorite of the local construction workforce. In fact, the Trupin site was such a money font that a member of the architectural review board was warned not to meddle if she "knew what was good for her."

Broken laws. Tax evasion. Threats. Harris was apoplectic. Her blood pressure soaring, she sat in her chair in the sunroom and dialed every single person she knew in Southampton. She spent hours on the phone, haranguing friends with an indignance for which there was no solace. "And where was the voice of authority while all this was happening?" she demanded of everyone she spoke to. "Why wasn't a stop-work order issued by the building inspector? Where was the mayor all this time?"

Doing Mr. Trupin's plumbing.

Roy Wines and Sons was Barry Trupin's plumbing contractor. It was Wines's company that installed the miles and miles of copper pipe needed for those waterfalls and grottoes. And it was Roy Wines Jr. who collected nearly $400,000 for doing the plumbing when Trupin didn't even have a building permit to begin with.

"I had no idea Mr. Wines was mayor of the village," Barry Trupin said, flabbergasted, when approached by the press. "How could I know? Our plumber, the *mayor?*"

Sitting in his high-backed chair in the mayor's offices at Southampton Village Hall, Roy Wines Jr. was completely unbowed. "I had no idea the building inspector hadn't given Trupin a building permit," Wines told the *Southampton Press*, despite the fact that the mayor was the village trustee in charge of the building inspector. His sons had been supervising the Trupins' plumbing, but the mayor did admit that he had been out to the worksite a couple of times. Wines also pointed out that there was nothing illegal in doing Mr. Trupin's plumbing — when his father was alive, he did the plumbing for half of the Summer Colony. "I have been very careful to avoid any conflicts of interest," Wines insisted. "I do not tell my building inspector what to do, and Mr. Trupin has never raised the issue with me. Charlotte Harris's personal attack on me is bringing village politics to a new low."

Labeling the story "Southampton's own Watergate," Harris launched into a one-woman media campaign. The Southampton Association took a full-page ad in the *Southampton Press* with the headline THE LAW IS BEING BROKEN IN OUR VILLAGE: "Did you ever — Build a house, Add a room, Erect a fence? . . . If you did, you know you had to get a building permit. . . . Why doesn't Mr. Barry Trupin have to do what you had to do?" In February, with Harris's encouragement, *W* magazine ran a piece called "How to Ruin the Hamptons." *Newsday* followed suit with an article titled "Turrets Called Height of Hideosity," using Harris's pet word in the headline. Even the *New York Times* took on the story, headlined, SOUTHAMPTON SPLIT WIDENS OVER MANSION.

It wasn't until June that *New York* magazine detonated the heart of Southampton with a cover story by Marie Brenner called "Mr. Trupin Builds His Dream House," in which Harris was quoted asking her now infamous "What if he's just another rich Jew?" question. (Trupin threatened to build a shul on Main Street in retaliation, a threat Evan Frankel had already made good on in East Hampton.) Harris said she wanted to sue for libel but claimed that she couldn't afford it. The following week *Dan's Papers* in Bridgehampton came out with an editorial deploring the open anti-Semitism of Charlotte Harris and praising the Trupins' pioneer spirit of wanting to build their dream castle. If that wasn't enough, in September Harris contributed heavily to another major piece in the *Washington Post*, in which she demanded of the reporter provocatively, "Did you know that Trupin has installed slot machines in the basement of Ocean Castle?" (He had not.)

Trupin was on his yacht in the Caribbean when a copy of *W* magazine was delivered to him and he first discovered that his house had become a national object of scorn. By the time he returned from vacation, Dragon's Head had become so notorious that tourists from all over Long Island were driving out to Meadow Lane to gawk at it. The Trupins had become media stars. "People look at us and say, 'They're the Trupins,'" Barry fumed. "We're the *Trupins*. The Trupins. That's the uncomfortable level. We hear it from people in Turkey, in England, all over the world. People don't like us who have never met us. People I never saw before in my life. What I would really like to do," he said, "is drop off the tax rolls and let the town blame Charlotte Harris. What's really going on here is that this is a Charlotte Harris witch-hunt."

In late May 1984 Charlotte Harris attended a standing-room-only meeting at Southampton Village Hall at which Bill Hattrick, the longtime chairman of the zoning board of appeals, issued a sixteen-page decision formally denying Barry Trupin's application for height variances, saying that Trupin had built the turrets with "intentional and knowing disregard" for the law and that a "stop work" order should be issued bringing all construction at Dragon's Head to a halt until it conformed with Southampton law.

Harris rejoiced after the meeting, walking around the hall shaking hands and congratulating friends. "It just goes to show what perseverance can do," she said. Later that night in a letter to the *Southampton Press,* she wrote, "Never go to bed mad. Stay up and fight."

But Barry Trupin also knew how to stay up and fight. In August 1983 he filed three lawsuits. The first was to force the village to give him a work permit to finish all Dragon's Head construction below the disputed roofline; the second was to legalize the height of the existing turrets; and the third was a federal civil rights lawsuit seeking $4.5 million in punitive damages, claiming that his constitutional rights had been violated intentionally, out of malice and prejudice. He claimed that he had become a political football between Roy Wines Jr. and Charlotte Harris in a village rife with anti-Semitism and that he sought retribution. Trupin sued not only the village but sixteen of its individual officers — members of the board of trustees, the zoning board of appeals, and the architectural review board. And because he knew that the village's insurance carrier, the Hartford Insurance Group, would cover the personal liability of the village officials, he specifically asked the court to hold each of the sixteen defendants *personally* liable for damages, because, he contended, this was personal. He wanted them to have to pay out of their own pockets like he had to pay, and if they didn't have the money, they would lose their homes, just like he had. Within days seven law firms were embroiled in protecting local citizens and the village of Southampton against the lawsuits of Barry Trupin.

One small irony was that Charlotte Harris didn't have an official capacity in the village, or Trupin would have certainly sued her too. Harris would have relished going head to head with Mr. Trupin, but friends and family were glad she wasn't involved any deeper than she was. Her health had grown much worse, and in recent months she had trouble walking. She began to see a pulmonary specialist in New York once or twice a month and was under a cardiologist's supervision at Southampton Hospital. Of course, she would not stop smoking — she never stopped smoking. She had slain a lot of demons in her time, but cigarettes would not be one of them. Mr. Trupin and Mr. Wines, however, were still in her sights. Indeed, if not for them to keep her going, Harris might have been a lot sicker.

In June 1984 Roy Wines Jr. was up for reelection for his fourth term, and Harris was determined not to let this happen. "It's going to take a lot of work to unseat our present government but it's got to be done," she wrote in the *Tradition Party Newsletter*. The key was to find somebody who was acceptable to the local people as well as to the estate crowd, and she thought she had just the man to bridge the gap, somebody everybody trusted — and a good Irish Catholic, to boot — in Bill Hattrick.

3

"DRAGON'S HEAD ruined my life," Bill Hattrick once said. He regrets saying it now, because he's had a good life, and Dragon's Head didn't ruin it, it just consumed him and the village of Southampton for five years. In 1985 he was a forty-nine-year-old stockbroker and the chairman of the village's zoning board of appeals. A soft-spoken man with a round face and easy smile, he went to mass every morning and said "Gee-dee" in conversation instead of "Goddamn." Many of his wealthy clients were members of the Southampton Association, who trusted and liked him, as did the local community, where his six children had grown up and gone to public school. Hattrick himself grew up in Riverhead and moved to Southampton twenty-five years earlier. "But living in Southampton for twenty-five years doesn't make you local," he said. "You're never really local unless you're born in Southampton Hospital."

That March Charlotte Harris paid a visit to Hattrick's unprepossessing farmhouse on Hill Street. Hattrick knew that Harris was having problems with her heart, but he was surprised at just how tiny and frail she looked that winter's day, fumbling for her cigarettes as she sipped hot black coffee in his kitchen. She was determined in her mission to oust Wines. Hattrick thought, How can anybody so fragile have such strong feeling about going to war? "But she had the heart of a tiger."

Harris said many people in the village believed that Hattrick was their best hope against Wines, and if the genial stockbroker agreed to run, she would throw her considerable support behind him. But Hattrick didn't think he had a good enough chance. "I thought Wines was unbeatable," he said. "Wines was entrenched, a talented politician who could get up in front of a crowd and make inspiring speeches. He could put on a cardinal's robe and walk on the water. I was just a guy trying to pay for the orthodontist."

On the other hand, as mayor, Hattrick could take on Barry Trupin. He was one of the local officials that Barry Trupin had asked the court to hold personally responsible in his civil rights lawsuit, and he was righteously angry about it. "If it gets to the point that my house and life savings are at risk," said Hattrick, "then, well, I've got some caveman in me someplace. What would a caveman do? He would say, 'You steal my ox, I beat you over the head.' Mr. Trupin better not come in person to take away my house." But Hattrick was not ready to run for mayor, and Harris left his house disappointed.

A week or so later a small article appeared in the *Southampton Press*, "Hattrick Declines to Run," and shortly thereafter Hattrick got a call from Roy Wines asking him to attend a meeting at his house with some of the village officials. "Wines beat around the bush for a while," Hattrick said, "and then he asked if I would consider running with him, as a member of his slate, for village trustee. Would I consider that?

"I said to Wines, 'My real problem is with the Trupin affair,' and Wines stood and pointed his finger at me and said, 'Don't give me that! As chairman of the zoning board of appeals, you're as guilty as I am!' "

Hattrick excused himself in a cold fury. "I went home, went upstairs to my office, picked up the phone and called Michael Meehan, the president of the Southampton Association, and said, 'Get out the horses, I'm ready to run for mayor!' "

A week later a gift-wrapped antique cane, with a hand-carved horse's-head handle, was delivered to his house. Attached to the neck was a note in Harris's unmistakable neat handwriting: "Speak softly," it said, "but carry a big stick."

Charlotte Harris never got to see Bill Hattrick become mayor of Southampton. By early spring her circulation was so bad that she couldn't walk more than a few yards without sitting down. She knew she was in a downward spiral, and she said to a young journalist helping her prepare one of her newsletters, "You are just starting out in life, I am coming to the end of mine." Perhaps the *coup de grâce* came when she was subpoenaed by Barry Trupin's attorneys to give depositions in his civil rights lawsuit. One of the assertions in the lawsuit was, in essence, that Charlotte Harris was the leader of a band of anti-Semites who intentionally deprived Trupin of building his dream house. Unable to smoke cigarettes, the videotaped depositions were a nightmare for her. When it was over, she wrote in her newsletter about her exhaustion after being "subjected to grueling hours of testimony." It took her several days to recover, and by then she was more preoccupied with getting voters out for the upcoming mayoral election than with seeing a pulmonary specialist in Manhattan, and she began to miss appointments.

On a bitterly cold Thursday, April 4, 1985, Harris went to work as a volunteer at a voter-registration drive at Town Hall. She had only just arrived when she began to have chest pains and feel short of breath. "She looked white as a ghost," said her friend Dorothy Brown, who was with her. Brown called an ambulance, but by the time Harris was rushed to the coronary care unit at Southampton Hospital, she was in full cardiac arrest and never regained consciousness. Her family was summoned to her bedside, and she passed away later that afternoon.

Just days before her death, Harris finished what would be the last edition of her *Tradition Party Newsletter*. It was a fretful missive. In it she worried about the Union Carbide chemical plant explosion in Bhopal, India, and what would happen if there was an explosion at the Shoreham nuclear plant that was slated to be built on Long Island? She worried that overdevelopment would deplete the water table. She worried that Roy Wines would go undefeated, and that Barry Trupin would win out.

4

ON JUNE 18, 1984, after the longest, dirtiest campaign in village history, Bill Hattrick defeated Roy Wines by a vote of 834 to 601. Wines admitted that he was "sore a bit" about the charges made against him during the campaign concerning his fees for work on the Trupin house, but he continued to protest his innocence. Wines told the *New York Times*, "Barry Trupin was more a victim than a cause. Charlotte Harris and the Southampton Association did a lot to create an atmosphere outside of the legal problem within the community for Mr. Trupin."

Six years after losing the election, Wines — still in public service, then chairman of the town planning board — filed for personal bankruptcy, listing $1.2 million in debt. In 1992, after he admitted that he took $10,000 in personal loans from a developer and a town engineer, the Southampton Town Board called for Wines's resignation. He had been a planning-board member for twenty-four years and its chairman for twenty. "I am not resigning for anything I've done or because of a question of ethics. . . . I happen to feel I have ethics equal to anyone in Town Hall." Wines died of cancer in 1994 at the age of seventy-one.

Ethics was also very important to the new mayor, Bill Hattrick. Some thought maybe too important, if that was possible. Hattrick's critics say he lost his distance and began dealing with the Trupin lawsuit not so much as a legal struggle but as a manifestation of the conflict between good and evil. Although Hattrick was a beloved mayor, the Trupin matter so obsessed him that he accomplished little in his two terms in office other than bringing summer concerts to Agawam Park or refurbishing the snack counter at Main Beach.

It was a great blow to Hattrick when in April 1986 Trupin won the first legal decision; a state supreme court justice ordered the village to allow Trupin to finish all of Dragon's Head *below* the disputed roofline. Hattrick was heartened three months later when Trupin lost his second lawsuit to have the height of the turrets legalized. At that point, in a strained effort to bring about peace and perhaps put an end to the mounting legal fees for the village, the mayor agreed to a bizarre compromise with Trupin: it was concluded that Trupin's turrets wouldn't be too high if the ground wasn't so low. In remedy, tons of sand and dirt were trucked out to Meadow Lane, and a twelve-foot hill was built along the road side of the house. The new hill was pushed in against a poured-concrete slab, blocking out the windows, turning the first floor into the basement. The house looked worse than ever. The village then agreed to give Trupin a building permit for all but the highest turret, clearing the way for him to resume construction.

But by then Trupin had no intention of continuing construction. "I don't know if I ever want to live there," he said of Dragon's Head the summer of 1986, wandering around the half-finished château wistfully. "I won't go into the pool," Trupin said. "I won't ever go into the pool until I know it's mine. Until there's peace. I've been crying about this house ever since it happened. This was my dream house. I don't have dreams anymore. . . ." Later that year Trupin moved to California and put Dragon's Head up for sale, listing it with Allan Schneider, who had the idea to advertise the house at $20 million for the completed renovation, or $12 million "as is." As the years passed, the price steadily dropped.

Trupin put Ocean Castle on the market as well, selling it in 1988 to Manhattan developers Jason and Julia Carter, a young couple with two young children, for $2.75 million. The day the Carters took title to the house, they were upset to discover that everything that wasn't nailed down — and even some things that were — was missing, like a $3,000 Sherle Wagner porcelain sink in the master-bedroom bath and a gazebo from the yard. Even the flower boxes had been ripped out. The Carters sued Trupin for the missing items and settled with him out of court.

On February 21, 1988, nearly five years after it all started, the civil rights lawsuit of *Barry H. Trupin v. the Village of Southampton, et al.* went to trial — not in Riverhead, as expected, but, because of a motion made by Trupin's attorneys, in Brooklyn, before Judge Charles P. Sifton in U.S. District Court for the Eastern District. This meant that every morning before the crack of dawn, all the defendants and their various lawyers had to make the two-and-a-half-hour trek from Southampton to downtown Brooklyn by 9 A.M. Trupin's suave attorney, Jacob Fuchsberg, a former New York Court of Appeals judge, presented his side of the case to a jury of six citizens from various middle-class neighborhoods in Queens, Brooklyn, and Long Island. For the five women and one man — a carpenter who wore white sneakers to court every day and lived at home with his parents — Southampton might as well have been Bali. "I took one look at the jury," Hattrick said, "and I knew we were in trouble."

Whatever fascination the jury might have found at first in the descriptions of Trupin's rags-to-riches story and of his lavish lifestyle, of his jade fireplaces and elaborate bathrooms, their attention soon dulled as much of the testimony turned to technical definitions, such as the description of a cupola being a "cylindrical transition to a point." The building and zoning laws and application process were not much more interesting, and at one point the young carpenter actually stretched out, put his head back, and dozed.

Judge Sifton ruled from the start that none of the sixteen town officials could be held personally liable for damages, but several were subpoenaed for the jury to see, including the chairman of the architectural review board, the town attorney, and the building inspector. Even Charlotte Harris threatened to make an appearance. Trupin's attorney tried to enter into evidence her videotaped deposition as an example of how anti-Semitism may have motivated the village's actions. After viewing the tape, Judge Sifton called Harris's comments "off the wall" and forbade it from being shown. Barry Trupin himself appeared in court each day in a conservative suit and tie, nodding his head at the testimony in his favor. The day of his testimony he was given lunchtime advice by his attorney to "act Anglo-Saxon on the stand." Trupin testified that he was "driven out of town" by the village and denied an assertion by one of the village's attorneys that he stopped construction on Dragon's Head because he had run out of money.

Twice during the trial Judge Sifton implored the village and its insurance company, the Hartford Insurance Group, to settle the suit out of court. Sifton even suggested a settlement scheme whereby in return for some payment, Trupin donated the mansion to the village, perhaps to be renamed the Barry Trupin Memorial. Bill Hattrick was angry enough to spit at that particular suggestion. There was no chance of settlement. "Trupin broke the laws with evil intent," Hattrick repeated. "I'm not going to say otherwise. I will not pay him a nickel." But as the days passed and a procession of witnesses testified, it began to look bad for the village of Southampton. In the hard light of a federal courthouse, they appeared an unsavory cast of characters — a slippery mayor who lined his pockets while his building inspector looked the other way and a Greek chorus of anti-Semitic blue bloods trying to tell a man how to build his dream house. "We sounded like a bunch of bigots who had put the wood to a boy from Brooklyn," Hattrick realized.

That's what the jury thought too. On March 4, 1988, after three days' deliberation, the jury awarded Trupin $1.9 million in damages, plus his attorneys' fees of $762,000. That, plus the $1.1 million the village owed for its own attorneys' fees, brought the village of South-ampton's liability to a grand total of $3.8 million. Since the Hart-ford Insurance Group was claiming the village's insurance policy was capped at $1 million, the remaining $2.8 million liability would be borne by the village. Southampton had a few options. It could declare bankruptcy, but then Trupin would have a lien against the municipality, thereby owning a piece of it, a bitter irony; the village could increase property taxes by 60 percent in one year to pay off the bill; or it could fight on in court, with an expensive appeal. At that moment an appeal was about the last thing the village wanted. Bill Hattrick immediately asked Judge Sifton to set aside the verdict pending an appeal.

Just a few nights after the jury's decision, Hattrick spoke at a standing-room-only meeting of the Southampton Rotary Club. He looked grim and ashen as he stood at a podium in the front of the hushed room. "It's a crushing and humiliating defeat," he ad-mitted. His eyes filled with tears. "The battlefield is strewn with carcasses. This is Armageddon — the final battle between good and evil. It's not money at stake, but our precious, hard-earned *reputation*." Hattrick's voice began to crack. "I pray you will join me in fighting this to the death. I'd rather die than lose this."

One year later, in March 1989, in a stunning reversal, a panel of three judges in the Second District U.S. Court of Appeals overturned the jury verdict and vacated the $2.7 million judgment, saying that Southampton officials had not violated Trupin's civil rights when they stopped construction of Dragon's Head because of noncompliance with the zoning laws. Trupin was outraged when he heard of the reversal and vowed to take the matter to the U.S. Supreme Court, but the case was turned down, and the verdict remained overturned.

That week Bill Hattrick's picture appeared on the front page of the *Southampton Press*, standing on the beach in front of Dragon's Head, as proud as a big-game hunter and his felled prey. "These are great tidings," Hattrick beamed. "Lazarus has arisen. We won! It's wonderful, really wonderful!" He was almost as happy to announce that he would not be running for mayor again that June, but would be returning full-time to being a stockbroker. He said about Barry Trupin, "History will show that this man has plowed a lot of people under. To me he is a filthy bastard."

6

EIGHT MONTHS LATER, in November 1989, Barry Trupin was holding a lavish, black-tie wedding for 200 guests at the Plaza Hotel in Manhattan to celebrate the marriage of his oldest daughter. Shortly after the Orthodox ceremony in the Terrace Room, one of the many photographers who had been taking pictures of Trupin and his guests reached into his camera bag and produced a stack of subpoenas five inches thick. The photographer casually walked over to where Trupin was standing with his family and handed him the papers. As soon as Trupin realized what he was holding, he dropped the bundle to the floor as though it had burned him. The photographer headed for the door, and Trupin herded his guests toward the grand ballroom; moments later two more men dressed in tuxedos handed Trupin several boxes, gaily wrapped like wedding gifts, filled to the brim with summonses.

Until that night, when a crack team of private investigators had been hired to infiltrate the Plaza Hotel, Trupin had for many months successfully evaded being served with over fifty *pounds* of summonses. The web of lawsuits and charges that followed Trupin for the next ten years was as dizzying and layered as his many corporate veils. Among the lawsuits, thirty-nine investors in Trupin's various companies were suing him in Manhattan Supreme Court, alleging that he lost $45 million among 600 investors in his various tax shelters and real estate deals, most of which had failed. Simultaneous to the private lawsuit, the Federal Bureau of Investigation launched an investigation into Trupin's interest in a Tustin, California, bank in which he had bought a 62 percent controlling interest and had introduced a number of loans that had to be written off as bad. The following year, in April 1990, federal regulators seized Constitution Federal Savings & Loan Association, a Monterey Park thrift in which Trupin had also bought partial ownership in 1986 for $2.6 million. It was alleged that Trupin bought into the thrift as a means of giving bad loans to his own ailing companies.

The next time Trupin made an appearance in New York was in May 1996, when he was convicted in federal district court of receiving, possessing, and selling a stolen painting. It turned out that *Le Petit Concert*, the Chagall that hung in his boat, had been stolen from the home of a Baltimore art collector. Trupin knew that the painting was stolen when he had one of his minions pay $100,000 for it in the backseat of a car on a deserted road near Kennedy Airport. He is appealing the conviction.

On February 11, 1997, Barry Trupin was indicted by the U.S. government as a tax cheat for the avoidance of $6.6 million in taxes. A grand jury indictment charged that he funneled the proceeds through various accounts until it wound up in his private stash in a bank in the British Virgin Islands. The indictment also charged Trupin with concealing the sale of his Hever Castle suit of armor for $1.5 million.

Barry Trupin currently travels a great deal and is often said to be on his yacht. He is understandably difficult to reach on the phone.

Visitors to Southampton sometimes drive off the road when they unexpectedly come upon Dragon's Head, it is still such a shock. In May 1992 Trupin sold the half-finished monstrosity to real estate developer Francesco Galesi, for the bargain price of $2.3 million. Galesi, a handsome silver-haired man, said he bought Dragon's Head to "take the curse out of it." He toned down the exterior, landscaped it, and tried to lower the towers to make the village happy, but they were fortified with cement and steel and couldn't be ripped out without destroying the walls of the original house. Eventually, the village granted Galesi the height variances he needed for the infamous southwest cupola that Trupin sought so long to have declared legal. Dragon's Head remains an eyesore and a wonder, a remnant of an ugly time.

The Pumpkin Prosecution

IN THE SMALL HOURS of December 3, 1993, advertising luminary Jerry Della Femina, fifty-seven, and his wife, Judy Licht, forty-seven, a reporter for WABC-TV in New York, were lying in bed in their ten-room, Fifth Avenue apartment, unable to sleep, waiting in silence for the sky to lighten. Later that morning, Jerry was scheduled to drive out to East Hampton and turn himself in to the police. A warrant had been sworn out for his arrest for the unlawful display of pumpkins in front of Jerry and David's Red Horse Market, a gourmet food store he co-owned on Montauk Highway. After a scare the day before about a carload of policemen coming into Manhattan to arrest him at his Madison Avenue offices, Della Femina's lawyer called the chief of police and promised that his client would cooperate and turn himself in the next day.

About five in the morning there was a timid knock at the bedroom door, and J.T., the couple's six-year-old son, appeared and asked if he could climb into bed with his mommy and daddy. "What's the matter, honey?" Judy asked, letting him snuggle under the covers with her.

"Are we going to lose everything when they put Daddy in jail?" J.T. asked. Jerry and Judy exchanged glances in the dark. J.T. had recently seen a live version of Charles Dickens's *A Christmas Carol* in which Scrooge's father is put in jail and the family is forced to live in a poorhouse.

"Of course not, J.T.," Judy said. "They're not going to put Daddy in jail, they're just going to arrest him and let him go. They don't keep you in jail for displaying pumpkins, honey." But the distinction was lost on the little boy, and he fell into a fitful sleep in his mother's arms.

Over the past few months Judy had watched in disbelief as the Pumpkin Prosecution had spun out of control. After twenty years in television journalism — and more than ten years being married to Jerry Della Femina — she had seen lots of kooky things, but nothing quite like this. It never for a moment occurred to either of them that the village would be stupid enough to actually arrest Jerry. But things had turned so nasty, no one knew what to expect anymore. "It got ridiculous," Judy said, "and frankly, I wanted out."

A lot of people were saying that Jerry brought it on himself, that when Larry Cantwell, the village administrator, told him to take away the pumpkins, claiming the design review board determined that, under the law, the pumpkins constituted an illegal sign because they were for sale (among the evidence they seized was a handwritten slate board that said, "29 cents a pound"), Jerry could have simply removed them.

After all, contrary to what Jerry claimed, the village officials insisted that he wasn't being singled out. The crackdown began months before, when they fined Espo's Surf and Sport $2,000 for displaying surfboards and beach chairs in front of the store on Main Street. Nine other stores had been warned to remove their outdoor displays of merchandise, including the A & P — and they all complied. If you didn't stop people from putting merchandise outside their shops, if the "signage" wasn't uniform, before you knew it, "East Hampton would look like Coney Island," said the architect and design review board chairman, Clayton Morey.

It was the very same Clayton Morey who had been Evan Frankel's bête noire on the town planning board. Frankel was long gone, but now Morey had Jerry Della Femina after him. After all these years, Morey had consolidated power as one of the most influential men in the village, in terms of how it looked. He had served almost forty-five years of cumulative time as chairman or member of the myriad different appeals, zoning, and design boards. Jerry described him as "the guy who's in charge of beauty. He tells people what's beautiful and what's not. If he doesn't think it's beautiful, they can't have it. This is a powerful post. He can make people squirm. He can keep them from opening a store and making a living. He can hold up their lives for months."

What pissed off Jerry most was the "Coney Island" remark. "Coney Island" is a code word among the Old East Hampton crowd. It meant the outsider, the ethnic, the newly rich. The "Coney Island" remark especially burned Jerry because part of the well-known, Jerry Della Femina Horatio Alger legend was that he grew up in Gravesend, Brooklyn, in the shadow of Coney Island; he took Morey's comment as a personal slur. Born Gennaro Tomas Della Femina, the son of Italian immigrants, he didn't even speak English until he was enrolled in school, where he was thought to be retarded and put in special classes. He went on to invent some of the most durable icons of American advertising. He created Fingerman, the talking finger that closed Ziploc bags for Dowproducts. He made the cats sing "meow, meow, meow" for Purina Cat Chow, an idea that came to him when he noticed one of the cats choking during an outtake. It was Jerry who turned Anne Meara into the Blue Nun, and it was Jerry's triumph to create Joe Isuzu, the smarmy auto salesman who turned Madison Avenue on its ear by lying about his client's cars and trucks while the truth was flashed in subtitles across the bottom of the TV screen.

He became rich and famous in the process. His audacious campaigns became Madison Avenue legend, and in 1969 he wrote a bestselling book about his adventures in the advertising trade, *From Those Wonderful Folks Who Brought You Pearl Harbor.* He became a national symbol of Madison Avenue cleverness; his partner, Ron Travisano, and he started to bill upward of $800 million a year. In 1986 he caught what seemed like the brass ring when a British advertising giant, WCRS, bought out his interest in the company for $30 million, plus a seven-figure-a-year employment contract to stay on and oversee U.S. operations.

Jerry was so clever that he even turned himself into an instantly recognizable logo. A lumbering six-footer, he had a shaved, egg-shaped dome and wore omnipresent nonprescription, dark-tinted glasses — even though he wore contact lenses — because he liked the way it looked. With his dark mustache and spreading goatee, he appeared to be one of those cartoon faces that you can turn upside down so the beard becomes hair and the smile becomes a frown. People mistake Jerry's hard stare from behind his tinted eyeglasses as menacing, but Judy says it's only the way his contact lenses make him focus. In fact, Jerry's not the least bit threatening, his friends discover. He's sweet and very funny and oddly shy. That's what made Jerry scarier to the village than, say, an obvious interloper like Barry Trupin; Jerry was insidious. Jerry gave to charities. He rescued decaying buildings. He created jobs. He opened up three major businesses: two restaurants and a gourmet food store. And his daughter, Jodi, owned part interest in a new weekly newspaper, the *Independent,* the first new paper in East Hampton in 300 years. ("When you're expecting a pogrom," Jerry said, "buy your own newspaper.")

To some, Jerry seemed rapacious. One letter writer to the *East Hampton Star* suggested that if Jerry bought any more businesses, the area might be renamed the "Della Hamptons." *New York* magazine ran a piece called "The Ad Man Who Ate the Hamptons," repeating an unfounded report that Jerry walked down Newtown

Lane one Saturday in a T-shirt that said, I'M JERRY. The most damning epitaph came from the acid pen of Michael Thomas, the "Midas Watch" columnist of the *New York Observer*, who named Jerry one of the Four Horsemen of the Hamptons Apocalypse, along with Martha Stewart, Mort Zuckerman, and publicist Peggy Siegel.

When the village administrator first ordered Jerry to remove the pumpkins from the triangle of grass in front of the Red Horse Market in October 1993, Jerry said, "No, I will not remove them. Pumpkins are not signs. Signs are advertising. Pumpkins are display. Don't tell me what advertising is." Furthermore, Jerry contended, the only reason the village was going after other outdoor displays of merchandise was so that it wouldn't look as though it was singling him out. "You are doing this to me because of *who I am*," Jerry told Clayton Morey and the design review board at one of their cantankerous meetings, a quote that appeared in the *East Hampton Star*. It's a mistake to say this in East Hampton — the hubris of "who I am." The phrase alone heats the air; everybody in East Hampton is somebody, each more privileged than the next.

Jerry not only kept the pumpkins displayed, he upped the ante by publicly taunting Clayton Morey and the design review board in the press. He took out a full-page advertisement in the *East Hampton Star*, demanding that Clayton Morey and the entire design review board resign. "I say you've let your hatred of me get in the way of your innate sense of decency," the body copy said. He invoked the American way and the Constitution, and insisted that he would continue with seasonal displays in front of Jerry and David's Red Horse Market, including Christmas trees and a Santa at Christmas, and an Easter display with an Easter Bunny. ("Oh my gosh," said the mayor, Paul F. Rickenbach Jr., "we have nothing against the Easter Bunny.")

Since the village trustees couldn't let Jerry flout the law, the East

Hampton Justice Court appointed a special prosecutor, Scott Allen, of a Brentwood, Long Island, law firm that handled the village zoning cases, to pursue the pumpkin matter. Jerry immediately dubbed the hapless Allen the "Pumpkin Prosecutor," and the name stuck. In late November 1993, after repeated requests to remove the pumpkins were ignored, the village sent a series of letters to Jerry and his partner, asking them to appear in East Hampton Justice Court before Judge James R. Ketcham as a formality, to resolve the issue. Instead, their lawyer appeared to complain that they hadn't been properly served. With Jerry and David seeming to thumb their nose at the court, in the heat of the moment, the Pumpkin Prosecutor demanded that Judge Ketcham swear out a warrant for Jerry and David's arrest. Ketcham concurred. "If we're going to do this," he said, lifting the lid on a Pandora's box, "let's go all the way." Suddenly Jerry Della Femina was a wanted man.

That balmy December morning when Jerry arrived at the Red Horse in his Range Rover, dressed in a multicolored knit sweater and tan slacks, there was a small group of reporters and photographers waiting for him. Jerry hotly contests the accusation that he had tipped off these reporters to be there, as several reporters claim. The presence of the media, and the ensuing news reportage of the Pumpkin Prosecution, became a matter of great significance to Jerry's adversaries. They pointed to it as proof of his insincerity, holding that his refusal to abide by the sign laws was part of a greater manipulation of a self-promoting huckster. Jerry was infuriated at the thought that the matter would not have been news without his having alerting the press. "How do you arrest a high-profile advertising executive, who owns three businesses in town, and not have it noticed by the press?" he demanded.

That being said, Jerry, "a walking sound bite," as Judy calls him, took full advantage of the situation. "My high school teachers voted me most likely to get the electric chair," Jerry smirked to the waiting reporters. "Thank God they did away with the death sentence in New York State." "Handcuffs will be slimming, don't you think?" he asked one reporter. Why did he want to be handcuffed? "A better photo op." "East Hampton is the only place you can get arrested for displaying pumpkins, except for Stalinist Russia," he told another. "The tangerines at the Red Horse market are on sale. They're sweet and at prices that beat the A and P."

He also openly gloated that Jerry and David's Red Horse Market was getting millions of dollars of free publicity. The market was the anchor of a handsome twenty-three-store, white-brick shopping complex on Montauk Highway and Cove Hollow Road, which lay 90 percent within the jurisdiction of the village. Jerry's partner, David Silver, fifty-four, was waiting for him inside the shop, casually dressed in a sweatshirt and sneakers. Silver wasn't very happy with all the attention, although he stood solidly with Jerry on the issue of the pumpkins. A small, pleasant man with a wry smile, Silver was the CEO of Regency Home Fashions Corporation, one of the largest home-furnishings manufacturers in the world. He lived most of the year in East Hampton with his wife and family, not far from Steven Spielberg's house. He was an alternate member of the village zoning board of appeals and an esteemed philanthropist with an interest in the welfare of local children. He got to know Jerry and Judy when he and his wife, Patti, cochaired the 1992 Planned Parenthood benefit held at Jerry's newly opened East Hampton Point restaurant, at which fireworks were supplied by the Gruccis. More than 1,000 people attended the event, a charity highlight of the summer; when Jerry asked Silver if he wanted to be his partner in a gourmet food shop at the Red Horse, Silver thought that it would be fun and wrote a six-figure check. "I came along for the ride," he said, "which I didn't expect to include being arrested."

Jerry called East Hampton police chief Glen Stonemetz from the Red Horse market to say that he and Silver were ready to be arrested and that the police could come get them. "That's not surrendering yourself," Stonemetz replied. He suggested that they just go on down to the court building on Pantigo Road and present themselves, and forget about being arrested.

"No, no," Jerry insisted, "I *want* to be arrested. I'm turning myself in at the police station."

With a caravan of reporters following, Jerry and David drove to the police station and presented themselves at the front desk. A young female police officer, Janice Beedenbender, escorted them into a small room, where she explained, somewhat apologetically, that it was the police department's policy to handcuff everyone. They extended their arms, and the officer fastened the steel bracelets lightly around each man's wrists. Then Jerry and David were led out a back door into the parking lot, where a police car was waiting to take them to the courthouse.

As soon as they stepped from the shadow of the police station, they could hear the camera shutters going off. Jerry began to take tiny steps to give the photographers time to get all the pictures they wanted. For a moment it seemed so surreal that he wanted to laugh, and he bit his bottom lip. But in another instant it stopped being funny; David Silver's nine-year-old daughter, Annie, who was watching from the sidelines with her mother, began to sob. Silver had promised his concerned child that despite what she heard from the other children in school, he was *not* going to jail and had promised her that she could come to court to watch and that he would drive home with her afterward. But the sight of her father in handcuffs overwhelmed the child, and her sobbing could be heard above the sound of the shutters clicking.

"It became a very bad feeling," Jerry said. "I tried to remember how ludicrous the situation was, but the only word I can think of to describe how it felt is *disgusting*." Jerry and David were put in the back of a police cruiser and were driven to the courthouse, the reporters and cameramen trailing behind. The image of Jerry being led away in handcuffs, biting his lip and smirking a bit, went out over the wire services that night, and the story about the wealthy man who was arrested by the uptight town for displaying pumpkins appeared in newspapers across the United States, and as far away as London.

In the police car, Jerry turned to David and said, "A few months from now you'll forget, and you'll stop being angry, but I'm going to kill those fuckers for this. They are really going to die."

2

EAST HAMPTON is the "Land of No." Its physical appearance is probably one of the most highly regulated in America. It is a trophy town, filled with trophy houses that are owned by some of the most opinionated tastemakers of the twentieth century. In East Hampton people are very self-conscious about the way things look. The reactionary, literate, and very vocal population gets stirred to noisy debate over things as small as whether the color of the bulbs on the Christmas trees that line Main Street should be blue or white. The stated raison d'être of almost every one of these debates has always been "to preserve the historical character of the town."

There are dozens of local organizations riding posse on taste offenders in East Hampton, from the Ladies Village Improvement Society to the town and village design review boards. The town would have instituted an architectural review board too, if it wasn't illegal to tell a citizen how to design his or her own house, and even some design issues are obliquely controlled through the town and village planning and zoning appeals boards, like denying homes taller than two stories. East Hampton is one of the only towns in America to have a resident architectural historian, whose responsibilities include driving around the village and looking at people's houses to make sure they're not changing them. There's even a woman whose sole job is to search out and tear down illegal yard-sale signs tacked on trees and poles. Backing up all this is a byzantine codex of rules and ordinances that govern the size, location, and appearance of almost everything in East Hampton — even the dress of people on the street. In 1954 the village adopted a law prohibiting the exposure of breasts, buttocks, or other body parts and disallowing any person from wearing a bathing suit farther than 500 feet from the water; in 1970 miniskirts were banned outright.

The signage law that Jerry Della Femina crossed is one of the most strictly enforced. The village passed its very first signage ordinance in 1921, just a year after it was incorporated. By that time the highway already had eighty billboards, and the women of the Ladies Village Improvement Society actually went out with saws and hatchets and cut them to the ground, so that by 1926 East Hampton was known as the "signless town." Currently the size, color, and placement of all signs in the village must be pre-approved by the design Review Board. A retail store's awning can have only the name of the store on the flap, not what it sells. Nothing sold inside the store can be placed outside, not even newspapers on a wire rack. Nor are florists allowed to have wagons of colorful flowers in front of their stores. Even roadside farm stands are regulated — they have to grow on their own land 80 percent of whatever is displayed.

Neon signs have also been banned, even those already in place are being slowly phased out. A neon sign inside a place of business in the village — for example, a sign for a brand of beer — has to be hidden so that it can't be seen through the window from the street and, in any event, at least four feet from the entrance. Stickers on the front door, including those for credit cards, must be orderly and leave 80 percent of the door unobscured. Vending machines with lights are forbidden. Bottle-redemption machines are banned from in front of the A & P. Except for ice cream, stores are not allowed to sell take-out food, on the principle that it would be unseemly for people to eat while walking up and down the streets. Entire kinds of businesses are outlawed in the village as well, including car dealerships, convenience stores, and gas stations, except for the ones already there. The design review board has also banned the display of outdoor art in the historical district; even Guild Hall, the repository of the town's artistic heritage, was once forced to remove the sculptures of artists William King and Tony Rosenthal from its front lawn. "East Hampton has an image to uphold," King griped. "Prissy and tearoomy."

All these strictures and covenants are imposed in an already contentious atmosphere. Lawsuits and legal brawls are rife between the town and its citizens, neighbor against neighbor, for many reasons similar to the causes of so many libel lawsuits in East Hampton in the 1600s: to define status and turf. Also there are so many "killers" in the Hamptons, as Jerry puts it. Not many of its denizens arrived there by being mediocre in their endeavors. A lucky few might have inherited their money, but most of the newcomers in the Hamptons made their money by being the toughest, most competitive in their fields. "It's very difficult to believe," Jerry said, "that people who work twenty-four hours a day Monday through Friday doing what they do, which includes screwing people out of things, would stop screwing people on Saturday and Sunday."

Inarguably, the summer weekend crowd finds it hard to leave the aggression of Manhattan behind. They arrive in droves each year with a sense of entitlement, and the level of rudeness and violence palpably rises. ("The Hamptons are so beautiful," sighed one fashion editor from Italy, "but so violent.") The local newspapers annually carry editorials beseeching civility on the streets and roadways, and in the late eighties the East Hampton Chamber of Commerce tried to launch a "Be Cool" campaign, which presumably failed. During the summer season the local papers are filled with reports of visitors in their $80,000 luxury cars having punch-outs over parking spots, or shoving matches at East Hampton's swanky foodstuffs store, the Barefoot Contessa, over who will get the last of the wheat berry salad. Motorists can't seem to be bothered to pull to the side of the road to let an ambulance through — and as for the local authorities, a few summers ago an irate Manhattan woman beat a police officer with a baguette for trying to give her a ticket.

Spoiled people get frustrated easily in East Hampton, in part because it is the great sociological leveler: Everybody is rich or famous. Celebrities and millionaires are chock-a-block, many richer and more famous than Jerry Della Femina. Fame has never proved to be an advantage with the establishment. Faye Dunaway found out how unmoved the village zoning board of appeals was by her acting ability when she made a tearful appearance at a meeting in an attempt to get permission to build a swimming pool in the wetlands behind her house off Egypt Lane. Standing at a podium in Town Hall, she spoke dramatically of her son's need to learn to swim, her eyes tearing. When she was finished, one of the board members, a Bonacker with fifteen generations behind him, said to her, "Miss Dunaway, we have a Maidstone Club up there you can join and let your son swim anytime he wants, you know? But we can't let you build a swimming pool in the wetlands." Of course, the Maidstone Club would never accept Faye Dunaway, not that she would join anyway. She sold the house and moved away.

The various boards sometimes seem guilty of caprice when confronted with power and unlimited money. Developer and onetime *New York Post* owner Peter Kalikow spent $40,000 to success-fully petition the zoning board of appeals for permission to build a floating dock in Three Mile Harbor to accommodate his 137-foot yacht, and then he was denied permission to build a catwalk to get to it. It took Paul Simon more than three years to find a sunny spot on his Montauk property to put a swimming pool that would satisfy the various zoning boards and environmental agencies, and the zon-ing board of appeals flat-out turned down violinist Itzhak Perlman's request to build a tennis court on a piece of property that didn't have a house on it. (Perlman has a sign in front of his house that says OLE KESEF, which loosely translates from Hebrew as "serious money.")

The zoning board of appeals frequently becomes the arbiter of disputes between neighbors. The zoning board of appeals denied resident movie stars Alec Baldwin and Kim Basinger a variance to enlarge their Amagansett farmhouse in anticipation of Basinger's be-coming pregnant. The Baldwins' neighbor's complained to the board that because the house stood only eleven feet from the property line, the new roofline would cut off their sunlight, and a taller chimney would spew soot in their direction. (A few years later, when Basinger did become pregnant, the couple sold the Amagansett farmhouse and moved north of the highway to a historical eighteenth-century, eight-acre farm called Stony Hill, which they purchased for the very good price of $1.7 million. This is the same farm on which Arthur Miller and Marilyn Monroe spent their honeymoon sum-mer together and is the setting of his play *After the Fall.*

A contingent from the village zoning board also once marched through the bedroom of Lee Radziwill, the sister of Jacqueline Onassis, and her husband, film director Herb Ross, to look out their window to decide whether a neighbor's wall was a "fence" or a "wall." Eighty-one-year-old Alice Lawrence, the widow of Sylvan Lawrence, the man who owned a good many of the office buildings on Wall Street, had built a vast, dramatic modern house of concrete and marble on the dunes right next to the Rosses. It had a sweeping gray roofline like the TWA terminal at Kennedy Airport and an ornamental wall that obliterated their western light and view. The house was so bizarre-looking that it quickly became one of the famous architectural atrocities of the Hamptons, like Dragon's Head, and all day long people would drive down the street to gape at it. Much to the Rosses' distress, after peering carefully out of the bedroom window, the board determined that because the wall had living space in it, it could stay. The Rosses planted trees, and Mrs. Sylvan put the house for sale at the reduced price of $12.5 million, with no takers in sight.

The ugliest of all Hamptons celebrity slugouts is the ongoing feud between Martha Stewart and the notorious real estate developer, Harry Macklowe, over their shared property line on Georgica Pond. Stewart and her daughter Alexis are ubiquitous in the Hamptons. Martha is a regular presence at fund-raisers and parties, frequently photographed in the local press; Alexis owns a motel and a gym. Martha owns two houses in East Hampton (in addition to a house in Connecticut). Her Lily Pond Lane house is an archetypical *Martha Stewart Living* showcase: a twenty-room Victorian-style shingled house that can be seen daily in the opening credits of her syndicated TV show. Located in the area known as Divinity Hill, this former 1878 home of Reverend DeWitt Talmage has become one of the most photographed and fussed-over houses in the Hamptons — and a giant tax write-off.

But the house that is really Stewart's passion is her second home, a stark two-bedroom residence that Gordon Bunshaft designed for himself on a wedged-shaped piece of land on Georgica Pond. This is the house that shares a property line with Harry Macklowe, a tough New Yorker who first came to public attention in 1985 when in the middle of the night he illegally tore down two single-occupancy hotels that he owned on Times Square, to beat a city ban on razing housing for the indigent. When Stewart moved into the Bunshaft house, she had workmen clear away dead brush between their properties, and it started a war. Macklowe claimed that Stewart cleared protected wetlands, some of it on his land, to better her view. He accused her of trespassing on his property and of violating village code and wetlands laws. In retaliation, he planted a stand of fourteen-foot evergreens and installed high-powered spotlights on the boundary line. Not only did the trees block Stewart's view of the pond, she claimed that some of them were on her property. When Stewart repeatedly had a surveyor mark off which trees were on her land, the surveyor's stakes mysteriously disappeared overnight. Macklowe's lawyers then moved to have Stewart evicted from her house by appealing her certificate of occupancy, claiming that she had illegally built a kitchen and bath in an accessory building on the property. While that battle continued in court, Stewart's lawyers asked the East Hampton zoning board of appeals for permission to remove fourteen of the offending trees and bushes planted on her property, and to tear out the lighting. Knowing that the moment the board granted her permission to cut down the trees, Macklowe's lawyers would get a restraining order, Stewart had a team of twenty landscapers with chainsaws and environmental consultants standing by. As soon as the board gave their okay, most of the trees were cut down and bushes ripped out before Macklowe was able to get an official notice to desist. One of the zoning board members called it "Showdown at the O.K. Corral."

The nastiness reached operatic status when in the summer of 1997 Stewart arrived at her house to discover a crew of landscapers building a fence between her property and Macklowe's and flew into a rage. While she was simultaneously cursing and making frantic calls for help on her cell phone, she backed her vehicle up against

Matthew Munnich, one of the workmen, pinning him against a fence pole and reportedly bruising his torso. The local police were called to the scene, but they declined to press charges. Munnich reportedly appealed to the district attorney's office to convene a grand jury and have Stewart arrested for attempted murder, but the D.A. declined without comment. The various matters with Macklowe over the property line are before a New York State Supreme Court of Appeals, and legal fees for each side are estimated to be approaching $500,000.

Other contretemps have been settled with finesse more worthy of the Hamptons reputation as a place of refinement. In 1985 Mort Zuckerman, then publisher of *U.S. News & World Report* and future owner of the *New York Daily News*, righteously offended his neighbors, Frances Ann Dougherty, the heiress to the Cannon bath towel fortune, and her husband, Frazer Dougherty, founder of the local television station, LTV, by installing an eight-foot-diameter satellite dish high on the dunes in front of his Lily Pond Lane house, which he bought from Pete Peterson, chairman of the Blackstone Group, for only $1 million because it was so exposed to the beach. (Peterson moved to Watermill, where he bought a $7.5 million waterfront estate.) Although having a satellite dish wasn't illegal, it stuck out on the horizon like a sore thumb. Zuckerman rebuffed the requests of the Doughertys and other neighbors to remove it, saying that the dish had to be positioned where it was for the best reception.

Mrs. Dougherty called the publisher "a spoiled brat" and, instead of phoning up her lawyers, turned to local sculptor William King. The Doughertys commissioned King to build and install on their property a forty-foot-high depiction of Don Quixote, complete with a soaring aluminum lance, from which was strung a thirty-foot-long assault banner of orange sailcloth, charging the offending satellite dish. It was a mocking comment, visible for all to see along the beach. "Don Quixote was chosen," Frazer Dougherty said, "because Quixote was the greatest champion of beauty ... against the philistines, and he never stopped trying."

Zuckerman knew when he was beat by a metaphor. His office issued the statement "Don Quixote has had so few victories over time that Mr. Zuckerman has decided to take down the satellite dish until the trees have grown large enough to shield it." The neighbors have lived in great harmony since.

3

IN 1988 a real estate broker took Jerry Della Femina and Judy Licht to see the house right next door to Mort Zuckerman's. It was a three-level brick mansion, a fixer-upper, high on a dune, with a bargain price tag of $3.4 million. The property had been purchased as an investment by Hartz Mountain CEO Leonard Stern and had been uninhabited for many years. When they first laid eyes on it, the house was so run-down that Judy wouldn't even get out of the car when the broker pulled into the driveway. Jerry dutifully climbed the grade to see the view. "When I got to the top," Jerry said, "the weeds were so high, you couldn't see over them, so I parted them, and there was the ocean." Not just the ocean, but a chunk of sand, water, and sky. Jerry didn't even bother to go inside the house. He turned around, climbed back down to the car, and knocked on the window. "You'd better get out," he said to Judy, "I'm buying the house."

There is a rare dynamic between Jerry Della Femina and Judy Licht, as much a synergy as it is a marriage. To experience the two of them together cajoling, adoring, interrupting, is like being in the presence of a legendary fit, like Molly and Fibber McGee, or Dagwood and Blondie. Jerry and Judy are so entertaining that they even taped five pilot episodes of a TV talk show together. Judy is the star, well spoken, irrepressibly candid, and always charming, with her trademark thousand-watt smile and giant blue eyes. At WABC-TV she's called the "sparkplug" of the evening newscast. She grew up in Brooklyn, not far from Jerry, and although warmer than Jerry, she has street smarts developed as a reporter on the streets of New York and does not suffer fools gladly either.

She met Jerry when she was a workaholic reporter doing upbeat human-interest stories for WNEW-TV in New York and Jerry was the wise-ass advertising executive who wrote the slogan "The Magic Is Back" for the New York Mets. ("The magic wasn't back," Jerry said. "They sucked.") They were both separated from their first spouses — Judy had been married six years to a Broadway stage manager — and were dating other people. She expected to loathe the smart-alec advertising mogul, but when she arrived at his offices with a camera crew in tow, she was struck by how shy he was off camera, and gentlemanly. After the interview they exchanged phone numbers and for the next three years became nightly phone pals, addicted to calling each other late at night to compare notes before falling asleep, all the time dating other people. It took her a while before it dawned on her that she loved the guy. "As corny as it sounds," Judy said, "this marriage developed as a friendship."

They married in 1983, in a penthouse overlooking Lincoln Center; not long after, Judy did something that she previously thought impossible; she stopped working to have two children, a daughter, Jessie, born in 1985, and a son, J.T., born in 1988. When the kids were old enough, Judy resumed her TV career, juggling being a TV personality, mother, and wife to a controversial advertising man — all with such aplomb that the National Mother's Day Committee named her an Outstanding Mother of America.

Judy wasn't a Hamptons person before they bought the house next to Mort Zuckerman's, but she fell in love quickly enough.

The house was just off Lily Pond Lane, the oceanfront "Park Avenue" of East Hampton, famous for its Gatsbyesque mansions set on towering dunes, with green lawns so vast that the semicircular driveways look like small racetracks. The wide lane, once almost exclusively the address of Maidstone Club members, now boasted a more eclectic assortment of neighbors, including corporate raider Carl Ichan; Westchester developer Lowell Schulman; New York developer Sheldon Solow; and TV gossip personality Claudia Cohen, who lives in the house she bought from her ex-husband, Ron Perelman, when their marriage ended. Lily Pond's most recent arrival is Howard Schultz, the CEO of Starbucks Coffee, who bought the Gwathmey-designed home of financier Robert Steinberg. The lane also boasts the home of Loida Lewis, an attorney and the widow of Reginald Lewis, the former chairman of TLC Beatrice International Holdings, Inc.

Judy and Jerry put a million dollars into the renovation of the house. They whitewashed the brick, restored the terraced walks and gardens, and installed an oceanside, gun-metal-blue gunite pool. The interior of the house was rebuilt, with six bedrooms, tented dining room, oceanfront kitchen, and wood-paneled den with large picture windows overlooking the beach. The first five years they lived there were sheer bliss for Judy and Jerry. "Nobody knew we were around," she remembered wistfully. "Jerry would cook funny, sloppy pasta dinners for friends and family, and we would stay home a lot. It was dreamy, and we fell more in love with East Hampton."

By the early 1990s, things were not going as dreamily for Jerry back in the city. The huge British conglomerate that owned him, WCRS, had sold his company to an even bigger French company, EuroRSCG, and Jerry had instant contempt for the elegant French advertising men who were his new bosses. He was suddenly one spoke in a very large international wheel. "The French reduced my role," Jerry said, "to being Ed Sullivan who introduced the acts." It didn't help corporate relations any when he began to publicly refer to the new French owners as "the Frogs." All this happened at a time when Madison Avenue was moving away from the kind of flippant, outrageous campaigns that had put Jerry on the map, and his agency began to leak accounts, including big spenders like Isuzu and Dow. In June 1992 Jerry was forced out of his own company by EuroRSCG. The French bought out the remainder of his employment contract for $3 million, and he was obligated not only to leave the business he had founded but to relinquish the rights to the name Della Femina as well. Jerry formed his own small agency, Jerry Inc., but the glory days were gone. He packed his bags and moved pretty much full-time to his Lily Pond Lane palace.

"I knew," he said, "and this was a real thought, that I had to reinvent myself. There were a lot of headlines in the *Wall Street Journal* and the *Times*. People see those headlines and then, maybe fifteen years later, they see you and say, 'Hey, I remember him.' So I decided to reinvent myself with another high-profile, high-risk business — my own restaurant. There's something about a restaurant that makes it . . . theater — your name is out there, people are talking about it, waiting for you to fail, waiting for you to succeed." When Jerry told Judy that he intended to open his own restaurant, she wanted to punch him. "Do you know the number of an all-night divorce lawyer?" she asked him.

In the summer of 1992, in short order, along with business partners Ben Krupinski, a successful local builder and speculator, and Larry Dunst, another wealthy advertising executive, Jerry went on an East Hampton spending spree. On June 29, 1992, he bought a down-on-its-heels 200-seat restaurant and forty-eight-slip marina situated on picturesque Three Mile Harbor, for $3.2 million, and completely refurbished it as the snazzy East Hampton Point; on July 29, he bought the Red Horse shopping complex, an abandoned, weed-covered eyesore on Montauk Highway, for $1.3 million, and tossed in another million or so to restore it; and he bought his favorite property, a building at Ninety-nine North Main Street in which to open Della Femina's.

It made perfect sense that Jerry would want to open a namesake restaurant just when restaurant life in the East End had taken on such desperate importance. For nearly 100 years, summer visitors hardly thought about going to a restaurant. Home-cooked meals were part of the summer weekend tradition, or summer visitors went to dinner parties at the homes of friends or to the club. Even if one was inclined to eat out, there weren't many restaurants to chose from, except for a few provincial grills that served local duck or Italian food. The economics of a four-month season made running a first-rate restaurant financially unfeasible. But as the decades passed, the East End slowly began to change from just a summer place to more of a year-round weekend getaway, and with the arrival of the socially ambitious baby boomers — a generation whose cultural life in Manhattan revolved around eating in trendy restaurants — there was a general champing at the bit to find a place to show off.

In 1988 restaurateur Pino Luongo, who owned Le Madri in Manhattan, kicked things into high gear by opening a handsome, high-priced Italian eatery called Sapore Di Mare, on Georgica Creek. When word spread that Sapore was grossing $2 million a year, other upscale, Manhattan-quality restaurants began to appear in every hamlet, most notably, Nick & Toni's on North Main Street, in East Hampton. Owned by Toni Ross, the daughter of the late Time Warner chief, and restaurateur Jeff Salaway ("Nick" was his college nickname), this small Italian restaurant in an unprepossessing wood-frame house managed to capture the Hamptons 1990s zeitgeist of high finance and show business royalty in much the same way Studio 54 became emblematic of its era. There are no velvet ropes, but for the new money, getting a table at Nick & Toni's, and sitting shoulder to shoulder with the big names of the new Hamptons — Steven Spielberg, Martha Stewart, Ronald Lauder, Ron Perelman, Wilbur Ross — has became a ticket to instant Hamptons social validation of its own sort.

Jerry knew there was room for another high-profile, A-list restaurant, and he wanted it to be his. The building he and his partners bought to refurbish on North Main Street had for many years been the home to a dingy Chinese restaurant, famous among certain circles as a place where it was easier to buy a gram of cocaine from one of the characters sitting at the bar than it was to get an egg roll. In the back of Jerry's mind he expected that he and his partners would be hailed as heroes for renovating and glamorizing this small corner of the village into a handsome redbrick-and-green-trim restaurant with large French doors. But when he appeared before Clayton Morey and the design review board for the final approval on the exterior, the dialogue was quite different.

Indicating a drawing of the plan, Clayton Morey said, "You know, there's this blank wall, and when you drive into town from Springs you see it. If you could cover it somehow, maybe you could keep it from being this big, cold wall."

Jerry thought to himself that it had been a big cold wall for as long as anybody could remember, but he kept his mouth shut. He came back to the board the next week with a new drawing and a new plan. "I said I'd put up a picket fence," Jerry recounted "with a lawn and flowers and vines covering the wall."

Clayton Morey said, "Wait a minute. If you put grass over here, somebody is going to take their drinks outside, and the next thing you know, there'll be outdoor dining. As you know, we can't allow outdoor dining in East Hampton. But if you sign a document saying that you'll never have outdoor dining, then we'll give you a certificate of occupancy to open."

"Wait a minute," Jerry said, "Does the design review board have the authority to grant me outdoor dining?"

"Well . . . no," Morey said.

"So then, you're not empowered to take it away either."

At this there was heated debate among the agitated board members; minutes later they grudgingly voted to give Jerry's restaurant a certificate of occupancy. Jerry went home triumphant, and the following week invitations were mailed for an opening party on August 8. Yet just two days before opening, Jerry was at home in Heaven's Gate when he was informed that the design review board had later reconvened in an emergency session and rescinded the restaurant's certificate of occupancy. He was told that Clayton Morey and the board felt railroaded, that they had second thoughts about giving the go-ahead, and that unless he signed a document stating he would not have outdoor dining, he could not open. If he hurried, he had just enough time to cancel the party.

Jerry was standing in the kitchen of his home, looking at the ocean, when he dialed Clayton Morey at his condominium on Pantigo Road. "*You fuck!*" Jerry roared at him. "I am going to *kill* you! I am going to *destroy* you!"

Said Morey, "That Jerry has got the biggest ego. There's nothing like his ego. He surrounded himself with yes men and when somebody said no to him, they got fired. Well, he couldn't fire me."

After things calmed down a bit, and Jerry threatened to take full-page ads in the local papers, Morey and the design review board decided to give Jerry his certificate of occupancy after all, without the no-outdoor-dining pledge, as long as he guaranteed he wouldn't enlarge his seating capacity. Della Femina's opened in August 1993 with a celebrity-packed gala, and it has been packing them in ever since. The *New York Times* awarded Della Femina's three stars, and the eighty-one-seat eatery generates an estimated revenue of $180,000 per seat annually. The ugly wall in question is covered by a trellis and vines and has never looked prettier, and there has never been any outdoor dining.

But there was blood of honor spilled on the streets of East Hampton. A little more than a year later, when Jerry was told to remove the pumpkins, he said no.

4

JERRY DELLA FEMINA and David Silver were arraigned by Judge James R. Ketcham on twenty-seven violations of the East Hampton village sign laws and were released on their own recognizance. The public-relations backlash was swift. Screenwriter-director Nora Ephron had T-shirts printed that said, FREE THE EAST HAMPTON 2. Writer Suzanne O'Malley offered to create a Della Femina Defense Fund, and a friend of Jerry's sent him a chocolate cake with a file inside. The upcoming trial, predicted *Newsday*, would be "East Hampton's version of the Scopes monkey trial."

It turned out that there was no trial. Several months later Judge Ketcham dismissed twenty-three of the twenty-seven counts against Jerry and David, saying that the pumpkins "failed to utilize letters, words, or figures" and under the law could not be considered signs. Ketcham later recused himself from the case, and the Pumpkin Prosecution was moved to neighboring Southampton, where on March 22, 1994, Judge Edward Burke dismissed the remaining charges "in the name of justice."

"A pumpkin is what it's been since the beginning of time," Jerry exalted outside the courthouse, "and that's a pumpkin."

But Jerry was far from finished with the village. Even before the charges against him were dismissed, he lodged two federal lawsuits, one challenging the constitutionality of the sign law, the other claiming that his civil rights had been violated by the village, charging "false arrest, malicious prosecution, and false imprisonment." He was asking $500,000 in damages and demanding a jury trial, saying that he hoped the village board members lived long lives, "because I'm going to sue them until either I'm dead or they're dead."

David Silver did not join Jerry in the lawsuit against the village. Although he was "behind Jerry from the start" on the issues, he felt that his point was made when the charges were dismissed. Silver instead turned his energies to raising $5 million to build a much-needed recreation center for local children. He was still punished for his involvement in the Pumpkin Prosecution. He was turned out of his seat on the village planning board, he was told, for having been party to an incident that was perceived to publicly embarrass the village.

"The cartoon version of what happened," Judy Licht said, "is that Jerry was the brash outsider, and the traditional people picked on him. But this was something deeper, this was happening long before we ever got there. Evan Frankel was possibly another example, and it was probably happening for thirty years before that. What was different about Jerry is that he's not very Christian when he's crossed. He became a lightning rod. He brought it out into the open. He became a symbol of every newcomer who ever wanted to do something in East Hampton and was told he couldn't. But what happened in the briar patch that is the Hamptons is, that like Tar Baby and Brer Rabbit, they wanted to stick it to him, and instead they got stuck."

In 1996, while his lawsuit was still wending its way through federal court, Jerry Della Femina decided that in the grand old American way of political dissent, he would run for village trustee. He noted that in the past 401 votes, the town board had voted unanimously 400 times and that the 1,500 residents of East Hampton village were so complacent with the status quo, the village board had been composed of practically the same men for the past fifteen years. In the last election, the races for trustee and mayor went uncontested. Two of the trustee seats were up for grabs in 1996, and although the election was a runoff, and candidates didn't run against anyone specifically, Jerry announced that he *was* running against one trustee in particular, William C. Heppenheimer III, one of the most respected and influential men in East Hampton.

5

VILLAGE TRUSTEE William C. Heppenheimer III — "Heppy," as he was known at the Maidstone Club, where he was a past president (1973–79) and third-generation member — lived in a large shingled house on Cove Hollow Farm, located on one of the knuckles of land that protrudes onto Georgica Pond. As a village trustee, he was always impeccably dressed in public, often in tan slacks and blue blazer, but at home dressed casually, like a gentleman farmer, in blue jeans, green sweater, and expensive hiking boots. Seventy-five years old, Heppenheimer had a ruddy complexion and cold blue eyes. Although he mumbled a little and mispronounced names (he repeatedly called Harry Macklowe "Matlow"), he was fit for his age, continuing to ski in the winter and vacation in Montana in the summer. His mother's family were Millers, one of the oldest names in the village, and his father's family, he said, have roots back to the *Mayflower*. Heppenheimer's aunt and uncle once owned all the land on which he sat, Cove Hollow Farms, which over the past ten years he has subdivided into an elite pondview community of homes in the $5–$10 million range. Before Heppenheimer went into real estate development, he was a retired executive at a printing ink company. It was from Heppenheimer that

Steven Spielberg and Steve Ross bought the stretch of farmland just across the pond from their homes to protect their view.

Heppenheimer was eager to be interviewed about the village and its problems but was wary of being quoted. This predicament is a little like that of the village itself: anxious to have its say in affairs, but not willing to take the responsibility that goes with it. Heppenheimer admitted he was, frankly, afraid of Jerry Della Femina and stirring up a hornet's nest that he believed was at rest. He handily defeated Jerry in the village trustee race, and the civil rights lawsuit had been settled. In any event, the village officials already had more trouble on their hands. Developer Harry Macklowe was suing them now, for much the same reasons Jerry did, saying that village officials had an "all-out vendetta against him," accusing them of favoring Martha Stewart in their property dispute.

Bad publicity. Heppenheimer believed it was that kind of bad publicity, and the publicity Jerry generated, that's really hurt East Hampton. He thought these new people were arrogant, that they had no respect for rules. He was astonished to be told that Jerry may have polarized the Them versus Us issue in East Hampton, because according to Heppenheimer, Them versus Us simply did not exist. "That's their vision," he said. "I'm objective and I don't see it. The new people could fit right in," he added. "They could go to the beach or join the tennis club."

"Are you married?" he asked a visitor to his spacious home, which was decorated in cheery white and yellows. The pond glittered just beyond the large windows of his book-filled den, the sun hard and bright, and across the way, Calvin Klein's mansion stood darkly against the dunes. An old yellow Labrador retriever stretched out on the carpet at Heppenheimer's feet. "The Maidstone Club is a family place," he said, for "families," and for "families with kids." He was affronted to hear that the Maidstone Club might be thought anti-Semitic, because as he said, there were now several Jewish members.

He was even more affronted when his visitor pointed out to him, after he suggested that East Hampton could "look like Coney Island" if rules weren't adhered to, that in some quarters "Coney Island" is believed to be a code word. Heppenheimer was outraged, in fact.

For two years before Jerry ran against Heppenheimer, ostensibly for trustee, the advertising executive had been excoriating him in a weekly column he began writing in the *Independent*, the newspaper his daughter, Jodi, had founded with several partners in 1993. Jerry bought a 20 percent interest in the newspaper in 1994 and awarded himself a column, called "Jerry's Ink." Although the circulation of the weekly *Independent* was less than 10,000 at the time, "Jerry's Ink" became some of the best-read 1,000 words in the East End. The column was just like him — clever, outrageous, and for many, too close to the bone. Some of the columns, although perhaps perfectly honest, seemed too ruthlessly mean, even nasty, and they began to divide public opinion about him. In describing his inspiration for the columns, he once wrote that a little devil alighted on his shoulder and said, "Go make fun of them."

"Them" were usually Clayton Morey, Bill Heppenheimer, and the village's respected mayor, Paul F. Rickenbach Jr., who was a former East Hampton police detective and onetime estate manager for Time Warner's Steve Ross and other wealthy residents. Jerry described Rickenbach as a former "house-sitter . . . a fine house-sitter from what I've heard, since nobody has reported their houses missing recently." In one column Jerry suggested that he might enlist his dog, Jackson, to run for mayor against Rickenbach in the next election, although Jackson bit people. Among other talents Jackson had that Rickenbach did not, Jerry wrote, was that "Jackson could lick himself. . . . Anyway, it would be better to be known as East Hampton the town with the dog mayor than East Hampton the town who handcuffs a merchant."

As for Heppenheimer, Jerry accused him of being "the man who pulls all the strings in the village of East Hampton." Jerry wrote a column in which he tried to enlist his Thanksgiving turkey to run for trustee against Heppenheimer. When the turkey reveals to Jerry that he's Jewish ("Reformed," the turkey explains), Jerry is unabashed. "I must confess," he wrote, "the thought of running a Jewish turkey against trustee Heppenheimer amuses me."

It did not amuse Heppenheimer. Indeed, the columns drove Heppenheimer and his colleagues "up the wall," he said. But no matter how nasty Jerry got, Heppenheimer and the other village officials made a pact not to publicly respond. They managed to keep a stiff upper lip for more than a year of taunting, until finally someone responded for them, if unofficially. Few could have had better credentials than Averill Dayton Geus, a woman whose ancestors founded the village of East Hampton, who was the manager of the Home, Sweet Home Museum, and who was the author of the elegantly written commemorative book *The Maidstone Club, The Second Fifty Years, 1941 to 1991* (Jeannette Rattray wrote about the first fifty years). Mrs. Geus wrote not to the *Independent*, where Jerry's column appeared, but to the *East Hampton Star*, and brought the issue of Them versus Us into the bas-relief of black-and-white. Mrs. Geus dubbed Jerry's column "Jerrysink," and Jerry himself, "Mr. DeMeena." She called him a "misguided, misinformed wannabe set loose in the Hamptons." She said he was a "short-term resident with a beach-baked brain" and called him "New York ego gone berserk." She lectured him on the sign laws and the town history, and added, "He should know we have been bullied many times through the years by more famous people.... We are still here. They are not."

The following week, Judy Licht responded on her husband's behalf. "Silly Jerry," she wrote. "He actually believes that hard work and democracy can take the place of years of refinement and good breeding. I'm sure the Indians felt the same way about your ancestors as you feel about my husband. It's called the 'there goes the neigh-borhood' syndrome. Certainly you can crush my husband the same way your ancestors crushed those ungrateful Indians. And believe me, he deserves some crushing. The man is a hopeless egomaniac who thinks that just because he employs over 100 village citizens in his establishments, he has the right to have some measure of control over his own life."

In the spring of 1996 Jerry officially announced that he was run-ning for trustee on his own ticket, the Village Party. The three men up for reelection, Heppenheimer, Mayor Rickenbach, and trustee Edwin L. Sherrill, a twenty-one-year veteran of the board whose family roots in East Hampton went back to the 1700s, marshaled forces and formed the Hook Mill Party. "We took his challenge very seriously," Heppenheimer said. "With Jerry, you had no choice. If Jerry had gotten on the board, he would have wrecked it." Another independent candidate, Tony Minardi, a local businessman and owner of a fish store, joined the race under the East Hampton Party banner. One small blessing was that as soon as Jerry announced his candidacy, he was obligated to stop writing columns about political issues in the *Independent*.

Heppenheimer still couldn't help but laugh out loud when he thought about the campaign. "You gotta say it was a comedy," he said, chuckling. "East Hampton had never seen anything like it. In the past, village elections were low, low key." So relaxed, in fact, that one year the incumbent didn't even bother to vote for himself. "I ran four times myself and never raised a penny," Heppenheimer said. "You didn't have to. But with Jerry coming into the picture, we raised thirty-six thousand dollars." That turned out to be only half the $70,000 campaign fund that Jerry put together, mainly from his own pocket. It was the most money ever spent on a village election in the history of New York State.

Jerry, whom the Hook Mill Party described as "unsuited" for

public office, characterized the campaign as "past nasty and headed for dirty" for the *New York Times*. Trustee Sherrill gravely warned the voters, "A former mayor once told me that once the outsiders take the village away from us, we'll never get it back." Rickenbach agreed that the situation was dire. "In some factions," the mayor said, "this is being looked at as a potential hostile takeover of the village." Everybody grumbled about "Madison Avenue muscle" taking over Main Street.

The campaign reached some sort of a nadir the night of the televised debate, shown locally on cable channel 27, LTV, one week before the June 18 election. The general tone of the evening was set in the opening moments when Heppenheimer, meeting Jerry face-to-face for the first time, refused to shake his hand. The bad feeling escalated after Edwin Sherrill called Jerry an "asshole" under his breath, clearly picked up by his lapel microphone and broadcast over the air. And the discussion completely disintegrated when Mayor Rickenbach contemptuously accused Jerry of running for trustee out of a "personal vendetta" over the Pumpkin Prosecution.

"I *won!*" Jerry insisted. "I don't have any vendetta! I *won*. People who *lose* have a vendetta. I won."

"The charges were *dismissed*, you didn't win!" Heppenheimer interjected.

"You alleged your civil rights were violated!" the mayor hissed at Jerry. "You *poor guy!* You *media mogul!* You *advertising guru!* You brought Madison Avenue onto Main Street in East Hampton, and that's not what we're all about. Learn to live in East Hampton and embrace and work with the community, Jerry."

A record number of voters turned out at the polls — 857 of them, more than half the population. People were so eager to vote that some turned up who weren't even registered. One determined man arrived at the polls in a wheelchair with an oxygen mask. Mayor Rickenbach won his uncontested election with 690 votes, and Edwin

Sherrill and Bill Heppenheimer won their trustee seats in a landslide, with 568 and 492 votes, respectively. Tony Minardi came in third with 280. Jerry was five votes behind, at 275. It cost him a grand total of $200 a vote in campaign spending. "It was worth every penny," Jerry insisted. "I showed my children how the American system of politics and dissent worked."

The Hook Mill Party may have won the election, but it still hadn't won the war with Jerry; his $500,000 civil rights lawsuit was still pending trial. Apparently, having learned a lesson from the Trupin affair in Southampton, the trustees decided that although it was a bitter pill to swallow, in March 1997, they agreed to pay Jerry $42,500 to cover his legal fees — $10,000 of which was the village's out-of-pocket insurance deductible. Presumably, the expense of the settlement will trickle down to the residents of the village in higher insurance premiums. In retrospect, the settlement seems like a small amount of money for such a big to-do. "It was never about money," said Jerry, "it was about principle, and I won."

Months later, sitting in his den, Heppenheimer didn't think anybody won. He mumbled that neither side was really happy with the settlement, but he couldn't comment further because of a court-imposed gag order. "If it was true that Jerry somehow managed to polarize the village," he said, "the results of the trustee election would have been very different."

Heppenheimer offered to escort his guest outside to his car, and the old yellow Lab waddled along by his side. The sky was cloudless and the air cool and still as Heppenheimer absentmindedly scratched the dog behind the ear. "To say that Jerry divided the community is way overexaggerated," he said, squinting. "What Jerry did is, he gave East Hampton too much goddamn publicity. Now everybody wants to come to the Hamptons, and it got worse since he started shooting off his mouth."

Fourth of July

BILL HEPPENHEIMER didn't go to the Maidstone Club to watch the Fourth of July fireworks over Main Beach, sponsored by the East Hampton Fire Department, even though the club has one of the best vantage points from which to watch the world-class display. Saturday night of the holiday weekend, 1997, nearly 20,000 spectators converged on Main Beach to see the 11,000 shell pyrotechnics, the largest crowd ever assembled in the village. They parked their cars and campers and RVs up and down the gilded lanes of the estate district, or on the grass fringes of the zealously guarded Maidstone golf links, and headed toward Main Beach, throngs of them gawking up at the great mansions as they went by, laden with children, blankets, strollers, and beach chairs.

Fourth of July brings with it a special delirium to the Hamptons, a lopsided New Year's Eve. It is so frenetic that many inveterate Hamptonites, like Heppenheimer, don't even leave their houses if they can avoid it. "The traffic is such a mess out there," he said. "It's a helluva job for the police department." Instead, he stayed at home with family and friends that weekend; if he stood on his back lawn, he could see the magnesium rockets and chrysanthemum starbursts lighting up the western sky just after dusk, two or three football fields wide, the percussion spreading in waves all over East Hampton.

That Fourth of July weekend, a few months after the village settled Jerry Della Femina's lawsuit, it really *did* seem like "everybody" had turned up in the Hamptons, as Heppenheimer had feared. According to official estimates, traffic increased by 8 percent that year, and the roads were reported to be "perilous" by the *East Hampton Star*. More than 2,200 emergency 911 calls were made to the East Hampton emergency services building on Cedar Street that weekend, so many that Police Chief Glen Stonemetz stood in the doorway of the room where the calls were coming in and shook his head in amazement. The Southampton Hospital emergency room experienced its busiest holiday weekend ever, attending to the victims of more than 100 automobile accidents, one pedestrian fatality, and the collision of a small private plane with a tree.

For the first time in memory, there were moments when the center of the five-square-mile village of East Hampton was gridlocked with cars, and during the day there was not a single unoccupied parking spot to be found. One frustrated local caterer, Brent Newsom, trying to make a delivery, rode in circles for more than an hour in the parking lot behind town trying to find a space, until he began to scream, red-faced, out his van window in frustration at all the visitors in their cars, "GO HOME! GO HOME!" To add to the general chaos of the holiday weekend, the sidewalks of all the hamlets were fairly teeming with day-tripping tourists, strolling along in rubber flip-flops and pastel-colored undershirts, sightseers who had made the long trip to the tip of Long Island, trying to find glamour and money on the streets, but mostly leaving disappointed to discover that the Hamptons are not a welcoming place for the uninitiated or uninvited.

For the cognoscenti willing to brave the roads, there was much to do. Novelists Rona Jaffe and Erica Jong held book-publishing parties at the same exact hour, both parties attended by Joan Rivers, and Lally Weymouth had a birthday party for her mother, *Washington Post* publisher Katharine Graham at the same time that cosmetics billionaire Ronald Lauder was throwing a birthday party for his daughter Jane. For those who were less connected, there was an 8K run in Southampton to benefit the Make-A-Wish Foundation, a North Sea fire department carnival, and a clothing sale at the Bridgehampton Community House to benefit the Design Industry Foundation Fighting AIDS. The Presbyterian Church in East Hampton was holding an antiques show, and the Amagansett Fire Department Ladies Auxiliary served up a pancake breakfast at the firehouse.

That weekend the restaurants were so crowded that the Bridgehampton Cafe was ticketed by the police because customers spilled out the front door, blocking the sidewalk. The owners of the American Hotel laid down the law and banned cell phones in the dining room but continued to keep an emergency pair of long pants in the checkroom so it wouldn't have to turn away men dressed in shorts, as they did John Kennedy Jr. the summer before. Dining at Nick & Toni's has become so sacred an experience that one woman who waited weeks for her reservation continued to eat her dinner even after her elderly husband passed out at the table and was taken away to Southampton Hospital by an ambulance, whisked out a door in the kitchen so as not to disturb patrons dining in the front room, who included directors Steven Spielberg and Nora Ephron.

Perhaps the East End claims a special affinity to this holiday, not only because it was originally part of Yankee New England, but because historians believe that the American flag sewn by Betsy Ross was a copy of the "Bridgehampton Original," designed by Lieutenant John Hulburt of Bridgehampton, used in raising a company of volunteer militia in 1775. One hundred years later, Independence Day festivities were supplied by young boys running through the streets with sparklers or setting off St. Catherine's wheels and Roman candles in the dunes with their fathers. For many years the Maidstone Club held its own fireworks display on the beach, with dancing on a wooden platform, and summer resident John Drew emceed a patriotic celebration on the East Hampton Commons, with Revolutionary War reenactments and a marching band.

The very rich held their own fireworks. Charlotte Harris's grandfather, Thomas E. Murray, set fire to the dunes with his own home-rigged fireworks display the very first Fourth of July that he and his family spent in Southampton, charring the dunes half a mile in either direction and royally enraging his neighbors. Nearly fifty years later, in 1972, writer and fireworks aficionado George Plimpton, who made pyrotechnics synonymous with the Hamptons, was arrested and handcuffed on the lawn of his own house by the town police, in front of guests who included Teddy Kennedy, for having a private fireworks display without a permit. Some years later another private fireworks display of Plimpton's went awry, and one of his guests was burned on the shoulder by a spark. The guest sued Plimpton for $11 million, and the author promptly stopped giving private displays and became instead the master of pyrotechnics at the annual benefit for Boys Harbor later in the summer.

In the old days, the Fourth of July was also a day of great revelry at The Creeks. The Herters gave visitors party favors of sparkler pinwheels and served pink lemonade. The guests were indebted to join the family in patriotic *tableau al fresco* while Albert read aloud descriptions of famous moments in American history. Modern-day Fourth of July at Ron Perelman's Creeks was just as festive, if perhaps more subdued. Actor Don Johnson and director Penny Marshall were guests, and among other weekend activities, Perelman fiddled with his drum set and screened movies for his guests. The Creeks' previous owner, Ted Dragon, resolutely stayed home on Fourth of July weekend, as he did for most of the summer. He ventured beyond the gardens of his house only in the early morning, to go to church or volunteer for the local hospice. He said he counts the days until

Labor Day, when summer is over, and his hometown gets back to normal again.

The lord of the manor, Robert D. L. Gardiner, was in residence again in his formidable stone mansion in the center of the village. He too kept a lower profile this summer, after last year's imbroglio on Gardiner's Island was reported in the press. As the walking legacy of East Hampton's rich early history, Gardiner is gearing up to take a prominent part in the 350th anniversary celebrations of the founding of the town of East Hampton that would consume the East End for most of 1998. His trips to Gardiner's Island this summer were less frequent, and his annual fall hunt to trim the herd of deer was called off. His nemeses, Robert Goelet and his family, have returned as well, celebrating Fourth of July weekend happily far from the mainland, by themselves in the luxury of the island's privacy.

Elena Prohaska lives contentedly most of the year in an Upper West Side duplex off Central Park, with her husband, Burt Glinn, and their teenage son, Sam. But every spring, when the weather begins to warm and the trees bud in the park, she is drawn, inexorably, back to the town where she was born. Elena and Burt own a white, contemporary home in Springs, set far off the road in an oak forest, its entrance marked only by a mailbox with a gamboling deer on top. Every Fourth of July weekend they hold a cocktail party on the back deck overlooking the pool, attended by an eclectic mixture of artists and writers and the local people she grew up with when she was a "townie." Not often, but at least once a summer, she drives down Hither Lane, past where Brigadoon once stood, and marvels that Evan's notorious swimming pool has been filled in with dirt and sodded over, as if it never was.

In Southampton Bill Hattrick, happily a private citizen again, has returned to being a full-time stockbroker. He was now a member of Southampton's posh Meadow Club, an invitation extended to him, he said, in thanks for his years of service as mayor. This holiday weekend he skipped the big parade down Main Street organized by the combined veterans organizations that he was obligated to attend for so many years as a village official, and went instead, along with many members of the Southampton Association, to a private fireworks display at a mansion on Dune Road, at a party to benefit the Fresh Air Home.

Perhaps the most talked about party that Fourth of July weekend was at Heaven's Gate, the home of Judy Licht and Jerry Della Femina, high on the dunes off Lily Pond Lane. The invitation called it "The Ultimate East Hampton Benefit," because it was free. "What you will receive," the invitation said, "is an incredible view of the fireworks, cocktails, hors d'oeuvres, dessert and coffee. And all it will cost you is a few hours on Saturday at 8 P.M." Jerry and Judy's fireworks party is always a big, convivial affair, with more than 100 guests spilling out of the house onto the patio and lawn. There were children everywhere, scurrying underfoot as the waiters circulated with hors d'oeuvres and splashing in the heated, smoking pool, because Jerry and Judy encouraged guests to bring their kids. "After all," Judy said, "this party is about *fireworks*." And what a night for fireworks. The sky was cloudless that Saturday night, ink blue and glittering with pinpoint stars. The air coming in from the ocean was cool and bracing, and in the distance the sound of Gershwin's "Rhapsody in Blue," emanating from speakers hidden in the dunes, was accompanied by the cadence of the waves thundering on the shore. There was a feeling of the perfect moment, perfectly played out.

Lauren Bacall was among the guests, as was actor Alan Alda, writer Ken Auletta, advertising executive Jay Chiatt, CBS News's Roone Arledge, and Mort Zuckerman, who wandered across the road from his own house for a better view. The checkout girls from the Red Horse Market were there too, as was the produce man, who proudly hoisted his three-year-old daughter on his shoulders. "This to me is the real Americana," Jerry said proudly. "It's not just rich people or famous people who are here, it's everybody. *This is the real East Hampton.*"

Just after 9 P.M. the fireworks started. They were so close, and the explosions so loud, that for a moment it seemed the stars themselves might shake out of the sky. The music segued to Ray Charles singing "America the Beautiful," and as the melody began to swell, Jerry and Judy began to sing along, shyly at first, and then more bravely. The people standing near them began to join in, and soon everyone was singing, their faces turned to the sky.

If there was anything to be gleaned from the sight of Lauren Bacall singing "America the Beautiful" at Jerry Della Femina's elbow, it was that the latest skirmish in the eternal Them versus Us struggle was already over. At the millennium, the score remained a shutout. As always, the invaders had won. If Wyandanch were around, he probably could have explained it. The establishment can hold off the newcomers for only so long; there are always more of Them than Us. Eventually you have to come to terms and make friends. But once you do, the newcomers' ills kill you. For the Indians, it was smallpox; for Evan Frankel, it was the desecration of the land; for Charlotte Harris, it was simply the invasion of bad taste. The way of life that Heppenheimer and company think they are protecting has already disappeared. There is no "fitting in" with the status quo, as Heppenheimer phrases it, because the status quo is the eclectic mixture of guests singing "America the Beautiful" at Jerry Della Femina's house. As to why each generation of newcomers was drawn here in the first place, well, there is little left to remind anyone.

Acknowledgments

I owe a great debt of gratitude to my supportive and loving friends, Rusty Unger and David Burr, Sophia Tezel and Frank Di Giacomo, Joseph Olshan and Barry Raine, Jonathan Canno and Jay Dagenhart, and Sydney Butchkes; and to Sue Pollock, whose canny suggestion it was that I write a book about the Hamptons.

Edward F. Dragon has not lost his ability to inspire. I am very grateful to him for entrusting me with his story of The Creeks. Mike Solomon of the Ossorio Foundation gave me unflagging support in the preparation of this book, far beyond the responsibilities of any director. I am also indebted to the family of Adele and Albert Herter, in particular Caroline Herter, who were kind enough to share with me their intimate family memories as well as Albert Herter's unpublished memoirs.

My deep appreciation also goes to Elena Prohaska, who took a leap of faith in sharing the story of her life with Evan Frankel with me. My thanks also go to Ernest Frankel, Andrew Sabin, Joan Cullman, Betty Marmon, and Harrie Ellen Schloss. Paul Brennan, Frank Newbold, Peter Hallock, Peggy Griffin, Rob Barnes, Rochelle Rosenberg, Ray Wesnofske, Mark Sene, and Charles Bullock, among many others, helped shape the Allan Schneider and real estate portions of this book. Clayton Morey, William Heppenheimer, William Hattrick, Dorothy and Sherburne Brown, Patricia Stewart, Patricia Murray Wood, Robert D. L. Gardiner, Judy Licht, Jerry Della Femina, Lona Rubenstein, Jen Rattiner, Fredric Mayer, Irving Markowitz, Bernard Zeldin, David Lee, Dan Rattiner, Nancy

Hyden Woodward, Bridget LeRoy, and Mary and Richard Cummings, among many others, are also owed a great debt of gratitude for their myriad contributions.

My thanks as well to Stephen Lamont, Peter Ogden, and Nicole Hirsh at Little, Brown, and to Dorothy King and Diana Dayton at the East Hampton Library. As always, this would be impossible without my intrepid editorial assistant and researcher, Martha Trachtenberg.

No author could ask for better advice, guidance, and creative nourishment than I received from my agent, Richard Pine, and from my savvy editor at Little, Brown, Bill Phillips.

Steven Gaines
Wainscott, New York
1998

Index